Corporate Europe

CORPORATE EUROPE

How Big Business Sets Policies on Food,
Climate and War

David Cronin

PlutoPress
www.plutobooks.com

First published 2013 by Pluto Press
345 Archway Road, London N6 5AA

www.plutobooks.com

Distributed in the United States of America exclusively by
Palgrave Macmillan, a division of St. Martin's Press LLC,
175 Fifth Avenue, New York, NY 10010

British Library Cataloguing in Publication Data
A catalogue record for this book is available from the British Library

ISBN   978 0 7453 3333 5   Hardback
ISBN   978 0 7453 3332 8   Paperback
ISBN   978 1 8496 4897 4   PDF eBook
ISBN   978 1 8496 4899 8   Kindle eBook
ISBN   978 1 8496 4898 1   EPUB eBook

Library of Congress Cataloging in Publication Data applied for

This book is printed on paper suitable for recycling and made from fully managed
and sustained forest sources. Logging, pulping and manufacturing processes are
expected to conform to the environmental standards of the country of origin.

10   9   8   7   6   5   4   3   2   1

Typeset from disk by Stanford DTP Services, Northampton, England
Simultaneously printed digitally by CPI Antony Rowe, Chippenham, UK and
Edwards Bros in the United States of America

Contents

Acknowledgements   vii
A short guide to the European Union   viii
List of acronyms   x

Introduction   1
   Strangling democracy in secret   4
   Heresy and hope   9

1. Wrecking the welfare state   11
   Ambushing the Irish   14
   The dogma of dynamism   17
   Eternal austerity?   21
   Greed v need   24

2. Bombarded by bankers   34
   A hug for tax havens   37
   Paying for access   41
   Serving the squid   42
   Betting on hunger   47

3. War is good for business   51
   Blood for breakfast   54
   Hijacking science   57
   The ethical afterthought   62
   Aping America   66
   Reinforcing the fortress   70

4. How we live and diet   73
   Waiting for a miracle?   78
   Breaking the traffic lights   84
   Under the influence   86
   Harmless to honey bees?   89

5. Smoke and mirrors   92
   Poaching the powerful   95
   Nicotine-stained nitpicking   97
   Downplaying the dangers   100
   Front groups and filibustering   102

6. Cheating on climate   106
   Addicted to oil   108
   Chemical brothers cry wolf   109
   Why offsetting is a scam   113
   Corporate capture and storage   115
   The wrong road   121

7. The malign legacy of Peter Mandelson   126
   Turbo-charged trade   127
   Eyeing up India   129
   Trampling on food rights   131
   Casino capitalism in Korea   135
   Sovereignty sabotaged   138
   Bleeding Canada dry   139
   Reserving medicines for the rich   141
   Africa's ally?   145
   Embracing oppression   147

Conclusion: Taking Europe back   150

Notes   158
Index   195

Acknowledgements

I very much appreciate the help received from the following people: Roger van Zwanenberg, David Shulman and everyone at Pluto Press, Pia Eberhardt, Olivier Hoedeman, Nina Holland, Martin Pigeon, Kenneth Haar, Yiorgos Vassalos, Paul de Clerck, Fiona Ryan, Mariann Skar, Dalindyebo Shabalala, Paul Goodison, Hans Muilerman, Henriette Christensen, Alexis Fremeaux, Dennis de Jong, Machteld Velema. A number of people also provided me with information on condition of anonymity; I'd like to thank them namelessly.

Needless to say, the people listed above do not necessarily share the opinions expressed in this book.

Extra special thanks to my wonderful wife, Susan Carroll, and our beautiful daughter Caitríona, whose arrival (in January 2013) helped me understand the importance of fighting for justice and equality.

David Cronin
March 2013

A short guide to the European Union

To outsiders (and even some insiders), the European Union institutions appear labyrinthine. There are all kinds of committees, acronyms and procedures that those following their work have to grapple with.

Having waded through this apparent complexity for years, I've come to the conclusion that the EU is actually quite a simple beast, albeit a multi-headed one. Most of its debates are ultimately about money and power.

There are just a few pieces of information you need to start understanding how the EU works. First off, there are three key decision-making bodies in Brussels: the European Commission, the European Parliament and the Council of Ministers. (Confusingly, the Parliament decamps to Strasbourg in France for a week each month at enormous expense to the taxpayer).

The Commission is the EU's executive. Its top table comprises of one member from each EU country (at the time of writing, there are 27). These members are nominated by their national governments: they are usually former ministers but are sometimes civil servants. Though they may have held elected office, voters are not given any opportunity to choose who should sit on the Commission. Portfolios of responsibility are assigned by the Commission's president, who is chosen by the prime ministers (or in some cases presidents) of countries comprising the Union. In theory, each commissioner is equal; in reality, some are more equal than others. Commissioners from the large EU countries tend to get 'sexier' jobs than those from smaller ones: at the time of writing, a Frenchman is in charge of banking regulation; a Briton in charge of foreign policy; and a German in charge of energy. Cyprus has been given education – a low priority for the Union – almost as a consolation prize.

The main thing you should bear in mind about the Commission is that it has the sole 'right' of initiative. This means that every piece of EU legislation begins its life as a proposal from the Commission.

Once the Commission has issued a proposal, it then forwards the text to the Parliament (the EU's only directly-elected institution) and the Council of Ministers (which brings together representatives of the Union's governments). This kicks off a series of negotiations, which are supposed to result in the three bodies reaching an agreement about the final shape of the law. (I say 'supposed to' because some dossiers can be deadlocked for aeons: it took a few decades, for example, before a deal to introduce an EU-wide patent system was secured in 2012).

Corporate lobbyists have been known to influence every stage of the EU's legislative process. The European Parliament has become a particularly important stomping ground for lobbyists in recent years. As members of the European Parliament (MEPs) have acquired new powers under the Union's treaties – its core rulebooks – lobbyists have been eager to influence them when they are voting to amend proposals.

The new powers have meant that the Parliament has some say in nearly all of the EU's activities. But this does not mean that the EU has become more democratic: in fact, the opposite is the case.

Not only have national assemblies ceded power to Brussels, the Commission has also encroached into political territory that used to be the preserve of national governments. Following the financial crisis that erupted in 2008, it successfully insisted that Brussels officials be involved in the preparation of budgets introduced in the capitals of EU states. Such a power grab would have been unthinkable under less trying economic circumstances.

Some of the EU's most important work is done outside of Brussels. The Frankfurt-based European Central Bank, in particular, merits careful monitoring. While its pronouncements on interest rates and inflation sound technical, the ECB is a deeply political outfit. Working in lockstep with the European Commission, it has effectively forced governments to implement measures that cause immense hardship to ordinary people.

In order to make things manageable, however, I have focused primarily on what happens in the Belgian capital. My hope is that this book provides a few snapshots of how an unaccountable elite has an unhealthy level of influence in matters that affect us all.

List of acronyms

ACP	African, Caribbean and Pacific
ACTA	Anti-Counterfeiting Trade Agreement
ADVENT	Adaptive versatile energy technology
AEA	Atomic Energy Agency
AIDS	Acquired immune deficiency syndrome
AIM	European Brands Association
AIMA	Alternative Investment Management Association
ALTER-EU	Alliance for Lobbying Transparency and Ethics Regulation
AMUE	Association for the Monetary Union of Europe
ASD	Aerospace and Defence Industries Association of Europe
BASCAP	Business Alliance to Stop Counterfeiting and Piracy
BAT	British American Tobacco
BDI	Federation of German Industries
BEUC	European Consumers' Organisation
BIOFRAC	Biofuels Research Advisory Council
BIT	Bilateral investment treaty
CCS	Carbon capture and storage
CCSA	Carbon Capture and Storage Association
CDM	Clean development mechanism
CEA	European Committee of Insurers
CECCM	Confederation of European Community Cigarette Manufacturers
CEDT	European Confederation of Tobacco Retailers
CEEV	European Committee of Wine Companies
CEFIC	European Chemical Industry Council
CERT	Canada-Europe Roundtable for Business
CETA	Comprehensive economic and trade agreement
CIAA	Confederation of the Food and Drink Industries of the EU
CL	Compulsory licensing
CO2	Carbon dioxide
CSR	Corporate social responsibility
DSEi	Defence Systems and Equipment International
EAHF	European Alcohol and Health Forum

EBF	European Banking Federation
ECB	European Central Bank
ECPA	European Centre for Public Affairs
EDA	European Defence Agency
EFCNI	European Foundation for the Care of Newborn Infants
EFPIA	European Federation of Pharmaceutical Industries and Associations
EFRD	European Forum for Responsible Drinking
EFSA	European Food Safety Authority
EPA	Economic partnership agreement
EPA	Environmental Protection Agency
EPC	European Policy Centre
EPF	European Patients' Forum
EPFSF	European Parliamentary Financial Services Forum
EMU	Economic and monetary union
ERF	European Risk Forum
ERT	European Roundtable of Industrialists
ESA	European Seed Association
ESF	European Services Forum
ESTOC	European Smokeless Tobacco Council
ETS	Emissions trading system
EU	European Union
EUFIC	European Food Information Council
Eurocare	European Alcohol Policy Alliance
EuropaBio	European Association for Bioindustries
EUROPIA	European Petroleum Industry Association
FAS	Future air systems
FIPRA	Finsbury International Policy and Regulatory Advisers
FOA	Futures and Options Association
GDP	Gross domestic product
GE	General Electric
GM	Genetically modified
GMO	Genetically modified organism
G20	Group of 20
HFC	Hydrofluorocarbon
HIV	Human immunodeficiency virus
HFSB	Hedge Fund Standards Board
IASB	International Accounting Standards Board
ICC	International Chamber of Commerce
IETA	International Emissions Trading Association

IIEA	Institute of International and European Affairs
ILSI	International Life Sciences Institute
IMF	International Monetary Fund
INSM	Initiative for a New Social Market Economy
IPR	Intellectual property rights
ISDA	International Swaps and Derivatives Association
KAS	Konrad Adenauer Stiftung
MAI	Multilateral agreement on investment
MEDEF	Movement of the Enterprises of France
MEP	Member of the European Parliament
MiFID	Market in financial instruments directive
NASA	National Aeronautics and Space Administration
NATO	North Atlantic Treaty Organisation
NHS	National Health Service
OECD	Organisation for Economic Cooperation and Development
OPARUS	Open architecture for UAV-based surveillance system
OPERA	European Observatory for Sustainable Agriculture
PR	Public relations
R&T	Research and technology
SCENIHR	Scientific committee on emerging and newly identified health risks
SDA	Security and Defence Agenda
SESAR	Single European Sky Air Traffic Management Research
SOMO	Centre for Research on Multinational Corporations
STP	Smokeless tobacco products
TABD	Trans Atlantic Business Dialogue
TINA	There is no alternative
TRIPS	Trade-related intellectual property rights
UAV	Unmanned aerial vehicle
UEHP	European Union of Private Hospitals
UNEP	United Nations Environment Programme
UNICE	Union of Industrial and Employers' Confederations of Europe
UKIP	United Kingdom Independence Party
WHO	World Health Organisation
WIPO	World Intellectual Property Organisation
WIMA²S	Wide-area airborne surveillance
WTO	World Trade Organisation

VideoSense	Virtual centre of excellence for ethically-guided and privacy-respecting video analytics in security
YAMS	Young adult male smokers
ZEP	Zero Emissions Platform

Introduction

Ferdinand de Meeûs stands upright. A slicked-back abundance of hair and trimmed beard give him a magisterial presence. The leaves on the trees sound like they are whispering to each other.

The bust of this nineteenth-century count is as good a place as any to begin exploring corporate power in Brussels. De Meeûs was a banker, entrepreneur and politician in his day. Aptly, the square bearing his name is now packed with offices of trade associations and 'public relations' firms. Their occupants straddle the nebulous divide between business and politics. The graffiti scrawled on another statue in this small park is mindless. Yet there is a greater vandalism underway behind the gleaming glass of nearby facades. Its perpetrators carry smart phones, instead of spray-paint.

The army of lobbyists headquartered here and on neighbouring streets follow a simple plan. Their objective is to slash and burn regulations designed to protect human health and the environment. The welfare state – one of Europe's finest achievements after the Second World War – will end up in a rubble heap if they have their way.

Of course, the army is a little more nuanced in outlining its strategy. Just as military propagandists refer to civilian deaths as 'collateral damage', the corporate army camouflages its real agenda by using terms like 'competitiveness' and 'consolidation'. Just as nations are bombed on 'humanitarian' pretexts, the corporate army claims that it is acting in the best interests of society; that it is providing jobs and stimulating growth. In reality, the corporate army is fighting a class war.

My choice of words may seem old-fashioned. But the type of class war I am referring to was brilliantly encapsulated by the slogan of the Occupy! movement that emerged in 2011. The corporate army is fighting for the interests of the 1 per cent against the 99 per cent. It is fighting for the interests of bosses against those of workers and the unemployed. There are two classes in this war. Them and us. As Warren Buffett – unmistakably one of 'them' – has noted, it's the 'rich class that's making war and we're winning.'[1] Buffett may have been referring primarily to the United States but his observation equally applies to Europe. The bank Credit Suisse estimated in 2012

1

that Europe hosted 22,000 'ultra-high net worth individuals' – with net assets of more than $50 million – while the US had 37,950.[2] It is in these pairs of hands – less than 60,000 on both sides of the Atlantic – that wealth and power is increasingly concentrated. For the sake of simplicity, I will refer to these 60,000 as the 1 per cent, although they represent a much smaller segment of the combined European and US population. It is these 60,000 that the corporate army serves.

Brussels is a key battleground for the corporate army. Outside of Washington, Brussels is generally accepted to have the highest concentration of lobbyists in the world.[3] Nobody is sure how many ply this trade in the Belgian capital. Estimates vary from 15,000 to 30,000. What is more telling than the overall number, however, is that more than two-thirds of these advocates represent private sector interests. The remaining one-third work for national or local authorities or organisations that can be broadly categorised as public interest (among them are trade unions and green and human rights groups).[4] So here's the breakdown to keep in mind: two-thirds of lobbyists belong to the corporate army. The rest fight for us.

I hasten to add the caveat that the picture is a tiny bit muddled. As I explain at various points in this book, there are some outfits in Brussels that give the impression they are on 'our' side or neutral, yet in reality are funded by corporations and either compromised as a result or engaged in covert advocacy. 'Think tanks', in particular, play an important role in ensuring that debate stays within clearly defined parameters, which effectively means that the only people taking part in it are the 1 per cent and their doormats. Edward Bernays, a pioneer of what has become known as 'public relations', explained this phenomenon in the 1920s as the 'conscious and intelligent manipulation of the organised habits and opinions of the masses'.[5] In twenty-first-century Europe, 'conscious and intelligent manipulation' means that we, the masses, are mostly excluded from discussions about issues of fundamental importance to our lives. Everything is left to the 'experts'. Either writing directly for the mainstream media or having a considerable input into its content, these 'experts' tell us what paths have to be followed by policy-makers. We are given no choice than to accept their 'wisdom'. This has particularly been the case since the financial crisis erupted in 2008. Harsh economic measures that widen inequality are sold as 'technical adjustments'. Those of us who object are treated as unreasonable for failing to show due deference to the goddess TINA ('there is no alternative').

Of course, lobbyists don't tend to recognise themselves as vandals. Time and again, I have heard lobbyists argue that they are contributing to the 'democratic process'; that they are doing nothing more sinister than representing 'stakeholders'. Many profess a devotion to the 'European project'. That phrase puzzled me when I first moved to Brussels in 1995 but I subsequently began to understand it (perhaps even to fall under its spell for a while). The 'project' refers to the construction of a political and economic union. Believers in it feel it has prevented war on this continent. I've no doubt that some of these believers are sincere. I also have no doubt that corporations have latched onto the 'project' for purely selfish reasons.

Located on Square de Meeûs, the Brussels office of Burson-Marsteller, one of the world's top 'public relations' firms, offers a case study into how lobbyists are either blinkered or severely constrained by ideology, whether they recognise it or not. The ideology in question holds that governments should be vassals of corporations; that regulations perceived as hostile to the accumulation of wealth must be scrapped. This ideology is often called neo-liberalism.[6] I prefer to call it vandalism.

David Earnshaw, head of Burson-Marsteller's office at the time of writing, is less than candid about the ideological role he serves. 'I'm a left-wing pro-European socialist and federalist and proud of that,' the one-time Labour Party election candidate told me in the spring of 2012. He listed some other sources of pride: how 75 per cent of his staff are women under the age of 30; how his company no longer works for the tobacco industry; how it was one of the first major PR agencies to publish details of its revenue (or so he claimed). Yet in between reeling off the firm's progressive attributes, he said: 'My own obsession is that we as an organisation don't believe in anything. We don't work just for the corporate sector. We don't work just for the private sector. We advise people on how to influence European public policy.'

Towards the end of our conversation, Earnshaw admitted that his firm does more than offer advice. His admission came after I asked him if Burson-Marsteller has a direct input in the writing of EU legislation. Does it prepare amendments to proposed laws that members of the European Parliament sign and put forward in their own names? He replied: 'Yes, as would any lobbyist.' Earnshaw justified this practice by saying that he had also written proposals for MEPs when he briefly worked for the anti-poverty group Oxfam a decade earlier. 'In principle, I don't see anything wrong with

David Earnshaw drafting an amendment. The problem arises when this becomes the norm, when this is the only way amendments get tabled. You get organisations like Oxfam and ExxonMobil doing exactly the same. You send 50 amendments to a politician and say "please table them" and the politician obliges. That's what is mad.'[7]

The equation made by Earnshaw is facile and fallacious. ExxonMobil has a much larger lobbying war chest than Oxfam or Greenpeace. In 2009 it spent over $27 million on lobbying in Washington.[8] These efforts persuaded the US to prevent a robust agreement being reached at that year's international climate change negotiations in Copenhagen. ExxonMobil's entry to a 'transparency register' run by the European Commission states that it shelled out around €5 million in activities directed at the Brussels institutions during 2011.[9] Greenpeace spent less than €1 million in EU-related campaigning that year.[10] Oxfam's EU affairs office had an annual budget of €500,000.[11] Burson-Marsteller, meanwhile, reported that its earnings from EU-focused lobbying in 2011 came to almost €9 million. Although it had a sizeable contract with the Polish foreign ministry, most of its clients were corporations (including ExxonMobil).[12]

I've heard several other PR specialists echo Earnshaw's reasoning. The standard response to questions about whether it is appropriate for corporate lobbyists to be effectively dictating legislation is that environmental groups also try to do so. ExxonMobil is the world's wealthiest corporation, according to the United Nations Conference on Trade and Development.[13] It can't seriously be compared to Greenpeace or Oxfam. A polluter can't seriously be compared to someone who campaigns against pollution, just as someone whose overriding ambition is to make as much profit as possible can't be compared to a charity worker. It follows that an amendment written by an oil firm or its 'drill, Baby, drill' cheerleaders can't be compared to one written by a conservationist. Failure to grasp this point amounts to a failure to understand power: how the strong and the wealthy have much more say than the weak and the poor, even if efforts are made to create an impression of fairness.

STRANGLING DEMOCRACY IN SECRET

Of course, we as citizens should have a right to know who advises politicians and civil servants, whether formally or informally. Despite some positive changes in recent years, the EU continues to work in an opaque fashion. This secrecy starts at the top. When presidents and prime ministers gather for summits in Brussels, they meet entirely behind closed doors. No recordings or transcripts of their deliberations are published. In September 2012, a report in *Le Monde diplomatique* provided a glimpse into how the leaders of France and Germany have been pursuing an anti-democratic offensive at these events. Both Angela Merkel and Nicolas Sarkozy recommended in October 2010 that governments should have their voting rights as EU member states suspended if they do not comply with the Union's rules on budgetary rigour, according to notes taken by diplomats attending a summit that month.[14] This means that the duo wished to install a new system, whereby entire nations could be punished as if they were errant teenagers for spending more on healthcare than the deficit hawks in the Brussels bureaucracy would allow.

None of the EU's institutions are immune from this opacity. The European Parliament might broadcast its key debates on the internet and on a satellite TV channel, yet there are countless decisions taken on the sidelines which we hear nothing about. Controversy can sometimes be a catalyst for reform. While I am loath to praise publications owned by Rupert Murdoch, the *Sunday Times* deserves credit for outing a number of MEPs as corrupt in March 2011 by revealing how they agreed to table amendments to a law then under discussion in return for payments from journalists posing as lobbyists.[15] Not only did the sting operation lead to a few resignations, it caused sufficient embarrassment for the Parliament to draw up a code of conduct for its members, forbidding them from engaging in the kind of practises revealed by the *Sunday Times*.[16]

But it should be emphasised that the Parliament is in no hurry to enable greater scrutiny of its activities. One of the measures considered after the 'cash for laws' scandal erupted was that the public should be able to examine MEPs' 'legislative footprints'. Under this idea, politicians tasked with preparing the Parliament's official response to new proposals for laws would have to fill out forms disclosing which lobbyists they spoke to. In May 2012 – more than a year after the controversy – I interviewed Dennis de Jong, a Dutch left-wing MEP who has been campaigning for greater transparency. De Jong stated that he had recently requested a 'legislative footprint' form from the Parliament's internal administration, only to be informed that no forms were yet available. 'This was a decision without a follow-up', he said.[17]

For all its flaws, the Parliament is at least an elected body. The same cannot be said for the European Commission. Although all EU laws begin life as proposals from the Commission, ordinary citizens have no say in the make-up of this institution. Sure, we are invited to participate every so often in 'public consultations' that it organises ahead of bringing forward legislation. We are not told, however, that views expressed by the 1 per cent during these exercises are treated with infinitely more respect than those from everyone else. Views that clash with those of the elite are simply disregarded. I have experience of this fact. After my book *Europe's Alliance With Israel: Aiding the Occupation* was published, I spent a lot of time trying to raise awareness about how companies making weapons that kill and maim Palestinian civilians are benefiting from EU grants for scientific research. A number of human rights organisations registered complaints on this matter when the Commission invited comments about the future direction of its research programmes in 2011. The complaints were extremely serious – they demonstrated how the Union was abetting war crimes under the pretext of encouraging 'innovation'.[18] Yet when the Commission issued an analysis of the 'consultation', it did not refer once to the concerns raised about EU support for Israel's arms industry.[19]

Corporations are involved in almost every stage of the formulation of the Union's laws and policies. When preparing new initiatives, the European Commission frequently relies on a network of 'expert groups'. As explained at various points in this book, most of the groups are comprised of private sector representatives, with one or two members from public interest organisations added in a tokenistic manner. Partly because of pressure from MEPs, a few piecemeal improvements have been made: more details of the groups' work can be found on the internet than was the case a few years ago, for example. Yet the Commission is refusing to concede that the nature of this network is inherently problematic. Maros Sefcovic, the EU's commissioner for administrative affairs at the time of writing, stated in 2011 that he and his colleagues paid 'attention to any possible conflict of interests that might arise in the course of a group's operations that could contaminate a group's objectives and jeopardise its effectiveness and efficiency'. Individuals found to have clashing interests can be excluded from some or all of a particular group's activities, he added.[20]

Sefcovic misses a salient point. Allowing a bank or a weapons manufacturer to shape the orientation of a financial services law or a 'security' blueprint is by definition a conflict of interests. Lobbyists for banks or arms companies are paid to seek the best outcome for their employers, not to work for the general good of society.

The conflicts of interests are especially egregious when subsidies are up for grabs. Yet there are many cases – some of them cited in this book – where the companies who help set priorities for spending programmes benefit directly from the eventual grants. To use Sefcovic's words, this enables the private sector to contaminate public policy. Beyond making some small gestures, there is no willingness on the part of the Commission to address this problem.

Who are the most influential corporate lobby groups in Brussels? Giving a definitive answer to this question is not easy. The advent of a 'transparency register' has certainly increased the amount of information available about lobbying. Companies and umbrella groups have been given clear incentives to subscribe. The provision of access badges to the European Parliament is conditional on signing up to the register, for example.[21] But the quality of the data contained in the register is sometimes of dubious quality. For a few consecutive years, Panavision has reported spending more on trying to influence the EU institutions than Shell, GDF Suez and ExxonMobil combined.[22] It is almost impossible to believe that a camera-maker would devote more resources to cultivating contacts in Brussels than the oil industry.

The lack of accurate data notwithstanding, most observers of corporate lobbying agree on who the big players are. In his book *Interest Representation in the European Union*, Justin Greenwood names the chemical industry 'family' – which comprises a few associations – as the largest, with 160 staff in 2010.[23] The European Chemical Industry Council (CEFIC), the main parent in this 'family', reported spending €6 million on making its case in Brussels' corridors of power between October 2011 and September 2012. It also stated, however, that its total annual budget came to €40 million.[24]

The Alliance for Lobbying Transparency and Ethics Regulation – a broad coalition of non-profit groups – has compiled a league table of top spenders among EU trade associations, based on figures from the 'transparency register'. CEFIC is at number two on that table, with the number one spot occupied by the European Seed Association (ESA). It, too, a lobby for chemical and biotechnology firms, ESA's reported expenditure on making its case to the Brussels elite exceeded €8 million in 2011. BusinessEurope was at number three, with €4 million.[25] The declared lobbying budget for that employers' federation should be treated with caution. According to its website, BusinessEurope has a staff of 49 and a network of 60 working groups with a total of 1,200 'experts'.[26] A survey published by 'headhunters' Ellwood and Atfield in 2010 found that lobbyists working for Brussels trade associations can command gross annual salaries ranging from €100,000 for a manager to over €400,000 for a secretary-general. These remuneration levels do not include additional benefits – a car, mobile phone, health insurance and pension contributions – that someone in those positions would expect.[27] With BusinessEurope's status as the most influential lobby group in Brussels undisputed and some of its top-level staff known for their ostentation, the group's claim to have less than €4 million per year in its war chest is simply not credible.

Size is not the only determinant of clout. The European Roundtable of Industrialists (ERT) stated that it had just three people on its payroll who were involved in 'direct advocacy' and a lobbying budget of under €800,000 in 2011.[28] Yet the ERT has been given credit for laying the foundations of the European Union as it is today. In his book *More Machiavelli in Brussels*, Rinus van Schendelen contends that the ERT's campaigning in the 1980s led to the development of a single market for goods and services.[29] The reason why it can flex its muscles with a lean operation is that ERT concentrates on the big picture, rather than poring over the minutiae of every dossier relevant to corporations. Moreover, it should be borne in mind that its small office answers to 50 of the top chief executives on this continent. As EU commissioners have attended its events right since its inception, the ERT hasn't needed to massively expand its full-time personnel in order to maintain its access-all-areas pass.[30]

The ERT has been home to some of the corporate army's top strategists. The tactics recommended by these strategists have been less than subtle but they are rarely subject to critical scrutiny. One of those strategists, Etienne Davignon, personifies the 'revolving doors' phenomenon between politics and business. In his capacity as Belgium's member of the European Commission in the 1980s, Davignon attended the inaugural meeting of the ERT in 1983.[31] After leaving the Commission, he was appointed chairman of the bank Société Générale de Belgique, a post once held by Ferdinand de Meeûs. This allowed Davignon to remain active with the ERT.[32] More recently, he has been head of the Bilderberg Group, a secretive invitation-only club that has aroused innumerable conspiracy theories.[33] The conspiracy theories are unnecessary because Davignon has given enough away of his real thinking to be regarded as a danger to democracy. In 2011, he stated that George Papandreou, then the Greek prime minister, had responded sensibly to the euro crisis but 'ended that course of action by calling a referendum'.[34]

Those few words say everything about the corporate army. Vicious austerity measures that are causing immense hardship in Greece are regarded as 'sensible'. Asking the people who are bearing the brunt of those measures for their consent is, on the other hand, perceived as daft. As a general in the corporate army, Davignon is determined to have his goals realised. Non-combatants are not allowed to stand in the way of his quest for corporate dominance. Once again, it is not necessary to be a conspiracy theorist to suspect that the ERT and similar groups are intent on conquering Europe. The ERT's own publications say so: in January 2012, it called for 'sunset screening' of all EU regulations with the aim of eliminating those which 'inhibit growth'. As the issue of 'flexible labour markets' was identified as a priority, the logical conclusion was that ERT was demanding a bonfire of laws and policies viewed as obstacles to profit.[35]

HERESY AND HOPE

Davignon has somehow found time in his packed diary to champion something called 'corporate social responsibility' (CSR).[36] He has been made president of CSR Europe, an assortment of weapons (Dassault), car (Toyota, Volkswagen, Renault) and food (Unilever, Danone, Cargill) companies formed in 2010.[37] Nobody should be deceived by CSR. It is not an effort by chief executives to get in touch with their inner tree-huggers. Rather, it is a deliberate ploy to make regulators back off by telling them that large corporations are perfectly capable of protecting human rights and the environment without interference. One of CSR Europe's first pamphlets indicated that corporate social responsibility relies on 'voluntary actions' and that it is a response to the 'partial redefinition of the boundary between the public and private sector' sparked by reforms to this continent's welfare states.[38]

Corporate social responsibility is an oxymoron. As Joel Bakan explains in his book *The Corporation*, the laws of most countries are clear about the role of big business. Under these laws, the overriding responsibility of corporate decision-makers is to maximise corporate gains. 'The law forbids any other motivation for their actions,' Bakan writes. 'Corporate social responsibility is thus illegal – at least when it is genuine.'[39] Worse, CSR is a distraction from the need to confront the power of big business. Predictably, EU policy-makers have allowed themselves be distracted. The European Commission has pledged to take action against corporate tax avoidance and evasion – a problem that deprives exchequers in EU countries of an estimated €1 trillion per year – under the CSR rubric.[40] For guidance on how to address this issue, it has turned to Michael Devereux, director of the Oxford University Centre for Business Taxation.[41] The centre names Vodafone as one of the companies providing 'vital' financial support to its research.[42] It is, to put it mildly, curious that Vodafone should be financing tax research: in 2011, this British company availed of various loopholes in order to pay no corporate tax in its home country.[43]

Having spent almost half my life in Brussels, learnt how to speak four European languages and travelled widely on this continent, it seems absurd to me that I can be called 'anti-European'. Yet that is the label which is routinely applied to those who criticise the 'European project'. The expatriate cocoon that has emerged in the 'European quarter' of my adopted city brooks no dissent. Neo-liberalism is treated as 'the one true faith' here. Questioning this orthodoxy is viewed as unholy (I exaggerate only slightly – senior EU officials have described those who do not respect their strictures as 'sinners').[44] The sordid irony is that it is the corporate army which is truly anti-European. Using brute force – and sometimes blackmail – it is jeopardising many of Europe's greatest achievements. By seeking to demolish our welfare states and our environmental laws, by convincing political leaders to behave in an increasingly bellicose manner in trade relations with the wider world, by promoting the development of war machines as tools of 'enterprise', the corporate army is determined to turn Europe into a carbon copy of the United States. If that is not anti-European, then I don't know what is.

I have written this book as an act of both heresy and hope. Heresy, in my view, is imperative when an inhuman ideology like neo-liberalism becomes all-pervasive. Yet the resistance to neo-liberalism that has been witnessed at mass protests in Athens, Madrid and elsewhere over the past few years suggests that the ideology will not reign supreme forever. These protesters – the *indignados*, to use that marvellous Spanish word – fill me with hope. By maintaining their momentum against many odds, these protesters are providing a rampart against the corporate army.

1
Wrecking the welfare state

Sometime during the last two months of 2011, the mask slipped off the European project. Elected governments in both Greece and Italy were replaced with hastily assembled administrations. Voters were given no say in the matter.

Most of the attention was focused on Greece, where George Papandreou resigned as prime minister because he had the temerity to suggest that a referendum be called, asking if ordinary people concurred with the terms of a 'bail-out' imposed on the country. His effective dismissal by Angela Merkel and Nicolas Sarkozy shattered the myth that the EU was a club of sovereign nations.[1] Perhaps the only mitigating factor was that the interim government in Athens wasn't in office for too long.[2] By contrast, the new regime in Rome stayed in office for a full year.

Mario Monti came to power in circumstances that resembled a coup. In the summer of 2011, Italy had a crushing national debt and found its banks under attack by speculators.[3] Jean Claude-Trichet, then the outgoing president of the European Central Bank, and his incoming successor Mario Draghi pounced on this crisis. Writing to Silvio Berlusconi in August that year, the duo complained that the prime minister's commitments to economic reform were 'insufficient'. It was 'essential', they added, for Italy to undertake 'large-scale privatisations' and to make it easier for firms to sack workers. A series of other measures must be introduced by decree within less than two months, Berlusconi was told.[4]

Though Berlusconi succumbed to the ECB's pressure and helped to bring in a package of cutbacks, he found his own position untenable. After many of his parliamentary allies deserted him, Berlusconi resigned in November 2011.[5] Monti promptly replaced him. No election was called. Like the other members of his hand-picked new cabinet, Monti was not an elected politician.[6]

Monti appeared in some respects to be the polar opposite of Berlusconi. Whereas Berlusconi had a penchant for risqué jokes and became synonymous with 'bunga bunga' parties, Monti came across as inscrutable and dour. Monti is routinely described as a 'technocrat', implying that as a university professor, he was not motivated by the base concerns of a career parliamentarian. The description was misleading: Monti proved not only to be highly political, he was in some respects more dangerous than Berlusconi. Monti quickly resorted to taking action by emergency decree; this effectively meant that he was ordering that the retirement age be increased and expenditure on public services be slashed.[7] As I hadn't heard any convincing explanation for why he was issuing diktats, I requested one when I approached Monti as he was leaving a conference in Brussels a few months later.

'Mr Monti, do you accept that you have no democratic mandate to introduce the reforms you are undertaking in Italy?' I asked.

'No, I do not,' he replied.

'What democratic mandate do you have?' I persevered.

'I have a huge majority in Parliament,' he said.[8]

I tried to enquire how his 'huge majority' compensated for the fact that he had not been elected but Monti had already walked away, surrounded by bodyguards and a smartly-dressed entourage.

Taking a more softball approach than I had, journalists with *Der Spiegel* soon learned how Monti actually regarded parliaments as something of an irritant. 'If governments let themselves be bound by the decisions of their parliaments without protecting their own freedom to act, a breakup of Europe would be a more probable outcome than integration,' he told the German magazine.[9]

Having monitored his work intermittently for more than a decade, I am convinced that Monti has long been seeking a fundamental transformation of the European economy. Because this kind of transformation (or 'integration', as he prefers to call it) necessitates social upheaval, it is not hard to see why he wants to avoid the oversight and checks and balances that parliaments are supposed to provide. Before I 'doorstepped' him, I had listened to Monti give a keynote address to an audience invited by the employers group BusinessEurope. Monti used this platform to spurn 'an old-fashioned Keynesian way of looking at the world', stressing efforts must be made towards 'budgetary consolidation'. He summarised his thinking as 'structural reforms – yes; ephemeral deficit spending – no'.[10] Didn't Margaret Thatcher adopt a similar outlook with the guidance of her economic guru Keith Joseph?[11] Just as Thatcher had done, Monti was wielding a machete at the big government policies favoured by John Maynard Keynes. Monti was urging the destruction of the welfare state not just in Italy but throughout the EU.

Between 1999 and 2004, Monti was the EU's commissioner for competition policy. He was best known during that period for blocking a merger between General Electric (GE) and Honeywell. Monti continued to spend much of his time in Brussels when his term as a commissioner expired. He was named chairman of Bruegel, an economic affairs 'think-tank'.[12] Ironically – or appropriately, depending on one's perspective – this outfit's activities have been partly financed by GE, as well as by Goldman Sachs, for whom Monti has worked as an adviser.[13] In an article published by Bruegel in 2005, Monti gave a useful history lesson. It is wrong, he argued, to equate the concept of a 'market economy' solely with Anglo-Saxon capitalism. Monti praised the German government of the 1950s – particularly Ludwig Erhard, the economics minister – for imprinting on 'the nascent European construction a solid market orientation', with the help of France. Twenty-first century France and Germany 'need quickly to reform and modernise their model, not repudiate it,' he added.[14]

It is telling that Monti's article was penned the year that Angela Merkel took over as chancellor in Germany. Ahead of her election, Merkel hired Paul Kirchhof as an economic adviser. An advocate of radical tax cuts, Kirchhof had been actively involved in the Initiative for a New Social Market Economy (INSM). Financed by trade associations representing the metal and electronics industries, the INSM was set up in 2005 to push for a weakening of the welfare state.[15] Merkel's scope for implementing the policies favoured by the INSM was limited in her first term in office. That was because she led a coalition with the Social Democrats, who were averse to Kirchhof's main recommendations.[16] Circumstances were to change dramatically after she was re-elected in 2009. Not only was Merkel able to form a government with the right-wing Free Democrats, the troubles besetting the eurozone helped her become the self-appointed empress of austerity. Largely at her behest, a number of European economies were remoulded to meet the requirements of the 'social market'.

The term 'social market' is a misnomer. The prefix 'social' has been attached purely as a form of sugar-coating to make painful adjustments appear palatable. In reality, 'social market' is a synonym for neo-liberalism, an ideology which holds that the most important purpose of the state is to defend private property rights.[17] Genuine social policies aimed at reducing poverty and inequality are anathema to this way of thinking. The INSM's vision of a social market is one where minimum wages are abolished and health insurance opened up to greater competition.[18]

To understand how the 'social market' involves a repackaging of old ideas, it is helpful to examine the report of a 2009 conference titled '60 Years of the Social Market Economy'. Held in Sankt-Augustin, a town near Bonn, the conference was hosted by the Konrad Adenauer Stiftung (KAS), a 'foundation' affiliated to Merkel's Christian Democratic Union, and the European Business Circle, a group dominated by German entrepreneurs and academics. The report traces the first use of the phrase 'social market economy' to a 1946 paper by the economist and anthropologist Alfred-Müller Armack. While the authors of the 2009 report contend that the concept is based on 'seemingly conflicting objectives, namely economic freedom and social security', they admit that it is 'a new variant of neo-liberalism'. What is particularly striking about the report is that it presented the economic crisis which erupted a year earlier as an opportunity to 'renew' the 'principles and fundamental ideas' behind the social market economy. Far from confining this debate to Germany, it urged that the concept be applied globally to 'reinvigorate the philosophical and economic standing of liberalism in general'.[19] Such thinking will be familiar to readers of Naomi Klein's magnum opus *The Shock Doctrine*. Among the numerous examples of market fundamentalists exploiting emergency situations cited by Klein was how the highly influential economist Milton Friedman urged the privatisation of the school system in New Orleans soon after the city was devastated by a hurricane.[20]

AMBUSHING THE IRISH

Towards the end of November 2010, the shock doctrine came to Ireland. I happened to be home in Dublin at the time that details of an €85 billion 'bail-out' were announced. It felt grimly appropriate that the news coincided with heavy snow. As the capital was covered with sheets of ice, it was a major challenge to walk the streets without breaking a leg. Parts of the city felt deserted, almost ghostly.

The Irish people were not bailed out on that bitterly cold week; they were ambushed. Those who had little, if anything, to do with the excesses of the Celtic Tiger era were forced to suffer the most now that the speculative bubble had burst. Most of the €85 billion was to be borrowed from the European Union and the International Monetary Fund under conditions that amounted to blackmail.

Just three years earlier, the largest business deal of the boom was clinched. At 2 a.m. on a Saturday in June 2007, Anglo Irish Bank issued a draft for €1.165 billion to allow a property developer to buy a chain of hotels. When the paroxysms in the global economy started the following year, it soon became clear that Anglo had been throwing gargantuan sums of 'other people's money' around like confetti. As Anglo's problems worsened, the Dublin government tried to 'rescue' it. Some €22 billion were pumped into it by May 2010. But this wasn't enough to cover its gambling debts and the bank's management conceded that the 'lion's share' of these billions wouldn't be seen again. In the words of Simon Carswell, author of the book *Anglo Republic*, the bank turned into a 'black hole for taxpayers' cash'.[21] The 'bail-out' prompted the Green Party to withdraw from a ruling coalition with the centre-right Fianna Fáil, leading to an election in 2011. Having been an active member of the Irish Greens in the 1990s, the party's performance in government had been unpleasant for me to observe, albeit from a distance; principles once held as sacrosanct were abandoned purely on the grounds of expediency. The decision to leave that government was accompanied by the ultimate act of betrayal. Rather than resisting the manifestly unfair terms of the 'bail-out', the Greens' leadership decided to facilitate its approval by the Oireachtas, Ireland's parliament, ahead of polling day.[22]

Although this treachery was to tie the hands of the next government, the main opposition party Fine Gael (slightly more right-wing than Fianna Fáil) went to the hustings with a promise it would 'burn the bondholders' (another popular term for refusing to repay lenders was to make them have a 'haircut').[23] The pledge was neatly summarised by Richard Bruton, then the party's spokesman for enterprise: 'We have to take the view that people who invested and invested unwisely have the consequences under capitalism of losing some or all of their investment.'[24] Internal European Commission documents I have seen indicate that Ireland's masters in Brussels were adamant that no bondholder would even by singed, regardless of how unwise his or her investments had been. A December 2010 'background note' prepared for Olli Rehn, the Union's economic and monetary affairs commissioner at the time, said that EU officials were already in contact with the leading opposition parties and believed that 'a high degree of policy continuity should be possible even in the case of a change of government'. As well as stressing that 'the main elements or goalposts of the ["bail-out"] programme should not be renegotiated', the paper explicitly stated that 'a possible involvement of banks' senior bondholders ("haircut") has been excluded and renegotiating this would run counter to the programme's main objective – restore confidence in the Irish banking system'. The same paper then went on to give a snapshot of the 'fiscal consolidation' and 'structural reform agenda' that would be implemented as a condition for the loans being released; among the key ingredients would be wage cuts and 'large reductions in welfare spending'. The country's corporation tax – at 12.5 per cent one of the lowest in the eurozone – would be left 'untouched'.[25]

The technical wording of the document does not eclipse its ideological bias. Other internal documents show that the Commission was perfectly aware that Ireland spent less on social welfare than many other EU countries. These papers nonetheless illustrated that the Commission preferred the slashing of payments on which people on the lower rungs of the social ladder depended to making bondholders pay their own casino bills now that their bets had gone belly-up. One such paper commented that Ireland's 'social safety net' was 'not very generous by EU standards'; an accompanying graph showed that in 2007, Ireland spent a little over 12.5 per cent of gross domestic product on social benefits. Germany, by contrast, spent 24.5 per cent that year, while the EU average was 19 per cent. While rising unemployment led to an increase in such spending over the next few years, Ireland's proportionate rate of expenditure on social benefits (18 per cent) in 2009 remained considerably less than Germany's (26.5 per cent) and the EU average (22 per cent).[26]

Even though EU officials had this very clear information at their disposal, they told Rehn that 'foreseen cuts in social payments and public sector pay appear appropriate'. Some months before the 'bail-out' was put together, Rehn was advised to tell Brian Lenihan, then Ireland's finance minister, that 'the Irish authorities should pursue further reforms to the social security system as soon as possible'.[27] The point was emphasised again later in 2010 when Rehn travelled to Dublin and met the politicians expected to comprise the next government. Rehn's core message was: 'The markets' trust in Ireland's ability to service and repay its sovereign debt is battered. Ireland needs to credibly convince markets of its commitment to fiscal discipline.' Calls by trade union leaders for a modicum of flexibility were rebuffed on the grounds that 'financial markets will simply not allow Ireland to kick the can further down the road'.[28]

Let's pause for a second and reflect on what all this means. Unless I am mistaken, it means that an unelected bureaucrat flew from

Brussels to dictate what path the next Irish government must take in order to please something called the 'markets'. The understanding was that the 'bondholders' who would feature so prominently in the subsequent election campaign were integral to these 'markets' and that it was not permissible to incur their wrath. For the most part, both Irish politicians and EU officials have behaved as if they do not know the identity of these bondholders. Yet a list of Anglo Irish Bank's bondholders can be found on the internet. The list includes many German and French institutions (BNP Paribas, Frankfurt Trust Investment, Société Générale, Deutsche Asset Management), as well as titans of global finance like Barclays, Pioneer Investments and Goldman Sachs.[29]

While in Dublin, Rehn claimed that he 'extended the dialogue to civil society'. This didn't involve visiting deprived areas of the city to meet those who would have their incomes reduced by the 'fiscal consolidation' he was demanding. Rather, it involved giving a speech to the Institute of International and European Affairs (IIEA).[30] Presenting itself as Ireland's leading 'think tank' on EU policy, the IIEA is financed by a number of banks and multinational firms such as Goldman Sachs, Pioneer Investments, Google, Diageo, Bank of Ireland, BT and Shell.[31] (Alert readers will notice that the first two of these names also appear on the list of Anglo's bondholders). The IIEA has branches in both Dublin and Brussels and at the time of writing is chaired by Brendan Halligan, a former MEP with the Irish Labour Party, who spent many years as a tobacco lobbyist.[32] Halligan seems to believe that Ireland should be obsequious towards the markets at all times. In his preface to the IIEA's 2010 annual report, he argued that a decision by his compatriots to vote against two EU treaties (Nice and Lisbon) in the first decade of this century had amounted to a 'near-death experience' for Ireland. He did not present any evidence to back up this ridiculous assertion but indicated that Ireland should follow the strictures set by financial bodies in more powerful countries like Germany. 'Monetary union can only endure if the economic union upon which it rests is imbued with the "stability culture" so painstakingly fashioned by the Bundesbank and if it is managed in accordance with the demands of that culture,' he stated.[33]

THE DOGMA OF DYNAMISM

The IIEA belongs to a plethora of think tanks dedicated to European policy. A search in the European Commission's 'transparency register' suggests that it has 268 entries in the 'think tank and research institution' category.[34] With some exceptions, these outfits rely on private sector funding, putting paid to the notion that they are hotbeds of intellectual enquiry. The most prominent think tanks are really advocacy organisations in disguise. 'Lobbying is often seen as a dirty word but exercising influence through a think tank is more respectable and discreet,' according to Dieter Plehwe from the watchdog Lobbycontrol.[35]

Significantly, a number of think tanks opened offices in Brussels in the early part of this century, with the specific objective of helping to shape the Union's economic policies. The Lisbon Council for Economic Competiveness and Social Renewal is perhaps the glitziest of these new kids on the block. It was formed in 2003 to advance the so-called Lisbon strategy – a goal set by the EU's governments in 2000 to transform the Union into the world's most dynamic economy. The husband and wife team who established it – Paul Hofheinz and Ann Mettler – had both previously worked for the World Economic Forum, which is best known for bringing the world's wealthiest and most powerful individuals together in Davos, Switzerland every January. Mettler, an ebullient German, is adept at concocting sound bites. 'We want to be to competitiveness what Greenpeace is to the environment,' she said around the time that the Lisbon Council was launched.[36]

'Competitiveness' is a buzzword heard so constantly in Brussels that I suspect few of us who live and work in the city stop to ask what the concept entails. According to the European Commission, competitiveness involves the 'ability of an economy to provide its population with high and rising standards of living and a high level of employment, for all those willing to work, on a sustainable basis'.[37] In theory, this sounds like a policy designed to help every individual reach his or her potential. Yet the official definition jars with the way that leading industrialists and groups like the Lisbon Council view the idea. They regard it as an excuse to attack the living standards of ordinary people in the pursuit of profit. More specifically, they see 'competitiveness' as a quasi-religious doctrine whereby labour rights and the welfare state are systematically eroded. To all intents and purposes, then, competitiveness is a synonym for neo-liberalism.

The Lisbon Council's statutes say that its principal purpose is to 'provide an objective, non-partisan forum' for those interested in turning Europe into the world's 'most competitive and dynamic knowledge-based economy'.[38] A careful reading of its publications exposes this claim as hogwash. Advised by representatives of large firms like IBM, Nokia and Philips, the forum is not objective but ideologically blinkered.[39] In 2008, for example, Ann Mettler issued something of a manifesto to mark the think tank's fifth birthday. Although she kicked off by quoting Karl Marx ('Philosophers have hitherto only described the world in various ways. The point is to change it'), she revealed her true colours by applauding Margaret Thatcher's dogma of 'there is no alternative' to neo-liberal reforms, without being frank enough to acknowledge the Iron Lady's influence on her outlook. The essence of Mettler's case was that believers in competitiveness should think more about how to sell their ideas. She recommended that a PR offensive be developed in order to depict defenders of the welfare state as unreasonable. The European Commission should 'try to shore up progressives and reformers' in all of the pressure groups working on issues relating to competitiveness, she argued, including groups 'hostile or indifferent' to her agenda. She added: 'Any group which opposes raising the retirement age should answer how pay-as-you-go pension schemes will be made sustainable for the future; any group that opposes private funding for higher education should answer how they are going to raise the necessary public funds in view of precarious public finances.'[40]

There is scant evidence to support claims that the welfare state is simply too expensive or that profligacy in public spending is at the roots of Europe's economic malaise. On the contrary, there is voluminous evidence that it was the private sector – and more specifically the financial sector – which has led the European economy to a precipice. The corporate-funded think tanks and trade associations in Brussels, however, are determined not to allow the facts to get in the way of their narrative. The Lisbon Council regularly organises conferences at which keynote speakers recite similar, if not identical, mantras. In 2004, Lucas Papademos, a European Central Bank bigwig who went on to become an unelected prime minister in Greece, delivered one of the Lisbon Council's earliest lectures, in which he contended that ageing populations will put welfare systems under strain and imperil economic growth 'unless remedial action is taken'.[41] The following year, Raghuram Rajan, a high-level economist with the International Monetary Fund, suggested that the secret behind making the public swallow painful measures was to flag them long in advance so that 'by the time the date draws near, the preannounced reform has a life of its own and it is too late to fight it'.[42] And in 2008, another ECB board member,

Lorenzo Bini Smaghi, warned that 'a high level of employment protection legislation may have a particularly strong negative impact on industries experiencing rapid technological change.'[43]

Ann Mettler has tried to give a modern slant on 'competitiveness' by extolling the virtues of 'eco-innovation'.[44] The most discernible contribution that she has made to environmental protection, however, is that she has recycled messages delivered a decade before the Lisbon Council set up shop. In 1993 high flyers from seven corporations – including Volvo, Nestlé, Unilever and Fiat – signed a 'charter for Europe's industrial future'. Bound together as the European Roundtable of Industrialists (ERT), the group argued that competitiveness should be at the top of the agenda for policy-makers, with a particular emphasis on handing over responsibility for public services to the private sector. The ERT stated that the move to strengthen workers' rights in some countries 'alarms industry'. Pushing for a 'standstill' on new rules, the charter added: 'industry insists that a radical change of direction is needed'.[45]

Although the pale blue cover of this document looks dated, the plan outlined in it is still being followed in Brussels. Many of its key recommendations have been implemented; after copying and pasting the core objectives of the document into the 'Lisbon strategy' in 2000, the EU's governments bolstered the agenda by setting up a ministerial body dedicated to competitiveness two years later.[46] Not content with merely dictating the agenda, the ERT has been adamant that tangible results be achieved. With Gerhard Cromme from the German steel firm ThyssenKrupp as its president between 2001 and 2005, the ERT lamented that the implementation of the Lisbon strategy was 'lethargic and sporadic'. The ERT was enthusiastic about the introduction of euro notes and coins at the beginning of 2002. Yet when it published a history of its work in 2010, the ERT contended that the single currency was weakened by the aversion of some EU governments towards reducing public expenditure and that this aversion contributed to a perception that 'Europe continued to regress, being outperformed by US and Asian economies'.[47]

The ERT has jumped on the opportunities presented by the economic crisis of more recent times. In February 2010, it unveiled a fresh – or, perhaps more accurately, reheated – manifesto, titled *ERT's Vision for a Competitive Europe in 2025*. The manifesto was wrapped in a metaphorical green ribbon as it identified 'sustainability', a concept normally synonymous with the environment, as a vital principle. Yet it was clear that the ERT had not turned into a polar bear conservation club. The first section of the manifesto implied that sustainability should be applied as much to public finances as to energy efficiency. One of its top recommendations was that an EU-wide audit of public pensions should be carried out and that a 'road map' be developed to 'guide their prudential reform'. Another call was that social security systems should be reassessed 'to strike a better balance between social cohesion and financial sustainability by, for example, placing greater emphasis on patients' responsibility for healthcare costs'.[48]

There was a chilling level of similarity between this manifesto and the 'Euro Plus Pact' agreed by governments belonging to the single currency little over a year later. Under the pact, governments committed themselves to reviewing wage indexation schemes (whereby workers' pay increases in line with inflation) and addressing the 'sustainability of pensions, health care and social benefits'. The reforms that may prove 'necessary', the pact stated, 'could include' raising the age of retirement.[49] Leif Johansson, a Volvo executive who was then the ERT's president, swiftly endorsed the pact, predicting that it would bring the attainment of the key objectives in his organisation's manifesto 'closer'.[50]

It is not hard to see why the Euro Plus Pact offers much lobbying potential for the likes of the ERT. While the pact sets a clear goal of eviscerating Europe's welfare states, it leaves some of the details of this evisceration open to further discussion. In order to fill in the gaps, the ERT has come forward with more demands. In October 2011, it issued a prescription to enable employers to sack workers and close down factories without having to worry about the impact this would have on families and communities. 'A re-balancing is required between unemployment benefits, transition support, redundancy payments and notice periods,' the prescription stated. 'Companies should not be forced to compensate former employees for their income loss through excessively high redundancy payments.'[51]

ETERNAL AUSTERITY?

One of the most frequent design flaws identified in the euro is that it involves a monetary union, without a proper fiscal union. The corollary of that argument is that it is now important to set common fiscal rules for all countries that have adopted the currency. While undoubtedly the euro lacked proper foundations, I am nonetheless convinced that the architects of the euro always hoped it would lead to the erosion of the welfare state. I have formed this belief after analysing the work of the Association for the Monetary Union of Europe (AMUE), a corporate club that drew up a blueprint for the currency.

The AMUE was formally established in 1987. According to the official narrative, it was the brainchild of Valéry Giscard d'Estaing, the former French president, and Helmut Schmidt, the former German chancellor.[52] Only a moist-eyed federalist could swallow that version of events. A document held by the French national archives indicates that the steering committee for the association was set up in 1986. Far from being a response to a polite request from two statesmen, the AMUE represented a ploy by leading industrialists to alter the nature of the European economy. Headquartered in the eight *arrondissement* of Paris, the association was composed of 400 private firms or trade associations. They included Goldman Sachs (of course), Deutsche Bank, Total, Siemens, Volkswagen and British American Tobacco. The employers' confederation UNICE (now called BusinessEurope) was there, too, along with some US companies such as the private health insurance behemoth Cigna.[53]

In 1988, the association came forward with an action plan for monetary union. Many of its points were rehashed by Jacques Delors, then the European Commission president, when he presented his 'vision' on this topic the following year. By calling for the complete liberalisation of capital movements, Delors set out to fulfil some of the bankers' wildest fantasies.[54] A foretaste of the anti-welfare measures approved by EU leaders more recently can be seen in the so-called 'convergence criteria' applying to eurozone economies. From an early stage, the requirement that public spending be cut so that deficits did not exceed 3 per cent of gross domestic product led to increased austerity for millions of Europeans. The AMUE used quasi-religious terms to justify the human suffering inflicted as its plan was put into effect. 'The convergence path to EMU [economic and monetary union] seems to have been a painful purgatory to a better life in EMU,' the association declared in one report. 'Whether paradise is eternal remains to be seen.'[55]

Safe in the knowledge that shiny euro coins would soon go into circulation, the AMUE declared its mission accomplished and dissolved itself in October 2001. Yet several of the association's staff members have continued to dispense their 'wisdom' at various forums. As its director of research, Stefan Collignon appears to have been the most prolific analyst in the AMUE. A few years after leaving that post, he wrote a 2002 paper for Harvard University in the US. In it, he advocated giving the European Commission the power to instruct national governments what their budgets should contain.[56] Collignon was still up to his old tricks a decade later, when he was contracted to advise the European Parliament on 'competitiveness'. In a 2012 paper for the Parliament's economic and monetary affairs committee, he concluded that a 'much more aggressive debate' about economic governance was needed. The primary area of focus for this debate should be wage restraint, he added.[57]

Despite the often turgid nature of his writing, Collignon's key recommendations chimed neatly with those of powerful clubs like BusinessEurope. Having been intimately involved in the deliberations leading to the euro's introduction, the employers' group continues to shape policies designed to shore up the currency. With almost no public debate, half a dozen new EU measures on economic governance came into effect in December 2011, having been shepherded through the Union's main institutions with a haste that has few, if any, precedents. Known colloquially as the 'Six Pack', these laws enabled the imposition of financial penalties on governments who spend too much on social services for the European Commission's liking. (The regulation puts things in a more arcane manner by referring to 'excessive deficit procedures'.)[58] To make the rules even more binding they were subsequently enshrined in the EU's core rulebook through the so-called 'fiscal treaty'. Ireland was the only country where this charter for austerity was put to the electorate; the Irish referendum was carried after the Dublin government warned that rejection would have dire consequences for jobs and investment.[59]

José Manuel Barroso, the European Commission's president, was in little doubt about the significance of these measures. After a decision paving the way for the 'Six Pack' was taken by the EU's governments in 2010, Barroso told a conference in Florence that a 'silent revolution' was in progress.[60] Given that the Brussels institutions have acquired more power in an anti-democratic fashion, it would probably have been more apt to speak of a coup. As befits coups, it involved both silence and stealth. The Commission has admitted that discussions about the 'Six Pack' took place between Olli Rehn and the BusinessEurope chief Philippe de Buck.[61] When I asked for details of these talks, the Commission stated that no minutes or records have been kept. If this is true, then it means Europe's welfare states are being dismantled partly on the basis of a few cosy chats between bureaucrats and businessmen.

We can get a flavour of what was likely to have been discussed by examining a few of BusinessEurope's policy papers. In February

2010, the group issued a 38-page 'action plan' for 'combining fiscal sustainability and growth'. Noting that public spending accounts for an average of 48 per cent of GDP across the EU, BusinessEurope argued that savings could be achieved if the private sector was given greater responsibility for providing essential services, including water and transport. A 'minimum requirement would be to ensure equal treatment of public and private operators,' it added, in an apparent call for widespread privatisation. Its section on medicine was especially troubling. According to BusinessEurope, there should be a higher 'degree of competition among providers of care and health insurance companies in order to make the system more efficient and innovative'. As part of this 'efficiency' drive, it urged an evaluation of regional hospitals, indicating that they should be subject to hard-headed cost benefit analyses, rather than a namby-pamby assessment of whether they are providing life-saving operations to people in small towns and rural areas.[62]

BusinessEurope fleshed out some of its recommendations a bit more in June that year. Demanding 'forceful corrective measures in case of indiscipline', it said that fiscal rectitude should 'privilege expenditure restraints' rather than tax increases.[63] It went further again in the Spring of 2011 by stating: 'In these times of fiscal entrenchment, business sees in most parts of Europe, the need to rethink the role of the public sector, readjusting its size and level to a new economic reality' and advocating that a ceiling on public spending be set in 18 countries, including France, Greece, Ireland, Britain, Spain and Portugal.[64] Whereas it generally offers a panoramic view of EU matters, BusinessEurope has become increasingly meddlesome in the internal affairs of national governments. Its annual 'benchmarking' report for 2012 stated that 'reform' of healthcare and pensions should be one of the top three priorities for the Netherlands, France, Finland, Belgium and Italy. Spain and Britain were told to put the emphasis on 'public sector efficiency'. To give its case some extra heft, BusinessEurope underscored that its country-specific recommendations were drawn up by national federations of employers. Peer pressure was vital to keep up the momentum for 'reform', according to BusinessEurope.[65]

GREED v. NEED

Spain offers a frightening insight into the results of the reforms being demanded. A study published by the journal *Clinical Medicine* in 2012 showed how Mariano Rajoy's centre-right administration had 'fundamentally reworked the healthcare system' within less than twelve months. Whereas all residents had previously been entitled to free medical attention, access to care has now been linked to employment. The upshot is that Spain is becoming more like the US, where medical entitlements are also connected to holding a job. In the measured words of Martin McKee, a public health professor, and the other academics behind the study, 'this creates a potentially serious situation in Spain, where over half of all youth are unemployed'.[66]

Rajoy has maintained that his overhaul of healthcare and other austerity measures have been motivated by 'common sense'.[67] Naturally, this begs the question: who benefits from this common sense? Jobless 23-year-olds obviously do not but there is a powerful private health industry that stands to gain if given greater control over health systems. The Spanish 'reforms' should be seen in the context of what is happening throughout the EU as part of a coordinated effort to privatise medicine in the name of competitiveness. While the Spanish case might be extreme, the groundwork has been laid for similar transformations elsewhere. Indeed, the crisis has allowed the Brussels institutions to acquire powers that they were unable to obtain under less straitened circumstances.

For most of the EU's history, responsibility for health issues has been guarded jealously by national governments. When the European Commission started dabbling more in health matters during the 1990s, it confined itself largely to awareness-raising activities on cancer and AIDS; the likelihood of it having a say in how hospitals would be run still seemed remote. This changed in the first decade of the new century when an attempt was made to have healthcare included in a controversial law aimed at opening up the services sector to greater competition. After a long battle with trade unions, healthcare was removed from the scope of the services directive in 2006.[68]

By the end of that decade, however, the European Parliament had voted to let greed triumph over need. In April 2009, the assembly approved a law on 'patient mobility', whereby someone in one EU country would be able to travel to another for medical treatment and then seek reimbursement from the social security schemes of their own home state. The most troubling aspect of the assembly's vote was that it agreed that the mobility dossier should fall under those provisions in the EU's treaty dealing with the single market, rather than those relating to health.[69] Though this may sound abstruse, it meant that MEPs were according more rights to people who can afford to travel abroad for operations than those who cannot.

By treating medicine as a matter for individuals and – at least partly – the market, the Parliament was giving an 'up yours' salute to the ethos behind the welfare state, under which healthcare is viewed as a question of collective rights. This ethos was explained succinctly by Nye Bevan, the Labour politician who played a vital role in setting up Britain's National Health Service in the 1940s: 'no society can legitimately call itself civilised if a sick person is denied medical aid because of lack of means'.[70] Indeed, it is no accident that some of the most gung-ho champions of the EU's patient mobility law in 2009 belonged to the Liberal Democrats, a party that would soon try to destroy the NHS when it formed a coalition with the Conservatives. Graham Watson, a long-standing Liberal MEP, spelled out a vision that was at odds with Bevan's when he told me: 'The best way to improve services for all is to make sure that the supply of treatment is of the best possible quality, and the best way to ensure this goal is to ensure that there is a healthy competition among suppliers, so that patients and authorities are free to choose the best offer among several.'[71]

Free to Choose happened to be the title of a television series narrated by Milton Friedman and first broadcast in 1980.[72] The views expressed by Friedman are broadly in keeping with those of Watson and his fellow Liberal MEPs, who are seeking that the principle of consumer choice should be equally applied to mobile phones as to heart surgery despite how they are radically different. As nobody's wellbeing depends on the number of 'apps' he or she can download, it is arguably not that big a deal for society if bog-standard mobiles are sold at £70 but the more sophisticated ones are sold at £700. The same logic should not be applied to heart surgery as the quality of this service on offer can literally be a matter of life and death. The 'healthy competition among suppliers' sought by Watson means that a richer heart disease victim could be prioritised over a poorer one.

It is no coincidence that when I asked the trade association Insurance Europe what it considered to be the most important dossier relating to healthcare in recent years, it pointed to the patient mobility law. Janina Clark, the group's spokeswoman, was not totally upfront about its agenda, though. She said: 'Insurance Europe does not advocate the privatisation of care of services currently provided by the public sector. It sees public and private healthcare provision as complementary.' Asked if there were any aspects of the American healthcare system that her group wished to see in Europe, Clark replied 'no'.[73] A markedly different message can be found in a 2011 policy paper by the same organisation, which was then known by the acronym CEA. After noting that more than 77 per cent of healthcare financing comes from the public purse throughout the EU (the figure is for 2006), CEA listed what it perceived as the advantages to private medical insurance. Among them were that 'consumers receive better access to healthcare and are offered better quality care as well as a higher level of reimbursement than with public healthcare systems' and that private insurance 'offers consumers more freedom of choice (e.g. when treatment takes place, by which specialist and in which hospital)'. The paper went on to exhort a 'level playing field' between the public sector and private firms in the provision of services. 'State intervention in a competitive market should be minimal,' the paper added, telling legislators to stay out of issues like 'product design' and 'risk assessment'.[74]

Despite Clark's claims that Insurance Europe does not want an American-style health system this side of the Atlantic, her organisation's rhetoric bears more than a passing resemblance to that of leading Republicans in the US. Here's the core message on medical insurance that Mitt Romney delivered when he ran – unsuccessfully – for president in 2012: 'Competition drives improvements in efficiency and effectiveness, offering consumers higher quality goods and services at lower cost. It can have the same effect in the health care system, if given the chance to work.'[75]

Wendell Potter, a former spokesman for the American insurer Cigna, has blown the whistle on what the kind of 'competition' favoured by Romney means. 'Insurance companies essentially have the power to make life or death decisions,' Potter has written. He has highlighted specific examples of insurers seeking to avoid covering operations recommended by doctors because of business considerations.[76]

I contacted Potter after being tipped off that Cigna was becoming more active on the EU scene and had turned to the Brussels office of the global public relations firm Fleishman-Hillard for assistance. Potter said that Fleishman had been hired by Cigna in the US while he was still with the company. 'It would not surprise me to learn that Cigna is using Fleishman-Hillard's offices in Europe to help advance the company's agenda in targeted countries,' he added. Potter had a pithy response when I asked him if he thought Cigna wished to see an American-style health system in Europe: 'Yes, without a doubt.'

He said:

The insurance industry and its allies in the US frequently talk about the benefit of competition in the US healthcare system. But competition has not led to expanded coverage of US citizens or controlled medical costs. In fact, there is plenty of evidence that our multi-payer system contributed to our most intractable problems. Europeans should become much more familiar with the US healthcare system and how it is failing more and more Americans every day. I learned when I was in London last year [2011] that people, even those who are leaders in healthcare, know little about the US system and are shocked when they begin to study it. European media should help educate people on just how bad things are because of the fact that private, for-profit corporations have taken over the healthcare system and are more interested in meeting shareholders' expectations than meeting the needs of American citizens.[77]

For its part, Fleishman-Hillard claimed that its relationship with Cigna was limited to 'a one-off project' relating to an 'acquisition in Belgium'. Anita Kelly, an associate director of Fleishman's Brussels office, said her firm did not have any reservations about working with Cigna, despite how Potter and other American campaigners had drawn attention to cases where private medical firms in the US put commercial considerations ahead of patients' needs. Cheekily, I enquired if Fleishman had any views on the ethics of healthcare and if it accepted that everyone should be entitled to the same level of service regardless of his or her ability to pay. 'Healthcare is indeed a human right,' Kelly replied. 'However, we are a communications consultancy – therefore, we are not experts in the best way to provide healthcare services.'[78]

John Bowis, on the other hand, is someone who presents himself as an expert on such topics. Following a stint as a health minister in Britain from 1992 to 1996, Bowis was elected a Conservative member of the European Parliament in 1999.[79] Although he ceased being an MEP in Brussels a decade later, Bowis has continued to shuttle between London and Brussels. Bowis has been recruited by several PR firms since leaving office.[80] These include Hanover, a consultancy which numbers the pharmaceutical corporation Merck among its recent clients.[81] They also include Finsbury International Policy and Regulatory Advisers (FIPRA), which had the insurer Axa and the drugs companies Eli Lilly and Pfizer on its roster during 2011.[82]

As if that wasn't keeping him sufficiently busy, Bowis heads Health First Europe, a discussion group run by Policy Action (another consultancy availing of his services).[83] Given his background in the Tories and his role as a corporate lobbyist, I asked Bowis if he was trying to dismantle the form of healthcare that can be found in many EU countries. 'Far from it,' he said. 'I am totally committed to our own welfare state [in the UK].'[84] Not only should any declaration of love for the welfare state emanating from a Tory mouth be treated with scepticism, it should be stressed that Health First Europe encompasses groups that are in favour of privatising medical care. This is particularly so with the European Union of Private Hospitals (known by its French acronym UEHP). In a contribution to a Health First Europe publication on how healthcare should be provided in the year 2050, two UEHP representatives, Max Poinseillé and Paolo Giardano, wrote: 'Financial sustainability has become a basic concept in the field of healthcare. There are too many public structures that benefit from a monopoly that does not work efficiently and that raises the public debt and by consequence taxation. Free competition and liberalisation of services are necessary to improve the European economy.'[85]

The UEHP acts on behalf of 1,300 private hospitals in France and 700 in Italy. 'These are real, pure hospitals, not aesthetic clinics,' Giardano said, explaining that many of their patients have their treatment bills covered by the national health authorities. The fact that some are located in working class areas such as the Saint Denis area of Paris means that 'there is no more discussion saying we are hospitals for the rich,' he added.

After trumpeting this willingness to treat the low-paid and the unemployed, Giardano laid out a more cut-throat vision:

All public hospitals can receive state aid without control. We think that this is a waste of money. We don't receive anything. At the end of the year, if we are negative [incurring a loss], we just close. Public hospitals still receive money. The delivery of services should be under the rules of competition. If you are bad, you close. Caring for patients is exactly the same for us as it is for public hospitals. But without competition, you don't have improvements. Without innovation, you don't improve the system. You need some rules so that only the best ones survive.[86]

This kind of thinking has been key to the debate over the future of Britain's National Health Service. As well as being instrumental in setting up the NHS, Labour (or, at least, that party's leadership) has plotted its downfall. It was Tony Blair who advanced the concept that healthcare should be treated as any other business by turning to privatisation advocates like Julian Le Grand and Paul Corrigan for counsel. As Colin Crouch discusses in his book *The Strange Non-Death of Neoliberalism*, these 'policy experts' tried to replace the public service ethos of the NHS with one guided more by financial incentives.[87]

Corrigan, a professor with Imperial College London, advised Blair between 2005 and 2007.[88] Before that he helped Alan Milburn and John Reid, both of whom served as health secretaries under Blair, hand over the running of many hospitals to foundation trusts. Corrigan has claimed that the reforms he helped design were not tantamount to privatisation and that backbench Labour MPs who revolted against the reforms were mistaken.[89] Yet pamphlets that Corrigan has subsequently written are less ambiguous. In a paper published by the think tank Reform in September 2012, Corrigan stated that 'two organisations' had the 'skill and capacity' to take over 'failing NHS hospitals'. The two organisations were his beloved foundation trusts and the private sector. The paper acknowledged that David Cameron's government had pledged to give the private sector a bigger role in health but had not delivered on this pledge as swiftly as Corrigan wanted.[90] Reform, incidentally, is financed by Sodexo and Serco, two firms that provide services to schools and hospitals, as well as by the insurer Aviva and the drugs-maker GSK.[91]

After learning that Corrigan visited Brussels to speak at a seminar in March 2012, I enquired if he was playing any particular role in the development of EU health policy. Corrigan responded by saying that he did not address EU health policy at the seminar and had 'no interest in it'. He said 'it was an accident of geography that the meeting was in Brussels and not because it is home to the EU'.[92] I don't buy his explanation: the seminar he attended was hosted by the Stockholm Network, which is part of a grouping of more than 100 'market-oriented' think tanks on this continent. The programme for the event stated that its purpose was 'to present to us a new vision of the healthcare future and to ask what Europe needs to do to make it a reality'.[93]

The Stockholm Network was founded by Helen Disney, a former *Times* journalist, who has argued that 'leaving the NHS unreformed will ultimately bankrupt it'.[94] I made repeated requests to Disney about who is financing the network's activities in Brussels, yet did not receive any reply. From checking its website in late 2012, it appeared that the network had not published its annual report online for a few years. The 'supporters' listed in its annual report for 2007 included Nuffield, a group of private hospitals, along with pharmaceutical companies like Pfizer and Merck.[95]

Health seems to be viewed as an increasingly hot topic among policy wonks. The European Policy Centre (EPC), perhaps the most prominent think tank in Brussels, runs a health programme in conjunction with Johnson & Johnson. 'Everything is quite transparent,' Annika Ahtonen from the EPC told me, adding that the centre decides what topics should be addressed at its events but checks with Johnson & Johnson that 'we're on the right line'.[96] To test out this transparency, I requested a copy of the contract signed between her centre and Johnson & Johnson. Although Ahtonen divulged that Johnson & Johnson contributed €55,000 to her health programme each year in 2011 and 2012, she could 'see no reason to provide you with a copy of the agreement' that the EPC had with the firm. Ahtonen wondered why I wanted to see the contract. I indicated that – in the absence of evidence to the contrary – I would have to surmise that her programme was a front group for the drugs industry. 'I'm sorry to hear that this is your assumption,' she replied.[97]

Luckily, Brussels has not been plagued with 'astro-turf' groups – fake grassroots organisations funded by corporations to give the impression that they have widespread public support – in the way that the US has been. I was shocked, all the same, to discover that some organisations purporting to defend the rights of people with illnesses are heavily reliant on private companies for funding. The European Patients' Forum (EPF) says that one of its main objectives is 'to combat discrimination on the grounds of illness and address health inequalities from the perspective of patients'. Over half of the EPF's 2011 budget of €790,000 came from pharmaceutical companies.[98] Nicola Bedlington, the EPF's director, said that her forum has never turned down money from a corporation. Asked if there were any types of companies that were not welcome to finance her activities, she said: 'We do not have a specific exclusion list but we would not accept funding from the tobacco, alcohol or arms industry.'[99]

The European Foundation for the Care of Newborn Infants (EFCNI), meanwhile, lists Nestlé Nutrition as a 'premium partner'. An advert for the Swiss multinational on the EFCNI website celebrates how Henri Nestlé's 'infants' flour' was first given to a baby born prematurely in 1867 and that the child in question lived for more than 60 years.[100] I was curious to find out why the EFCNI was in a partnership with Nestlé, when that firm remained the target of an international consumer boycott campaign over reports that it had used aggressive tactics to convince mothers in poor countries that buying baby milk is preferable to breastfeeding.[101] Silke Mader, the ECFNI's chief, told me her foundation was committed to transparency but did not answer my question about how much it receives from Nestlé. I requested that she supply me with the minutes of all meetings held by an 'interest group' that the EFCNI runs within the European Parliament. According to her, 'no formal minutes' had been taken.[102]

I'm not alleging that a foundation focused on babies has an ulterior motive. Yet any organisation that is less than frank about its activities leaves itself open to suspicion. With a debate as important as the future of healthcare, the least we should be able to expect is full disclosure about who each participant in that debate represents and what its real intentions are.

Warriors against the welfare state have achieved a great deal in just a few years. Based on the evidence that is available, there are solid reasons to believe that corporations and their lackeys in EU institutions have their minds set on achieving a decisive and lasting victory for capital over labour. By favouring cutbacks to public services and the compression of wages instead of corporate tax hikes, the austerity agenda has led to a 'formidably regressive redistribution of income', in the words of Greek economist Costas Lapavitsas.[103]

The worst may still be to come. Ryanair, the no-frills airline, has been badgering the European Commission to propose a law that would ban strikes among air traffic controllers. So far, the Commission appears to have resisted this pressure on the basis that the right to strike is a fundamental right.[104] It would be comforting to dismiss Ryanair and its chief executive Michael O'Leary as attention-seekers. It would also be foolish to do so. Budget airlines are not simply interested in making our flights cheaper and our lives hell if we try to check in items of luggage that they deem as surplus to requirements. Rather, they are striving to wreck as many regulations that they perceive as hostile to business as possible. This much was underscored by John Hanlon from the European Low Fares Airline Association when I listened to him spar with a trade union activist. 'I heard competition described earlier as some kind of evil ideology,' Hanlon said. 'Well, if it is, I'm all for it.'[105]

Ryanair's machinations follow a series of rulings by the European Court of Justice that were hostile to workers' rights. Nor should it be forgotten that one of the first concrete steps taken by Ronald Reagan in his neo-liberal crusade was to crush a strike by air traffic controllers.[106]

The welfare state is at the core of everything that makes Europe decent. Without it, we would not have the 'values' to which EU politicians constantly profess attachment. But we know from history – much of it recent – that hard-won gains can be rapidly unravelled and that rights mean little unless they are defended vigorously and relentlessly.

2
Bombarded by bankers

By an intriguing historical quirk, one of the politicians who has been most successful in giving practical effect to the teachings of Margaret Thatcher is an Irish Catholic. Charlie McCreevy spent the 1980s on the back benches of Dáil Eireann, the lower house in his country's parliament. To reveal himself as a staunch admirer of the Iron Lady would have been unthinkable at that time as the County Kildare man belonged to a republican family.[1] It wasn't until 2005 that he plucked up the courage to fully emerge from the closet by praising Thatcher for how she had 'effectively transformed' the British economy. Europe needed leaders like her, he argued.[2]

By that time, McCreevy was the EU's commissioner for its single market in goods and services. His portfolio gave him responsibility for overseeing a project that was dear to his heroine's heart. Despite her reputedly fractious relationship with the Brussels institutions, Thatcher has described the complete removal of restrictions on trade within the then European community as her 'one overriding positive goal'.[3]

McCreevy used his stint with the Union's executive to assert the primacy of competition over such irritants to enterprise as rights for workers. Earlier in 2005, he declared it 'extraordinary' that MEPs had the temerity to question him over how he rallied to the support of the Latvian construction company Laval, which interpreted EU law as an invitation to flout Swedish pay agreements while building a school near Stockholm.[4]

As Ireland's finance minister from 1997 to 2004, McCreevy had stimulated a property boom by dramatically reducing capital gains tax.[5] This encouraged a speculation binge that was patently unsustainable and ultimately led to the crisis that later hit Ireland without mercy.[6] McCreevy behaved in a comparably irresponsible manner after he moved to Brussels. Few other EU commissioners displayed the same deep-rooted aversion to regulation and oversight that he did. Few others had the chutzpah to brag of how they deliberately failed to perform duties required of them, as McCreevy did in 2009, when he admitted ignoring how Spain was using a form of accounting for banks that concealed the real profits and losses made by companies.[7] (The reason cited by McCreevy for how he gave the nod to 'dynamic provisioning', as the type of accounting practised in Spain was known, was that he remembered fondly the days when Irish banks were more secretive.)[8]

McCreevy sold his philosophy as being prudent. 'We should not and cannot prescribe rules for every conceivable situation,' he wrote in a 2007 opinion piece for the *Wall Street Journal*. 'There is a difference between accountancy and rocket science. The latter is science; the former is not and shouldn't be. As an accountant by profession, I might be expected to empathise with the urge some regulators seem to have to control every detail. But I think that box-ticking alone doesn't work.'[9]

His straight-talking provided a cover for an ideological conviction that capitalist buccaneers should be free to amass profits regardless of the consequences. This attitude was taken to an extreme when it came to hedge funds.

Contrary to what McCreevy hinted, it was not necessary to be a rocket scientist to realise that the type of activity hedge funds engaged in was bound to prove catastrophic, especially if it was not subject to strict controls. Short selling is an abstruse practice whereby a financial whizz-kid borrows shares and sells them based on the prediction that their value will drop, then buys them back once the fall has materialised, making a tidy profit. The activity predates blackberries and the other paraphernalia of modern finance. Short selling had been undertaken in the 1920s but was deemed 'too racy' by investors nominally taking care of other people's savings after the stock market crash of 1929, according to Sebastian Mallaby's book on hedge funds *More Money Than God*.[10]

The flourishing of hedge funds in recent times can largely be traced to the tax cuts for rich Americans introduced by Ronald Reagan in 1982. These wealthy folk had to do something with the gargantuan sums at their disposal; gambling on markets proved a popular option. When Jack Nash founded a prototype hedge fund in 1983, he had $50 million worth of capital. By 2007, there were 10,000 hedge funds in the world, with total assets nearing $2 trillion.[11]

The concentration of so much money in the hands of such a small number of people did not trouble McCreevy. Shortly after he stepped down as a commissioner in 2010, McCreevy vigorously defended his record at a conference in London. He accused left-leaning MEPs of treating hedge funds as 'scapegoats', insisting 'there was no evidence whatsoever' that hedge funds contributed to the economic crisis in either Europe or the US.

'The managers of these funds were presented as locusts and asset strippers – descriptions that won the kind of easy headlines that were and are part of the bread and butter of life for socialists seeking to appeal to their domestic, home member state audiences,' he said. 'Resisting this pressure required firmness, doggedness, consistency and determination. But resist it I did because I was not convinced – and I am still not today – that either hedge funds or private equity need intrusive regulation.'

In that speech, McCreevy distanced himself from José Manuel Barroso, an ideological kindred spirit who had been his boss a few months earlier. According to McCreevy, Barroso had hurriedly introduced proposals to regulate hedge funds as his first term as European Commission president drew to a close. This was because Barroso was 'desirous of a second term' and was 'sharply attuned' to the wishes of the European Parliament and some EU governments, McCreevy added. Because it was prepared so hurriedly, McCreevy added, the proposal probably caught hedge funds 'off guard' and 'without the kind of lobbying resources and know-how that are a feature of many other parts of the financial services industry.'[12]

He was wrong on two counts. First, there were strong reasons to believe that hedge funds helped spark the economic crisis. Hedge funds may not have been the originators of the subprime-backed 'securities' that proved to be toxic in the US in 2007. Yet there could not have been a mass market for these securities without hedge funds.[13] The problems of lax regulation were compounded by the false financial picture painted of some hedge funds. This was recognised by America's Securities and Exchange Commission in 2008 when it charged two former senior asset managers in Bear Stearns with fraudulently misleading investors over the state of the bank's two largest hedge funds.[14]

And secondly, the hedge fund industry was able to marshal considerable resources to counter the perceived threat posed by the proposal demanded by Barroso. The industry was also quite familiar with how Brussels worked: McCreevy and the department he headed helped it to be. Niall Bohan, an EU official known as loyal to his compatriot McCreevy, coordinated an 'expert group' on hedge fund regulation in 2006. Its 16 members all hailed from the financial services sector. Among the banks represented were Goldman Sachs, Morgan Stanley and Deutsche Bank. Predictably, the group's report advocated a hands-off approach.[15]

The hasty preparation of the alternative investment fund managers directive – as the law on hedge funds was called – worked to the financial sector's advantage. MEPs sitting on the committees handling the dossier found themselves deluged with requests to table detailed amendments. An internal European Parliament document indicates that many of the amendments were sent to MEPs within an extremely tight timeframe – possibly as tight as within one week of draft papers outlining the assembly's likely response to the proposal being circulated.[16]

Anyone who attempted to read through these amendments – as I did – would be struck by how technical many of them were. The only people who could have provided that level of specific detail at such short notice are financial service insiders. In total, 1,600 amendments were considered by the Parliament's economic and monetary affairs committee; a large number of amendments also went before its legal affairs committee, which was tasked with assessing part of the dossier.[17] A Parliament source who followed the hedge fund debate closely told me that about 80 per cent of these proposed amendments were written by financial service lobbyists and then signed by MEPs.[18]

The Commission's proposal was by no means radical. It was designed to ensure that there would be some scrutiny of fund managers handling portfolios exceeding €100 million. Yet it left the hedge funds and private equity industries free to develop their own investment policies. Interfering in policies would be 'unnecessarily restrictive,' according to an explanatory memo from EU officials.[19]

Moreover, the new rules would be easy to circumvent. Poul Nyrup Rasmussen, the former Danish prime minister whose vociferous criticism of hedge funds and private equity led him to being branded their most 'dangerous opponent', pointed out that managers would be able to escape supervision by chopping up their portfolios so that each one would contain less than €100 million.[20] (Rasmussen was an MEP from 2004 to 2009, during which time he presented the Parliament with an 'own-initiative' report – a policy paper that is not a formal response to a specific legislative proposal – on hedge funds and private equity.)[21]

A HUG FOR TAX HAVENS

The moderate nature of the Commission's proposal did not prevent some financial interest groups from depicting it as a threat to Europe's economy. Deutsche Bank prepared a response which it marked 'confidential and not for distribution'. It predicted that the 'proposed rules would negatively impact economic growth in the EU'. No sources were cited to back up that prediction.

Deutsche Bank's scaremongering zoomed in on a requirement in the proposal that funds located in 'offshore' centres would have to sign agreements on taxation in order to do business in the EU. As 'not all third country regimes will be able' to comply with such provisions, 'the consequence of this would most likely be a dramatic decrease in choice for EU professional investors which will not be in their interests,' Deutsche Bank warned.[22]

The provisions in question were of particular relevance to the Cayman Islands, a tax haven officially classified as a British overseas territory which has the dubious distinction of hosting three-quarters of the world's hedge funds and 'one cinema', according to the investigative journalist Nicholas Shaxson.[23] Each hedge fund registered with the Cayman Islands Monetary Authority has been given a 100-year exemption from tax.[24]

With close links between the City of London and the Cayman Islands, the battle against EU hedge fund regulation was largely interpreted as a battle to defend the Anglo-Saxon model of capitalism. Boris Johnson, the flamboyant mayor of London, was the best-known figure who hopped on the Eurostar to Brussels as part of efforts to dilute the proposal.[25]

A core argument used by City lobbyists was that the new rules would hamper efforts to 'innovate'; this case relied on the flimsy assumption that new financial 'products' could be presented as benefits to humanity in the same way as breakthroughs in medical research. The Hedge Fund Standards Board (HFSB) is an alliance of fund managers who stated that they wish to 'minimise the need for restrictive regulation' of their industry.[26] In a discussion document, it suggested that the new rules would hamper its efforts to fuel 'the Darwinian process' in the financial sector and implementation of the rules would lead to 'not the kind of Europe we want to achieve'. Describing the proposal as 'protectionist' (a dirty word in Brussels circles), the HFSB contended that its clauses aimed at tax havens contradicted the policy of the Group of 20 (G20) leading economies to keep markets open.[27] Thomas Deinet, the board's director, played down the importance of his lobbying when I contacted him. 'It is not our role to draft amendments,' he said, although adding that if MEPs were influenced by the HFSB's recommended standards 'we welcome that'.[28]

The Alternative Investment Management Association (AIMA) – which represents hedge funds throughout the world – also tried to have the tax havens clauses erased from the rules. 'Tax issues do not belong in a directive aimed specifically at a small section of the asset management industry,' said its director Florence Lombard.[29]

Sharon Bowles, an MEP with Britain's Liberal Democrats, signed a large number of amendments to the proposal. When I put it to her that the arguments she made to justify them resembled almost verbatim those in position papers from the financial sector, she replied that she was 'in communication with all sides'. She added: 'so the answer to your questions as to whether any amendments have parts that may have been written or promoted by interest groups is yes, but this is never done blindly or from a point of ignorance. When the subject matter is complicated, it is essential to get technical advice.'[30]

Bowles is an influential figure within the Parliament. At the time of writing, she holds the coveted position of chairwoman of its economic and monetary affairs committee. Her claim to consult with 'all sides' does not tally with information contained on her own website. A list of meetings that she holds indicates that she and her staff spend far more time talking to financial lobbyists, EU officials and politicians than to fighters for social justice. A sample for one particular month (May, the year is not specified) gives details of 15 meetings; it shows that her office welcomed representatives of Goldman Sachs, Insurance Europe and the International Swaps and Directives Association but did not meet anyone who could be viewed as hostile to capitalism during that period.[31]

Klaus-Heiner Lehne, a long-standing MEP with Germany's centre-right Christian Democrats, organised a 'mini-hearing' within the Parliament on the hedge fund rules. The programme for the event featured two speakers: one from Deutsche Bank; the other from the 'think tank' Re-Define.[32] Like Bowles, Lehne cannot be dismissed as an isolated figure. At the time of the discussion on hedge funds, he was chairman of the Parliament's legal affairs committee, which was formally tasked with presenting a response to the proposed rules. A more impartial chairman would surely have made sure that the speakers at his hearing offered different perspectives. Re-Define's team of 'experts', however, includes Chris Rose, formerly of Goldman Sachs, who has helped run a number of hedge funds and John Fullerton, previously a managing director with J.P. Morgan.[33] These are not the kind of 'experts' likely to offer a searing indictment of Wall Street and the City of London.

Another key argument used by financial lobbyists was that the proposed new rules were too broad. Investments by charities and pension funds could be affected by this breadth, the argument went. 'The financial services world is not like chemicals, where there is a chemical signature for everything,' a lobbyist who drafted some of the amendments tabled by MEPs said, on condition of anonymity. 'It is a lot more disorganised than people give it credit for.'[34] The same lobbyist claimed that hedge funds and private equity were the victims of 'vendetta politics' as Poul Nyrup Rasmussen was angered by how private equity firms had taken over the Danish telecommunications company TDC, incurring significant debts.[35]

Lehne proved especially receptive to arguments made by Deutsche Bank and other big players in global finance. Several amendments under his name sought to weaken the suggested clauses that were ostensibly aimed at reducing tax avoidance by hedge funds. Unless the rules were altered, he contended, they would harm Europe's pensions industry.[36] His case was unconvincing: savings made by ordinary people in preparation for their retirement should not be vehicles for gambling and corporate tax avoidance. I asked Lehne if private sector interest groups drafted the amendments which he signed; he did not reply.

As well as being an MEP, Lehne has been a partner in the Dusseldorf office of the law firm TaylorWessing since 2003.[37] TaylorWessing's website says its 'top-rated corporate lawyers' have a 'recognised specialism in venture capital and private equity' and that it acts for 'many of the world's wealthiest families'.[38] While Lehne may not be directly involved in such activities, his second job with a firm that brags of its deep knowledge of private equity would appear problematic, considering he has been involved in regulating that industry.

The bombardment of MEPs paid dividends for the hedge fund industry. During a crunch vote in May 2010, the Parliament's economic and monetary affairs committee decided against demanding stronger rules than those recommended by the Commission. On some key issues, MEPs capitulated – with only minor caveats – to pressure from the lobbyists. They agreed, for example, that hedge fund managers should be allowed to appoint their own valuators to assess how much their funds are worth. The Commission, by contrast, had sought to forbid fund managers from being their own valuators.[39]

It is frightening that a directly elected institution (the Parliament) can be just as amenable – if not more so – to persuasion by the super-rich than an unelected one (the Commission). Yet this is the logical consequence of a situation where the views of banks and other financial service providers are treated as having a greater weight and validity than those of their less wealthy critics.

The antagonism which McCreevy detected towards the financial sector from Social Democrats (misleadingly called Socialists) should not be exaggerated. Some centre-left MEPs who fancy themselves as power-brokers have proven quite accommodating to the masters of money.

PAYING FOR ACCESS

Pervenche Berès, an MEP with France's Socialist Party, preceded Sharon Bowles as chairwoman of the Parliament's economics committee. In 2008, *AccountancyAge* placed her at number eight on its 'Top 50 Power' list. Berès, the magazine noted, had 'ruffled feathers' at the International Accounting Standards Board by querying its moves to converge business reporting norms in the US with those of the rest of the world. Her willingness to challenge the 'accountability' of the IASB meant she was likely to remain a 'thorn in the side' for the board, *AccountancyAge* added.[40]

Established in 2001, the IASB was run by 14 men and one woman in 2012. Most of the 15 have spent their professional lives with accountancy giants like Deloitte & Touche or KPMG, banks, credit rating agencies or Volvo (Jan Engström, previously a senior manager with the Swedish car and truck maker, appears to be a token representative of the real economy at the time of writing).[41] Although it is a private firm, governments and public institutions have allowed it to stipulate what information companies throughout the world should and should not make public. Given its partisan nature, it is not surprising that the board has been in no hurry to pressurise corporations to disclose how much – or how little – tax they pay in each country where they operate. The absence of transparency has deprived poor countries of about $160 billion in tax revenues per year, Christian Aid has estimated.[42]

Berès was certainly more combative towards the IASB than her apparent nemesis McCreevy, who was viscerally opposed to greater transparency. 'Published accounts will always be like bikinis – much more interesting for what they conceal than what they reveal – regardless of more exacting accounting standards,' he once said.[43]

Yet Berès also belongs to a private club that has been clearly designed to bolster the financial services sector. The European

Parliamentary Financial Services Forum is a body that brings together MEPs with corporations who pay an annual membership fee of €8,000. Its office is located in the same building as the European Banking Federation, which coordinates its activities. Companies who are not fully signed up to the forum can nonetheless take part in its meetings – space permitting – if they fork out €200 each time.[44] This means that corporate lobbyists are guaranteed a chance to cajole key law-makers provided they pay for it.

SpinWatch, an organisation that monitors the public relations industry, has argued that there may be a conflict of interest between Berès' participation in the forum and the lead role she played in drawing up the European Parliament's position on insurance legislation. This is because Insurance Europe is part of the forum and may have had 'undue access' to Berès as a result. When questioned about this matter, Berès told Andy Rowell, who undertook the SpinWatch investigation, that she was 'not an active member' of the forum's board and 'therefore don't have a direct influence on its agenda and regulations'.[45]

Information contained on the forum's website, however, appears to contradict her assurances. Reports of its activities show that she chaired at least five of its meetings between 2003 and 2008 (a relatively large number, considering that the forum only lists about five or six events per year on its published calendar). At a 'lunchtime discussion' in September 2005, for example, she listened to Alain Gourio from BNP Paribas speak about boosting mortgage lending across borders.[46] As Berès was in charge of the Parliament's economics committee at the time and was overseeing the debate on many dossiers likely to be of interest to BNP Paribas, questions must surely be asked about whether it was appropriate for her to be involved in a private club administered by the European Banking Federation.

SERVING THE SQUID

Dick Durbin, a member of the US Senate, declared in 2009 that the 'banks are still the most powerful lobby on Capitol Hill. And frankly they own the place.'[47] The same observation can be made about Brussels, despite how the 'ownership' is slightly more subtle. Banks do not give donations to European election candidates in anything like the same amounts as they do in the US. State funding of political parties fortunately rules out this possibility in many EU countries. Banks have nonetheless been intimately involved in every stage of drafting regulations on this side of the Atlantic.

The European Banking Federation, in particular, had sufficient clout ahead of the economic crisis to demand that the financial services sector should be deregulated. In 2005 and 2006, the EBF exerted pressure on the European Commission to challenge a German law that restricted the name *Sparkasse* (savings bank) to publicly-owned institutions. According to Guido Ravoet, then the EBF's secretary-general, the situation in Germany was an 'impediment to the free movement of capital' and could no longer be defended on the basis of the 'general interest'.[48] Based largely on his arguments, the Commission initiated legal proceedings against Germany in the summer of 2006 before reaching a settlement – under which Germany effectively pledged to facilitate greater competition in its banking sector – later that year.[49]

Goldman Sachs has attracted more attention over the past decade than at any time in its history. The vivid description used by *Rolling Stone* journalist Matt Taibbi of the investment bank as a 'great vampire squid wrapped around the face of humanity, relentlessly jamming its blood funnel into anything that smells like money' has certainly helped raise awareness of the harm it causes.[50]

Just as it was part of the European Commission's 'expert group' on hedge funds, Goldman Sachs was part of a similar 'working party' on derivatives assembled by McCreevy in 2008. True, the name Goldman Sachs did not appear on the list of the working party's members when it was announced. But Goldman Sachs belonged to several of the umbrella groups that comprised the working party. These included the International Swaps and Derivatives Association (ISDA), the Futures and Options Association (FOA) and the EBF.[51]

Derivatives – instruments that enable investors to bet on the future price of commodities or shares without actually buying the underlying investment – were famously labelled 'weapons of mass destruction' by Warren Buffett. In the 2002 annual report of his firm Berkshire Hathaway, Buffett warned that parties to derivatives have 'enormous incentives to cheat in accounting for them'. Because there is no real market involved, the model used to account for derivatives 'can bring on large-scale mischief,' he wrote.[52]

In most walks of life cheats are distrusted. It is unlikely that an athlete caught taking performance-enhancing drugs would soon afterwards be invited to draw up new ethical rules for sport. In its wisdom, though, the European Commission invited the cheats of the financial world to advise it on drawing new rules on derivatives, a product synonymous with cheating. (A US commission of inquiry into the financial crisis concluded, in effect, that major investment banks had availed of the incentive to cheat: derivatives were found to be means to conceal the full extent of bank borrowing.)[53]

Like many cheats, large investment banks were in denial about their habit and protested that they were treated as scapegoats. 'We are the red-headed stepchild of Europe,' a lobbyist who represents a number of banks told me, on condition of anonymity. 'The most politically convenient thing in the world to do is to kick the financial industry. Another analogy is a bar fight. If you are in a bar fight, who do you turn around and punch? You punch the guy who is not holding a chair.'[54]

The major investment banks may not have been holding a chair in this 'fight'. But they were holding a pen. After some initial discussions among the members of the EU's working party, Goldman Sachs, Barclays Capital, Deutsche Bank and Morgan Stanley told McCreevy they could be relied on to act responsibly from now on. In their letter, the banks made a commitment to ensure that credit default swaps – the fastest growing type of derivatives traded before the crisis – would pass through a clearing house.[55]

The European Commission soon announced it was holding a 'public consultation exercise' on how derivatives should be regulated.[56] The consultation was a sham. It was based on a paper drawn up by McCreevy's minions; that document began by saying there is 'broad agreement about the benefits and risks of derivatives markets'. The key source cited to support the contention of 'broad agreement' was a 'high level group' report written at the Commission's own request.[57]

This 'high level group' was headed by Jacques de Larosière, a managing director of the International Monetary Fund in the 1980s, who had more recently been a senior adviser to the French bank BNP Paribas. Callum McCarthy also sat on the group; as chairman of Britain's Financial Services Authority, he had dismissed calls for tighter supervision of banks as a 'mad dog' overreaction in 2007. Another member of the group, Otmar Issing, had gone straight from being chief economist with the European Central Bank to counselling Goldman Sachs. He is a devotee of Friedrich Hayek, the Austrian economist who preached an extreme version of capitalism that has become known as neo-liberalism.[58] This meant that the ideological hue of the group's members was almost identically narrow, so by definition their report could not provide evidence of 'broad agreement' about something as controversial as derivatives.

Capable of wearing several hats simultaneously, de Larosière is also a chairman of Eurofi, a 'think tank' whose two 'lead sponsors' for its 2012 'high level seminar' were the insurance giant Axa and (you've guessed it) Goldman Sachs.[59] Speaking at a 2010 Eurofi conference, Lloyd Blankfein, the Goldman Sachs chief executive, underscored that Europe was vital for his bank before sounding the alarm bells about 'mismatched regulation'. By stating that 'operations can be moved globally', his message was interpreted by the *Financial Times* as a 'veiled warning' that Goldman would quit the EU if rules were introduced that were not to its liking.[60]

The combined effect of cajoling and threats is that banks have been left free to play with derivatives as before, subject to a few minor restrictions. A blueprint for a law on derivatives published by the Commission in 2010 did little more than seek to give formal effect to the commitments on having a clearing house made by major investment banks a year earlier.[61] Otherwise, the Commission permitted the proliferation of these weapons of mass destruction, without curtailing some of the most harmful uses to which they had been put. Short selling – where a speculator gambles with shares he or she does not own – would still be allowed. In July 2012, the Commission approved rules enabling national authorities to restrict short selling under exceptional circumstances.[62] It is important to underscore that any bans would be optional and almost certainly would only be imposed after much damage had already been done. This is tantamount to only allowing gun control measures after enough psychopaths have gone on killing sprees.

Not long ago, there were indications that the EU's authorities were furious with Goldman Sachs. In 2010, the Union's number-crunching agency Eurostat visited Greece to probe allegations that the data it had been processing on that country's debt was inaccurate. Eurostat noted that at the beginning of that year 'it became known that Greece had entered in 2001 into currency off-market swap agreements with Goldman Sachs, using an exchange rate different to the spot prevailing one.' Athens neither notified Eurostat of this agreement nor requested an opinion on what 'accounting treatment' should apply to it. Worse again, the Athens government had lied to Eurostat in 2008 in explicitly stating that it did not engage in off-market swaps.[63]

In theory, its secretive manoeuvres with the Greek authorities should have led to it being blacklisted in Brussels. The currency swap arranged by Goldman Sachs was designed to enable the Greeks to borrow $1 billion on top of a $10 billion loan without this extra sum showing up on the declared public accounts. This implied that a Manhattan bank was helping Greece to find ways around the expenditure rules set down in the EU's Maastricht treaty, which are supposed to be of fundamental importance to the euro.[64] EU officials tend to speak of these rules (the 'convergence criteria' in Brussels parlance) as if they are sacred.

Far from blacklisting it, the EU has held Goldman Sachs even tighter than before. Lucas Papademos was head of the Greek central bank at the time of the deal with Goldman Sachs. In 2011, he was installed as Greece's unelected prime minister. Mario Monti became Italy's unelected prime minister the same year; since 2005 he was a paid advisor to Goldman on 'European business and major public policy initiatives worldwide'.[65] Completing a triumvirate, Mario Draghi, president of the European Central Bank, was a managing director with Goldman Sachs between 2002 and 2005.[66]

Goldman Sachs bounced back rapidly from the jittery autumn and winter of 2008. The following year it had the cash and chutzpah to award over $16 billion in executive bonuses.[67] Lumbered with the 'vampire squid' analogy, it seems nonetheless to be striving towards a partial rebranding.

One of the main topics of correspondence between it and the European Commission in 2011 related to the concept of the 'social economy and entrepreneurship'. Michael Sherwood, who heads the bank's operations in London, has tried to dispel the squid image. In one letter to Michel Barnier, who succeeded McCreevy as the EU's single market commissioner, Sherwood lauded the Goldman board as an 'extraordinary group of professionals'. He wrote: 'We are conscious of the responsibility our industry has not only to uphold prudent and robust risk management and governance practices but also to ensure our sector remains an engine for entrepreneurial and sustainable growth, innovation and recovery in the European economy. We are not complacent on either of these points.'[68]

Sherwood has been promoting a lending scheme ostensibly designed to help small businesses in Britain as a model that could be replicated elsewhere.[69] The scheme has received a positive response from Barnier. He invited Goldman to help EU officials prepare a plan on making social entrepreneurship 'a mass phenomenon'.[70] The plan to which Barnier referred was published later in 2011. Titled the Social Business Initiative, it bears more than a passing resemblance to the 'big society' idea pedalled by David Cameron's government, whereby services traditionally performed by the state are taken over by private companies. A brochure produced by Barnier's services went so far as to suggest that education for children with learning difficulties could be provided by the private sector.[71]

Goldman Sachs' professed passion for the 'social economy' should be treated with a little scepticism. Soon after it was courted by Barnier, Goldman Sachs threatened litigation against the Lower East Side People's Federal Credit Union, which caters for New Yorkers refused services by commercial banks on the grounds they are too poor. Goldman Sachs had originally promised a small donation to a fundraising event run by the credit union in 2011. Yet it took umbrage at how the credit union supported the Occupy Wall Street movement, which called on customers to transfer their accounts from mainstream banks to small not-for-profit ones, serving local communities.[72] So while the vampire squid was pretending to caress community initiatives on one side of the Atlantic, it was flapping its tentacles menacingly against similar initiatives on the other.

BETTING ON HUNGER

There are indications, too, that Goldman Sachs has been eager to show concern for the world's hungry. Isabelle Ealet has been called 'the most powerful woman' in Goldman Sachs.[73] She has also been described as the 'queen of commodities' for her prowess in betting on the prices of food and other raw materials.[74] Under her leadership, the commodities department became the most profitable division of Goldman Sachs in the first decade of this century.[75]

In August 2011, Goldman Sachs requested an appointment between Ealet and her French compatriot Michel Barnier. The purpose of the appointment, according to an email message from the bank, would be to inform Barnier about 'an initiative on which we are working to assist developing countries with managing high food prices'.[76]

The idea that Goldman Sachs would wish to help poor countries manage high food prices would be comical, if the issues at stake were not so serious. One year earlier, the World Development Movement, an anti-poverty organisation, published a study explaining how Goldman Sachs was making billions out of exacerbating global hunger. Citing estimates that Goldman Sachs had amassed $5 billion from commodities trading in 2009 alone, the study explained how the bank was one of the main originators of commodity index funds. The orgy of speculation in which these funds were involved essentially meant that banks were betting against their own clients. Banks would both arrange to buy derivatives contracts, charging a hefty fee to do so, and sell the contract that the index fund was buying.[77]

Relying heavily on computers and mathematical formulae, the gambling had profound impacts in the real world. Rising prices of wheat, rice and vegetable oils meant that the food import bills for the world's 48 poorest countries increased by 37 per cent between 2007 and 2008. The United Nations pinpointed food speculation, climate change and the growing use of agricultural crops for biofuels as major contributing factors to a 'perfect storm' which pushed 125 million people into extreme poverty and saw the number of people categorised as hungry swell by an extra 75 million.[78]

Given its innovative approach to food price gambling, it seemed reasonable to surmise that Goldman Sachs wished to convince Barnier that it was capable of shielding the vulnerable from the effects of its activities and that stringent rules against speculation were not required. So I contacted the bank's government affairs team in the City of London, asking if the real intention of the initiative it was discussing with Barnier was to tell him to back off. 'Your assumption couldn't be further from the truth,' said its spokeswoman Joanna Carss. Yet when I asked for a summary of what the initiative entailed, she said: 'I am not in a position to divulge that kind of information. The initiative wasn't designed for public consumption.'[79]

Can it be a coincidence, though, that Ealet has been part of an elitist group that has indeed told policy-makers to back off (albeit politely)? She was a member of the commodities task force with the International Institute of Finance, an alliance of top banks, which delivered a set of policy prescriptions in 2011. While the institute's paper was primarily directed at the G20, it zoomed in on the EU's market in financial instruments directive (MiFID), that was then under review by the Union's key bodies. The paper argued that investment in commodities has 'considerable social utility', particularly for pensioners who benefit from 'well-diversified portfolios'. Positioning themselves as well-placed to address political concerns about an ageing population was a clever way to insist that 'broad-brush regulation' could lead to even worse price volatility and interfere with the 'market's inherent equilibrating forces'.[80]

It is, of course, bizarre that adults who presumably realised some time ago that there was no Santa Claus or tooth fairy should still spread the myth that markets have some magical, self-correcting power. Faith in the masters of finance, unfortunately, remains strong in Brussels' European quarter.

When Michel Barnier was appointed the EU's single market commissioner in 2010, Nicolas Sarkozy hailed the elevation of a Frenchman to this post as a major defeat for Anglo-Saxon capitalism. The *Daily Telegraph* pondered the implications of Barnier's new post for the City of London by asking if he was the 'most dangerous man in Europe'.[81]

Like many conspiracy theories, the notion a plot was being hatched in Paris to annihilate British bankers was not supported by evidence. It is true that Sarkozy denounced the 'crazy system' of modern finance when it was politically expedient to do so in 2008.[82] This did not mean that he had undergone a road to Damascus-type conversion from his 2007 position of advocating that France should deregulate itself to resemble America, where, in his view, easy access to credit encouraged home ownership. As it happened, Sarkozy continued to deserve the nickname 'president of the rich' throughout his term in office. Under his leadership, France was the most strenuous opponent of all EU states to a proposed cap on bankers' bonuses in 2010.[83]

Equally, it should be stressed that Barnier has been more emollient towards the City of London and in general more guarded in his public comments than Sarkozy. Barnier has taken a number of trips across the English Channel, where the titans of finance queuing up to meet him have proclaimed themselves 'reassured' by his openness to dialogue.[84]

Compared to McCreevy, Barnier looks hyperactive with his regular flow of policy announcements. On issues of substance, the difference between the two men is considerably narrower. Barnier has maintained McCreevy's practice of giving banks privileged access to the Berlaymont and the Borschette, two of the buildings where some of the most important legislative discussions take place in Brussels. It is especially disconcerting that Barnier turns to discredited figures for counsel. In February 2012, he announced the establishment of a new 'expert group' on potential reforms to the structure of banks.[85] The group included Carole Sergeant, who had been head of risk at Lloyd's when it was Britain's largest mis-seller of payment protection insurance.[86] Following a High Court order, Lloyd's agreed to pay out a total of £3.2 billion in compensation to customers affected by the scandal.[87]

'Scandal', as it happens, is precisely the word that Barnier used to describe speculation in basic foodstuffs 'when there are a billion people starving in the world'. At the time he delivered that clear message he was trying to convince MEPs to approve his nomination to the European Commission at a confirmation hearing. 'I am fighting for a fairer word and I want Europe to take the lead on that,' he added.[88]

The fighting spirit has been sadly absent when Barnier has got around to proposing new initiatives. When he put forward a revamped version of MiFID in 2011, he proved receptive to the demands made by the City of London. One major concern identified by the City related to high-frequency trading, which has been made possible by advanced technology. This can allow speculation on commodities by exploiting price differences within a fraction of a second. While the proposal published by Barnier advocated some risk control on this form of trading, it did not grapple with the fundamental problems posed by it.[89] According to the Centre for Research on Multinational Corporations (known by the acronym SOMO) in the Netherlands, the provisions were 'dangerously weak'.[90]

Nonetheless, the City has been pressing the EU institutions to make the provisions even weaker. An unpublished paper drawn up by City lobbyists and sent to Barnier acknowledged that EU officials were concerned about 'rogue algorithms' that could threaten the 'orderly function of markets' yet argued against robust rules on high-frequency trading. The 'fluid and evolutionary nature of technological and market changes' made it unlikely that legal certainty could be provided by any proposed rules, the paper argued.[91] Goldman Sachs has had the temerity to describe high-frequency trading as a 'natural evolution'.[92]

In private meetings with banks, EU officials have tried to allay concerns that Barnier is a regulation junkie. During one such meeting with Goldman Sachs, Tim Binning, a policy officer in the Commission's single market department, acknowledged that there was pressure from 'some politicians' in Europe to ban high-frequency trading. Binning assured Goldman that Barnier had no such plans up his sleeve; rather, Barnier was 'likely to look closely at the US approach so we are not out of step'. Translated into plain English, this meant that some of Europe's financial rules are being modelled on those set in Washington – a city that has long been under Goldman's spell.[93]

At the time of writing, it is more than two years since Barnier voiced his revulsion at the links between speculation and hunger. He has still not brought forward measures to outlaw or put major restrictions on a single form of betting on commodity prices. Rather than fighting for a fairer word, he has worked to preserve the status quo.

3
War is good for business

Selling weapons to a regime accused by Amnesty International of 'gross and widespread human rights violations' is no laughing matter.[1] So I was a little taken aback when a British civil servant answered my question about what role he played in an infamous arms deal with Saudi Arabia with a jovial chuckle.

I was even more astonished that Nick Witney, the giggling mandarin in question, had listed working on al-Yamamah – as the weapons contract is known – as a career highlight on his *curriculum vitae*.[2] Most mortals try to avoid drawing attention to past embarrassments when detailing their work experience. Yet here was someone parading his association with a deal so controversial that Tony Blair's government intervened in 2006 to block an investigation into claims that it was flanked by huge bribes to the Saudi royal family.[3] Once he had stopped chortling, Witney said he had 'nothing to do with the money' and had merely managed part of the export contract for the Ministry of Defence. Admitting that he was 'aware that in Saudi Arabia, there is remarkably little distinction between the public and private purse', Witney added, 'I can't say I lost any sleep over the thought that some proportion of the revenues went to Saudi princes rather than the Saudi exchequer'.[4]

Witney's cavalier attitude brought to mind the explanation offered by Alan Clark over how – as a trade minister in the 1980s – he had authorised the export of arms that the Indonesian military junta used in its acts of genocide against the people of East Timor. 'My responsibility is to my own people,' Clark told the journalist John Pilger. 'I don't really fill my mind much with what one set of foreigners is doing to another.'[5]

When Clark spoke of 'my own people' was he really referring to the arms industry? The main beneficiaries of both the deliveries to Indonesia and Saudi Arabia were the executives of British Aerospace (now BAE Systems). Never mind, then, that the company's Hawk jets were observed on bombing runs in East Timor.[6] And never mind that armoured vehicles bought by the Saudis would eventually prove handy in repressing pro-democracy protests in Bahrain.[7] The politicians and officials who rubber-stamped the sales were fulfilling a responsibility to their 'own people'.

In early 2004, Nick Witney was tasked with preparing a blueprint for the European Defence Agency, becoming its first director later that year. Witney had, in his own words, been given 'a bit of a blank screen'.[8] The formal guidance given to him consisted of one paragraph in a declaration made by the Union's presidents and prime ministers at a meeting in Thessaloniki, Greece, the previous summer. According to that paragraph, the new body should strive towards 'strengthening and promoting and enhancing European armaments cooperation, strengthening the European defence industrial base and creating a competitive European defence equipment market'. The agency was also tasked with encouraging scientific research 'aimed at leadership in strategic technologies for future defence and security capabilities'.[9]

The 'blank screen' did not go unnoticed by weapons dealers. Shortly before the EDA was formally established, the heads of Europe's three largest arms companies – BAE, Thales and EADS – took the rare step of signing a joint letter to selected newspapers. It declared that the agency had a 'vital role' to play in addressing the gap in military expenditure between the EU and the US. Special attention was drawn to how America outspent the EU by eight times on 'defence R&T [research and technology] investment'. While praising the EU's stated commitment to beefing up its arsenal, the trio warned that 'this must not once again be a fig-leaf to cover the nakedness of any real efforts to improve European defence'.[10]

BAE is the world's second largest arms company; with annual weapon sales exceeding $32 billion only America's Lockheed Martin has outperformed it in recent years.[11] As Andrew Feinstein demonstrates in his book *The Shadow World*, BAE is so powerful that British prime ministers act as its salesmen. In the second half of his decade in Downing Street, Tony Blair named the fight against poverty in Africa as a top priority. At the same time as he was encouraging increased spending on AIDS and malaria, Blair harried the authorities in Tanzania, one of the world's poorest countries, into forking out $40 million on a BAE-manufactured air radar system for warplanes.[12]

David Cameron has kept up the dishonourable tradition set by his predecessors. Reflecting on the popular uprisings in a number of Arab countries in 2011, Cameron spoke of a 'responsibility to stand up to regimes that persecute their people'.[13] That comment was made to the UN general assembly in the autumn of that year. Shortly after the courageous crowds in Cairo's Tahrir Square forced the resignation of Hosni Mubarak that February, Cameron undertook a trade mission to the Middle East. He was accompanied by Ian King, BAE's chief executive, and a few other arms company chiefs. The purpose of the trip was to ensure that Britain got a 'healthy slice' of the international arms business, Cameron said.[14]

Once he was back in England, Ian King received a visit from Claude-France Arnould, who had recently been appointed the third head of the European Defence Agency. In a follow-up letter, Arnould – a Frenchwoman – told King it was 'most appropriate' that BAE should be the first British firm with which she held discussions in her new role. Arnould found 'the geographic spread of your company enlightening', adding: 'I note there is a significant footprint in Europe and here I believe that some of our work can assist in one of your key priorities of growing the exportability of your products.'[15] The stilted phrasing should not be allowed camouflage what she was really saying: Arnould wished to help Europe's largest arms dealer get an even healthier slice of international business.

BAE has been hired by the agency to take the lead in drafting several studies. At least two of these studies warrant careful scrutiny: one concerns unmanned aerial vehicles (UAVs), those cutting-edge warplanes generally called drones; the other 'precision-guided' ammunition.

Arms industry analysts sometimes mock BAE's history of drone development. BAE's Phoenix has been nicknamed the 'bugger off' because a large number of these pilotless drones went missing when they were deployed as part of NATO's attack on Serbia in 1999 and the Anglo-American invasion of Iraq between 2003 and 2006.[16] That unflattering sobriquet overlooks how BAE was able to test out its products during two wars that were probably illegal under international law (neither was mandated by the UN nor could be justified on the grounds of self-defence; their conduct, therefore, appears to have involved the crime of aggression, as defined by the Nuremberg principles).[17]

The 'bugger off' setback does not appear to have damaged BAE's reputation in Brussels; a 2007 analysis paper written by consultants Frost & Sullivan for the European Commission stated that BAE was 'one of the few European companies to have developed and sold a considerable number of UAVs'.[18] Nor did the loss of drones in Basra prevent the British government from helping to finance BAE's Taranis and Mantis programmes since late 2006. Prototypes of both these drones have subsequently been unveiled;

the Mantis is a noteworthy innovation as it is intended to make the business of warfare even more automated than it already is. Unlike conventional drones, the Mantis is not remote-controlled but follows a pre-programmed flight path.[19]

As work on these programmes advanced, BAE was chosen by the European Defence Agency in 2008 to head a consortium for developing a plan to enable military drones to be flown 'routinely' (the EDA's own word) in civilian airspace by 2015. Displaying a less-than-complete understanding of irony, the EDA described the plan as a 'road map'.[20] David Kershaw, the leading BAE representative on the consortium, has also been in charge of soliciting subsidies for the Mantis and Taranis.[21]

Not content with plotting to overcome the hurdles that currently save commercial air passengers from having to fly alongside pilotless warplanes, BAE has also led a team counselling the EDA while it prepared a strategy for 'precision-guided' weaponry. The conclusions of the final report, delivered by the team in late 2011, can be summarised crudely: Europe needs more 'smart' bombs. Pieter Taal, a senior European Defence Agency official, has claimed that the increased investment in such weaponry is necessary to 'avoid casualties amongst friendly forces and non-combatant third parties'.[22] Yet in public comments, he has overlooked how the extensive use of 'smart' bombs in recent military exploits have frequently led to the spilling of innocent blood; the Bureau of Investigative Journalism has found, for example, that as many as 889 civilians were killed by CIA drone strikes in Pakistan between 2004 and 2012.[23] Taal has been so determined to promote BAE's work that he was a special guest at a briefing the firm organised as part of its contribution to the Defence Systems and Equipment International (DSEi), Britain's largest arms bazaar, in 2011.[24]

BLOOD FOR BREAKFAST

The Swedish corporation Saab has worked in tandem with BAE on a number of arms deal. Some of them have been controversial: in 2011, Saab admitted that a large bribe was paid to bag a contract that would enable it and BAE sell fighter jets to South Africa.[25] The main defence offered by Hakan Bushke, Saab's chief executive, when faced with the allegations was that its subsidiary, the South African National Industrial Participation, was effectively managed by BAE at the time the deal was negotiated in the late 1990s.[26]

Bushke's confession does not appear to have harmed Saab's relationship with the European Defence Agency. With sales of about \$3.6 billion in 2011, Saab could be viewed as a minnow in comparison to BAE.[27] Still, Saab has a better knack for winning EU grants than its British competitor. In 2011, Saab received over €1 million from the Union, compared to €800,000 for BAE.[28] Anecdotal evidence – some of it backed up by documentation – further indicates that Saab lobbyists have been assiduous in developing strong bonds with EDA personnel. On at least one occasion, individuals working for the EDA have been asked to contribute when a whip-around was organised to buy a retirement gift for a member of Saab's Brussels team.[29]

Venturing into a realm of activity usually reserved for think tanks, Saab began hosting regular early morning confabs for a select gathering in 2012. Invitations to the inaugural 'Breakfast at Saab's' event that January promised it would address the impact of 'economic austerity' on the 'European defence technological and industrial base'.[30] Having a few like-minded folk around for coffee and croissants may not appear troubling *per se*. But it takes on a greater importance when examined in the context of how Saab has been contracted to advance an agenda with the ultimate goal of greater militarisation in the EU.

During ILA Berlin – a biennial air show – in March 2012, Claude-France Arnould drew attention to a study prepared by a Saab-led grouping which concluded that Europe's warplane industry is 'now losing capabilities'.[31] What the statement she issued didn't say, however, was that Saab had been explicitly encouraged to sound an alarmist note by her agency. Named FAS4Europe, the 'future air systems' study was commissioned by the EDA, with Saab paid to perform a coordinating role. Internal EDA documents that I have obtained show that the bureaucrats in the agency were even more adamant that the economic downturn's effects on military-related innovation should be underscored than the companies supposedly driving that innovation. Whereas, for example, Saab had recommended that the study should warn of how reductions in financing for weapons development will 'potentially' affect 'competitiveness in the long term', the EDA advocated that the word 'potentially' be erased. To make the matters sound more urgent, its preferred wording stressed that less spending on military research 'will impact long-term competitiveness'.[32]

To a layperson, these differences probably look subtle. But it should be noted that there is a determination on the part of the EDA insiders that their chums in the arms industry should be allowed to get their hands on as much public cash as possible, even if the overall amount of available cash is shrinking. As part of this battle, participants in a strategic discussion on the FAS4Europe study held at the EDA's headquarters in March 2011 concurred that 'how the report is written is important' as 'it needs to have sufficient impact to influence policy-makers', according to the minutes of that meeting.[33] Another EDA document suggested that the financial crisis afforded an opportunity to promote more joint activities between rival arms firms. Advocating that the FAS4Europe project tell a 'waterproof story', it added: 'This might be the time to sell collaboration, particularly if it can be demonstrated that the result will be the more effective use of scarce military resources.'[34]

One factor that helps explain why Saab's advice is so valued in Brussels is that the corporation has been known to compete directly with US firms for contracts. Diplomatic cables made public by WikiLeaks have shown that the US government was sufficiently worried that Norway would opt to buy Saab's Gripen fighter planes, instead of American F-35s, in 2008 that it delayed approval of a Saab request to integrate US-made radar equipment into the Gripens. Washington was perturbed by the prospect that a long-standing NATO member like Norway would buy European and that other countries in the alliance – notably Denmark and the Netherlands – might be inspired to spurn F-35s when shopping around for military hardware.[35]

Preserving a strong manufacturing capacity for war equipment on this continent is one of the EDA's chief preoccupations. In one document exchanged between the EDA and Saab, the agency bemoaned how Poland and other countries in eastern Europe had bought American fighter jets such as F-16s in recent years. The document warned that the 'future air systems' strategy pursued by the agency was at risk because of 'overwhelming political and commercial pressure from the US'. Describing the consequent failure to develop a 'homogenous EU industrial base in this sector' as an 'unfortunate turn of events', the paper urged a response involving 'joint efforts by government and industry alike'.[36]

It would be wrong to deduce from these concerns that EU officials are striving towards a more ethical alternative to the US. As Saab has been eager to sell its Skeldar drone to the US Navy, its participation in discussions about countering American influence in Europe should be viewed with a large degree of scepticism.[37] Efforts to increase the use of drones throughout the world are intimately linked to US foreign policy, especially the 'war on terror' declared by George W. Bush's administration. The Pentagon's 2006 Quadrennial Defence Review recommended a doubling of America's drone capacity 'to increase persistent surveillance' and safeguard that nation's 'scientific and technological advantage over potential competitors'.[38] Saab has shown great interest in the results of decisions taken in the Pentagon and the Oval Office. An email message sent by a representative of the company to the European Defence Agency in 2012 requested statistics on the use of drones as 'a percentage of all operational sorties in Afghanistan and Iraq' and as 'a percentage of all flying time in the same theatres'. The Saab lobbyist (whose name has been redacted from the copy of the email I've seen) added: 'I have been trying to find this data with no success. I think it would be useful if we could show this to our CE [chief executive].'[39]

HIJACKING SCIENCE

Although it does not receive much scrutiny by the mainstream media, scientific research is one of the single largest areas of expenditure from the European Union's budget (in allocations for 2011, it was surpassed only by agriculture and regional aid).[40] With a total of over €8 billion per year earmarked for a plethora of research projects, arms manufacturers have been understandably determined to take part in as many subsidised initiatives as possible. As I argued in my previous book, *Europe's Alliance With Israel*, arms industry representatives have milked the opportunities presented by the 'war on terror' diligently. Following the 11 September 2001 atrocities in the US and the 2003 train bombings in Madrid, the EU's institutions decided that 'security' would become a theme in the Union's multi-annual research programme. As Israel is the most active non-European participant in this programme, its arms companies have benefited handsomely from the grants on offer. The involvement of the same companies in crimes against humanity – such as the three-week offensive against Gaza in late 2008 and early 2009 and the construction of an 'apartheid wall' in the West Bank – was not deemed problematic by Brussels officials.[41]

Whenever I have challenged representatives of the European Commission about the surrounding issues, they have always insisted that the research being financed does not involve the development of new weaponry. In July 2012, a director in the Commission's enterprise department, Lluís Prats repeated a mantra I had heard many times when I confronted him at a conference. Prats told me it was 'very clear' that the Union's research programme was 'exclusively civilian'.[42]

Towards the end of that same month, Prats' department issued a blueprint on the future of 'security' research. It stated that the 'global security market' had 'grown nearly tenfold' over the preceding decade: from €10 billion to about €100 billion per year. While EU-based firms enjoyed a 25 per cent share of this market in 2010, that could fall to 20 per cent by 2020 if 'no action is launched to enhance the competitiveness of the EU security industry'. The blueprint stated that there was 'ongoing coordination' between those security research activities handled by the European Commission and those handled by the European Defence Agency. 'The aim is to synchronise this research with a view to avoid duplications and to profit from possible synergies,' the blueprint stated, adding that the Commission 'intends to continue and expand this cooperation'.[43]

The blueprint is so heavy on jargon that its authors should have been inducted into the Plain English Campaign's hall of shame. But it does expose the assurance given to me by Prats as hollow. The European Defence Agency, it should be recalled, was given explicit instructions by EU governments to work towards strengthening the arms industry. Given that its core activities relate to military technology, it would be naive to think that its discussions with the European Commission only relate to civilian matters.

Moreover, the assurances that Prats and his ilk have given me in public are not reflected by what EU officials are saying in private. Unpublished records confirm that the EDA has been examining how research funded by the EU can help air forces. One member of the agency's staff has referred to 'increasing interest in the impact of SESAR on military aviation'.[44] SESAR stands for Single European Sky Air Traffic Management Research. As its title suggests, this initiative is designed to modernise air traffic management; dominated by corporations, the project has been allocated some €350 million by the EU between 2008 and 2014.[45] Some of the participants in SESAR may have either been unaware of the Commission's apparent proviso that it only finances civilian research or else chose to ignore that proviso. John Clark, a captain in Britain's Royal Air Force has sat on SESAR's administrative board. In an interview with the project's in-house magazine, he insisted that SESAR will 'need to accommodate the needs' of the military 'because they won't go away'. Clark said that 'wide military involvement [in SESAR] is important' in order to study how militaries use airspace, given that 'missions often launch with very short notice'.[46]

The EU's Lisbon treaty – which came into force in December 2009 – appears to allow the innovation of new arms to be financed directly from the Union's budget. The largely unintelligible treaty contains a clause saying that the EU may promote 'all the research activities deemed necessary'.[47] The insertion of this article in the Union's core rulebook does not, of course, mean that the activities resulting from it enjoy democratic legitimacy. The treaty was rejected by voters in Ireland – the only country where it was subject to a referendum – in 2008. 'No' was deemed an unacceptable response in Brussels, however, so my compatriots were browbeaten into accepting the treaty in a second poll.

Theoretically, the European Parliament could refuse to sign off budgets in which money is allocated to weapons development. It would nonetheless be foolish to place much confidence in our elected representatives. At the time of writing, the final contours of Horizon 2020 – the EU's latest multi-annual science programme – are still under discussion. But an indication that MEPs may prove acquiescent towards funding weapons development comes in a 2011 briefing paper marked for 'European Parliament internal use only!' (exclamation mark included). Drafted by the assembly's policy department, the paper recommends that the 'present strict limitation [on civilian research] should be removed'. The 'standard approach' for research activities should be to address the 'requirements' of the military 'together with non-defence related requirements,' the paper added.[48]

Why does the Lisbon treaty mirror the hopes and desires of arms dealers? One explanation is that part of the treaty was – to all intents and purposes – written by arms dealers. The key provisions on military capabilities in the treaty were copied and pasted from the draft EU constitution. Rather than being binned after it was defeated in French and Dutch referenda in 2005, the constitution was recycled and repackaged as the Lisbon treaty. Valéry Giscard d'Estaing, the erstwhile French president who chaired a 'convention' tasked with drafting the constitution, has confessed that the branding exercise was deceptive. 'Public opinion will be led – without knowing it – to adopt the policies we would never dare to present to them directly,' he stated in 2007. 'All of the earlier proposals will be in the new text but will be hidden and disguised in some way.'[49]

To be more specific, the heavy military focus of the Lisbon treaty was the result of nine meetings of the defence working group in Giscard's convention during 2002. A total of 13 'experts' were heard by that group. Two of them represented Europe's largest arms-makers, BAE and EADS; others belonged to the European Defence Industries Group and Sweden's Defence Equipment Agency. The remaining 'experts' were army generals, civil servants and politicians known to have a pro-military outlook. The group's final report contended that 'it is essential to step up investment in military research'. Many of those who took part in the group's discussions favoured the establishment of a special EU office to oversee such research and coordinate improvements to the EU's military 'capabilities'.[50]

Wishes do come true for arms dealers. By 2004, the idea for a special EU office for military affairs was given flesh in the form of the European Defence Agency. With an annual budget of over €30 million, the EDA is now acting as a puppet for the companies who pushed for its creation.[51] Secret talks facilitated by the agency often turn into brainstorming sessions about what future demands arms dealers should make on the average taxpayer. During such talks in January 2012, arms dealers mulled over the question of 'would a European military framework programme be possible?' This indicates that the dealers are pushing for a multi-annual research fund to be earmarked exclusively for weapons development. The rationale behind this proposal, according to minutes of the secret meeting, was that it would help 'European nations coordinate their work' and free up the EDA to be 'more active in sensitive areas'.[52]

Minutes of an earlier secret meeting hosted by the agency confirm that the European Commission – despite all the assurances it has given me to the contrary – would be happy to hand over some of my tax to the arms industry. Participants in that September 2010 meeting learned that 'discussions are ongoing' between the EDA and the Commission about giving EU research grants to drone and military helicopter projects between 2014 and 2020. The allocations 'should be possible given that primarily dual use technologies are involved,' they learned, too.[53]

'Dual-use' is a euphemism for those tools of war that can sometimes have benign applications. Understandably, arms dealers seldom gloat in public about how many children have been killed by their wares. Rather, they tend to accentuate the life-saving potential of the technology they champion. The same goes for politicians. Antonio Tajani, the EU's enterprise commissioner at the time of writing, opened a 2010 'security research' conference in the Belgian coastal town of Ostend by applauding how European satellite images had helped rescue-workers reach earthquake victims in China and Italy over the preceding couple of years. 'The EU must be in the forefront of security research in order to guarantee the best possible protection of its citizens,' Tajani added. A few moments later, he tried to give the impression that 'security' is something of a cottage industry. One fifth of the €500 million allocated by the EU on 'security research' between 2007 and 2010 had gone to small and medium-sized enterprises, he noted.[54]

Tajani's attempt to portray 'security research' as a form of philanthropy was a little ham-fisted. Scrutiny of the 'advisory group' set up by the European Commission to guide its activities in this area leads to the conclusion that the arms industry is in the driving seat. When the group first met in 2007, it had 16 members from outside the Commission. Half of the 16 represented companies or trade associations that were directly involved in weapons or surveillance technology production: they included Thales, the Belgian gun maker FN Herstal, Italy's Finmeccanica, Britain's QinetiQ (a supplier of bomb-detecting robots to British troops in Afghanistan) and two firms (Siemens and Petards) active in the closed circuit TV market.[55] The group also had participants from the European Defence Agency and the Technion in Haifa, an institute which appears proud of inventing a remote-controlled bulldozer to help the Israeli military demolish Palestinian homes.[56] With all that hard-headed nous to draw on, the group couldn't really be expected to limit its focus on improving the wherewithal for responding to disasters. Rather, the group has recommended that 'is there a market?' and 'is someone going to buy it?' should be the first questions asked when proposals for EU funding are being addressed.[57] Rules on conflicts of interest applying to members of the group are laughable. While these rules state that the members may not evaluate requests for EU grants, they may belong to consortia which benefit from these grants. The only stipulation is that they 'should' be open about their participation when issues relating to particular grants are discussed by the group. In those cases, the members 'can be requested to abstain from the deliberations'.[58]

Having the firms that ultimately benefit from EU security research advise on setting its priorities involves – by definition – a conflict of interests. The profitability of these firms depends – on creating what Colin Powell, the former US general and secretary of state, once called a 'terror-industrial complex'.[59] There would be scarce demand for their products if there wasn't a climate of fear. The companies, therefore, have strong reasons to talk up – even to exaggerate – threats. Their business model depends on selling 'techno-fixes' to address the symptoms of 'terror', while leaving the causes of modern political violence to fester. Whereas common sense indicates that the threat of buses or trains being blown up would be dramatically reduced if the US ceased invading other countries or the Palestinians no longer had to live under a system of apartheid, I have yet to find such thinking in official EU papers on 'security research'.

One of the most comprehensive of such papers was a 'catalogue' published by the Commission in September 2011, giving a summary of the 123 'security research' projects it had approved since 2007. Thales, the French arms company, was involved in no fewer than 22 of these projects. Given that Thales was also part of the 'advisory group' setting the priorities for this research, its ability to benefit from almost one-fifth of the subsidies on offer seems problematic, to put it mildly.

Some of these projects clearly have military applications. Nearly €1.2 million have been allocated to the project OPARUS (open architecture for UAV-based surveillance system); its objective is to promote standardisation for computer equipment used in drones. Both Thales and BAE belong to the consortium implementing this project, which has a particular emphasis on border monitoring. Thales, meanwhile, is coordinating WIMA²S (wide-area airborne surveillance); with a budget of almost €4 million, this project is designed to encourage the greater use of drones in addressing the 'urgent need to control illegal immigration and human trafficking by sea'. (This 'urgent need' is a subject to which I will return).

THE ETHICAL AFTERTHOUGHT

It is true that the EU makes the occasional nod to civil liberties. Thales is taking part in a €6.4 million scheme called VideoSense (virtual centre of excellence for ethically-guided and privacy-respecting video analytics in security).[60] Nobody should be fooled, however, by the inferences that EU officials wish to have more politically correct forms of surveillance. Thales (previously Thomson-CSF) is not a credible authority on ethics. In 2011, the corporation announced that it would pay a fine of €170 million over a bribery scandal that bedevilled its supply of frigates to Taiwan.[61] Thales had unsuccessfully appealed against the fine ordered by a Paris-based tribunal of arbitration in 2010 – about 19 years after the original frigate contract was signed. Some €500 million– 20 per cent of the contract's total value – found its way to an intermediary with multiple identities (Wang Chan Poo; Andrew Wang; Dédé; Mr Shampoo).[62]

Ethics are no more than an afterthought in the EU's security research programme. Security is a multi-faceted concept. A truly ethical approach would not duck such questions as whether genuine security can ever be achieved when there is so much inequality between and within the world's countries or whether an arms industry with a great degree of political clout jeopardises security. Such questions are not receiving the attention they deserve in Brussels' corridors of power, where security research is viewed from a narrow economic perspective.

It is significant that the security research programme is administered by the European Commission's enterprise department, rather than its science department, which is in charge of most other research activities financed by the EU's budget. The Aerospace and Defence Industries Association of Europe (ASD) – which binds together many of the largest arms companies – has been adamant that the enterprise department (directorate-general in Brussels parlance) must remain in control of security research. In 'speaking notes' prepared for the association's then president Allan Cook ahead of a 2009 meeting with senior EU officials, ASD stated that one of the 'behind the scenes drivers' of the EU's security research programme was to support measures 'that are of benefit both to security and defence' (in this context, the word 'defence' appears to be a euphemism for weapons production). The enterprise department was described as 'the guardian of the dual-use principle' as no other part of the Commission could have 'as pronounced an interest'. The paper also pointed out that the enterprise department had a seat on the European Defence Agency's steering board. While 'power struggles concerning the future responsibilities for security affairs' in the EU executive 'may weaken the role' of the enterprise department, it was 'of prime importance' that security research continued to be handled as an enterprise issue, the paper added.[63]

Rather than acting as a guardian for the war industry, it might be more accurate to think of the enterprise department as a sugar daddy. By giving privileged access to weapons makers, the European Commission can have its sense of importance inflated as it draws up strategies for enhancing 'competitiveness'. The economic case for indulging the war industry is threadbare: only 0.2 per cent of the British jobs depend on arms exports.[64]

A glimpse into this cosy relationship is afforded by one of the 'tomorrow's world' initiatives underway. In 2009, the Commission decided to set up a 'high level group' on 'key enabling technologies' for industries of the future. It was charged with recommending steps to nurture nanotechnology, the manipulation of matter so tiny it is measured in nanometres (a nanometre is one billionth of a metre). During December that year, ASD was asked to suggest representatives from the arms industry who would sit on this board. The trade association recommended two people, one of whom was selected for the overwhelmingly male group when it was inaugurated the following year. He was Richard Parker, a director with Rolls-Royce.[65]

The group's final report contained some militaristic language: it referred to a gap between 'basic knowledge generation' and the 'commercialisation' of that knowledge as the 'valley of death'. But it generally depicted the activities being supported as benevolent: as some of the technologies have energy applications, they were hailed as 'crucial in the battle to combat climate change'.[66]

Should we really believe we can find the heart of a dolphin lover beneath the tough exterior of a Rolls-Royce executive? In its 2011 annual report, the corporation says it is the world's second largest provider of engines for military aircraft and applauds the use of its equipment during NATO's attacks on Libya earlier in the year. It adds: 'Our engineers in Indianapolis are working on key enabling technologies for the US Air Force ADVENT contract. This work focuses on developing and demonstrating variable cycle engine technologies aimed at incorporation in future generation US military aircraft.'[67] When the US military unveiled the ADVENT (adaptive versatile engine technology) programme in 2007, its stated objective was to develop a replacement to the fixed engines in today's warplanes. Variable cycle engines are supposed to offer potential for saving fuel, as well as providing the capacity to fly further and faster. Jeff Stricker, a senior figure in the Ohio-based Air Force Research Laboratory, contended that more fuel-efficient engines are needed because weapons and sensors gobble up large amounts of energy.[68]

In simple terms, this means that Rolls-Royce is helping America build up a more lethal arsenal for future wars of aggression. This fact has been conveniently omitted from the EU's 'key enabling technologies' plan, to which Rolls-Royce contributed.

At least some details have been made public about the high level group on key enabling technologies. Other clubs which bring together EU officials and the arms industry are more clandestine. The Defence Stakeholders Group is a case in point. From studying material acquired using freedom of information rules, I understand this club is run by a few EU officials, who invite arms industry lobbyists to occasional discussions. The club is so exclusive that its mailing list seems to have only about 20 subscribers. A question flagged for discussion by the club in 2009 reveals much about its thinking. It asked what 'obstacles' weapons producers need to overcome so that they can do business across borders in a way 'comparable to civil industries'.[69] Unless I am mistaken, this can only mean one thing: the officials who drafted this paper want it to be as easy to sell bombs as it is to sell any other product. In their twisted worldview, bullets should be traded as if they are no different to tomato ketchup or denim jeans.

It would be comforting if this club was merely a talking shop. But a letter written the same year by Paul Weissenberg, then a director in the Commission's enterprise department, emphasised that the group 'has been invaluable in supporting our preparations' for two key pieces of EU legislation.[70] Originally proposed by the Commission in 2007, the 'defence procurement' and 'intra-community transfers' directives aimed at prising open the Union's weapons markets to greater competition. Among other things, they introduced a common system of licenses for sales of weapons between the EU's countries and stipulated that most tenders for military equipment should be published across the Union. Arms industry lobbyists gave a rapturous welcome to these laws. Bill Giles, BAE's point man in Brussels, argued in 2008 that such measures would have been unimaginable five years earlier. 'For governments and an industry accustomed to believe the final authority in all defence equipment matters lies in national capitals, these directives represent something of a revolution,' Giles wrote.[71]

Paul Weissenberg has been determined to turn apparent problems to the arms industry's advantage. When speaking in public, some EU officials such as Claude-France Arnould have almost implied that weapons makers face destitution by describing the downfall in military expenditure as 'alarming'.[72] More upbeat noises have been made in the privacy of Weissenberg's office, where he has been holding 'brainstorming' sessions in order 'to take a fresh look at European defence industrial policy'. In an invitation to one such session, Weissenberg wrote: 'I would like to consider whether the financial crisis provides a new opportunity to examine ways forward in the sensitive area of consolidation.' The 'consolidation' to which he was referring involved possible mergers between weapons producers or their subsidiaries. Although he stated that this area was primarily the responsibility of EU national governments, he argued that 'it is in all our interests to ensure that any serious moves towards consolidation should take into account the long-term viability' of a technologically-advanced military industry.[73]

Two years after Weissenberg penned those words, news broke that BAE Systems and EADS were in talks about merging the two firms. Though the merger did not go ahead, supporters of the kind of 'consolidation' envisaged present it as a no-brainer. The gist of their argument is that there is too much duplication of efforts among Europe's weapons producers and an inability of these producers to get their act together is holding the continent back. Frank Haun, head of the German tank maker Krauss-Maffei Wegmann encapsulated this line of thinking when he asked: 'Is there really a necessity for six different types of 8x8s [eight wheel drives] vehicles [to be] developed and produced within the European Union?'[74]

APING AMERICA

The usual reason given why Europe 'needs' a stronger arms industry is to keep up with America. The EDA's staff regularly sift through data from both sides of the Atlantic. Such data indicates that in 2010, the US spent €520 billion on the military, compared to €194 billion for the EDA's 26 countries (all of the EU's states, bar Denmark, take part in the agency's activities). Of particular concern to the EDA was that its members spent a total of €2.1 billion in military-related research and technology that year, whereas the US spent €10 billion. The mismatch is even greater when you examine how the EDA countries allocated 3.2 per cent of total government spending (or 1.6 per cent of gross domestic product) to the military, while America allocated an enormous 11.2 per cent (or 4.8 per cent of GDP). This breaks down at roughly €390 for every man, woman and child living in the 26 European countries in question but at €1,676 for every American. And although overall military expenditure has stagnated or fallen slightly during recent years in Europe, it rose in the US under Barack Obama's presidency (by 5 per cent between 2009 and 2010).[75]

Contrary to what the EDA insinuates, there is nothing 'alarming' about cutting military budgets from the perspective of ordinary people. Rather, such cuts are one of the few – and perhaps the only – positive consequences of the wave of austerity sweeping over Europe. The truly alarming aspect of this debate is that even with these cuts, the EU still accounts for about one-quarter of the world's military spending.[76] The argument that Europe must have an arms industry comparable to that of the US is both weak and dishonest. We will not be safer in this continent if we try to stay abreast of America. Being a trigger-happy superpower did not save New York from the attacks on 11 September 2001; more than likely, the attacks were a response to US imperialism. How, then, could an arms race or a military technology competition be expected to shield us from what policy wonks call 'asymmetric threats'?

The same argument is dishonest because – far from acting as a rival to the US – Europe's war industry cooperates frequently with its counterpart across the Atlantic. This cooperation should be seen in the wider political context of how the EU's status as a vassal of the US has been reinforced through the Lisbon treaty. It stated plainly that the Union would be under the thumb of NATO, which 'remains the foundation of the collective defence of its members'.[77] NATO has been a US-led alliance ever since its inception; the likelihood of America relinquishing that leadership is remote.

American and European arms companies have even been known to join forces in order to lobby the White House. In December 2009, for example, BAE's Linda Hudson signed a letter to Barack Obama drafted by the Aerospace Industries Association of America, urging that the controls on exports of military technology be weakened.[78] A briefing document circulated among the arms industry elite said that multilateral rules introduced to halt the proliferation of weapons of mass destruction 'needlessly restrict' the sale of surveillance and reconnaissance equipment that 'are in very high demand by the US military and our coalition partners'. Subjecting drones intended for spy operations instead of dropping bombs to 'the same restrictions as cruise missiles is unnecessary and inappropriate,' the document added.[79]

A separate paper from ASD noted that the trade association had developed a 'close dialogue' with chief executives in the US arms industry 'on issues affecting the so-called trans-Atlantic defence marketplace since at least 2005'. ASD has been seeking that the EU institutions support its efforts to have a relaxation of controls on the exportation of military components from the US. In particular, it has sought that European weapons programmes – such as Saab's Gripen project – should be exempt from the requirement of having an export licence issued by the US authorities each time they wish to use an American item.[80]

Barack Obama's administration has faced rumours that he is not as interested in Europe as many of its predecessors. The rumours are, in my view, exaggerated. It was not an accident that Robert Gates, who served as defence secretary under both Obama and

George W. Bush, chose to give his final policy speech in Brussels during June 2011. On that occasion, Gates bemoaned how 'total European defence spending declined by nearly 15 per cent in the decade following 9/11' and how the US now accounts for 75 per cent of military expenditure by NATO members. Unless Europe became more militaristic, US policymakers 'may not consider the return on America's investment in NATO worth the cost,' he said.[81]

It was not an accident, either, that Gates issued this warning at a conference organised by Security and Defence Agenda (SDA). His patently ludicrous warning that Europeans must pull their weight or they will no longer have a supporting role in helping America remain a superpower echoed the myth that this outfit has been peddling since it was formed in 2002. SDA styles itself as 'the only think-tank in Brussels focusing exclusively on security and defence issues'.[82] Regardless of whether that it is strictly accurate, SDA has certainly attracted the powerful. Two former secretary generals of NATO – Jaap de Hoop Scheffer and Javier Solana – routinely chair SDA events, sometimes jointly.[83] Its advisory board at the time of writing boasts Claude France-Arnould from the European Defence Agency, Tony Blair's one-time foreign policy adviser Robert Cooper and Scott Harris, previously a senior representative of the American arms giant Lockheed Martin.[84]

As if there weren't enough alpha males (and the occasional woman) jostling for attention, SDA is directed by Giles Merritt, who, according to his erstwhile employer the *Financial Times*, is one of the 30 most influential people in Brussels.[85] As a journalist-turned-lobbyist, Merritt has dabbled in a variety of subject matters. In the 1990s, he ran the Philip Morris Institute, which tried to cultivate an aura of sophistication around cigarettes by promoting debates on global affairs.[86] Along with championing Big Tobacco, he poses as a friend of the downtrodden by presiding over the Development Policy Forum, which focuses on aid nominally intended to reduce global poverty.[87]

In 2010, Merritt put his name to an opinion piece, arguing that the 'credibility' of many European governments on military matters 'leaves so much to be desired'. Also signed by Narcis Serra, previously a Spanish defence minister, the article labelled governments with relatively low levels of military spending as 'free-rider EU countries'.[88] I asked Merritt how he could reconcile his campaigning for higher spending on both armaments and the fight against poverty. Despite having authored a rant against 'free-rider EU countries', Merritt replied: 'I do not myself advocate higher defence spending, and certainly there would be no need to increase spending if nations worked together more closely and pooled resources. By working together and avoiding duplication and waste, resources could be freed up for areas like development. These ideas are not as contradictory as you seem to think.'

In return for an annual fee of €7,500, weapons producers 'receive visibility and speaking opportunities' at SDA events, Merritt told me. 'But our editorial independence and balance is contractually guaranteed, and all our events are the subject of reports that are widely disseminated and can be found on our website. I don't think you would be able to point to any SDA documents as "lobbying material". Panellists at SDA debates are questioned by moderators and audiences, ensuring that all possible questions, polite or tough, get asked.'[89]

The tough questions do not necessarily get answered, however. That is what I discovered when I accepted Merritt's invitation to attend an SDA debate about the future of NATO in a royal Belgian palace during May 2012. My questions were prompted by an advertisement from Lockheed Martin in a brochure prepared especially for the event. Headlined 'Bringing our Best to Trans-Atlantic Partnerships', the ad stated that 'Lockheed was proud to have contributed to smarter defence with products such as the F-35' jet.[90]

After Chad Fulgham, a Lockheed vice-president, had given a presentation, I raised my hand and requested the floor. Noting Lockheed's pride in the F-35, I asked: 'Are you proud that in 2010, your company signed a contract to supply 20 of these fighter jets to the state of Israel? Are you proud that other weapons manufactured by your company have been used by Israel to butcher Palestinian civilians?[91] Are you proud that your pay slip is stained with the blood of Palestinian children? And if you are not proud, can you give me one good reason why your company should not be prosecuted for crimes against humanity?' My query did not elicit any response, so I stood up in protest. 'Is he [Fulgham] going to answer?' I persisted. 'I very much doubt it,' Merritt interjected. 'It has little to do with the topic we are discussing.'[92] Challenging the arms industry for facilitating and profiting from human rights abuses is not what gentlemen do, it would appear.

Lockheed Martin is no stranger to European affairs. During the 1990s Lockheed stalwart Bruce Jackson led a campaign to have a grouping of ex-communist states admitted to NATO, despite explicit promises made by Ronald Reagan in 1989 that the alliance would not attempt to encircle Russia. Jackson proved similarly meddlesome in 2003, when he drafted the 'Vilnius Ten' letter, an expression of support from leaders in central and eastern Europe for George Bush's preparations to occupy Iraq. Lockheed was 'one of the biggest beneficiaries' of the invasion, as William Hartung writes in his book *Prophets of War*. Perhaps its most deplorable contribution involved supplying rocket systems to launch cluster bombs, which will more than likely continue to slice limbs off Iraqi civilians for many years, if not decades.[93]

REINFORCING THE FORTRESS

Away from the glare of public opinion, Lockheed has been advising Frontex, the EU's border management agency, about how its warplanes can help to keep foreigners out of Europe. In 2011, Frontex invited Lockheed to stage a demonstration titled 'UAVs: the potential for European border surveillance' in conjunction with the Greek authorities. The purpose of this workshop, according to Edgar Beugels, the head of research for Frontex, was 'to present industry with the chance to demonstrate the capabilities of currently available technological solutions'.[94] Lockheed not only grasped the opportunity; it sent the agency a €30,000 bill for its services.[95]

The cooperation between Frontex and the Greek authorities is troubling in itself. Human Rights Watch has investigated the detention of almost 12,000 migrants who entered Greece at its land border with Turkey between November 2010 and March 2011. During that time, the European Court of Human Rights in Strasbourg issued a judgment, which declared that Greece's asylum system was dysfunctional. The country's detention facilities were found to be so shabby that they violated human rights laws prohibiting ill-treatment and torture. Guards deployed by Frontex regularly apprehended migrants and brought them to the detention centres, frequently in buses provided by the agency. In some of these centres, unaccompanied children were held for long periods.[96] This means that an official EU agency helped flout international law. Under the 1951 Refugee Convention, all signatories are supposed to guarantee the protection of minors, particularly children who are not accompanied by a parent or another adult.[97]

Fleeing persecution and poverty is no crime. Yet Frontex is making plans to deploy warplanes against people who are doing nothing more sinister than trying to reach Europe in the hope that they might be able to have a better life here. Frontex was established in 2004; another eight years passed before the agency got around to appointing its first fundamental rights officer.[98] Throughout its history, then, the Warsaw-based body has been treating poor, unarmed migrants as a quasi-military threat. At the time of writing, the agency is headed by Ilkka Laitenen, a Finnish brigadier general.[99] He has commanded a budget that has risen from €6.5 million in 2005 to €112 million in 2011. Originally, Frontex had to rely on equipment borrowed from EU governments but in 2011 it was given the green light to buy its own equipment. America's Department of Commerce was quick to take note of this decision, predicting that 'this new purchasing freedom may provide those US companies with European subsidiaries with new export possibilities'.[100]

Well before the 'freedom' was granted, Europe's own arms companies were in cahoots with Frontex. ASD has been having discussions with the agency about 'anticipation of future threats'.[101] The uprisings that ousted dictators in Tunisia and Egypt during 2011 prompted Finmeccanica, the Italian corporation, to contact Laitenen. Pointing to 'increased migratory flows' towards Europe from North Africa, Finmeccanica requested an appointment to explain how one of its maritime patrol aircraft (the ATR42/72) 'can perfectly represent the "core" for a fully integrated, custom tailored project to meet the specific Frontex requirements in the current Mediterranean scenario'.[102] Paolo Pozzessere, a 'senior vice president' with the company, was so eager to stress the perfection of his products that he neglected to mention Finmeccanica's role in propping up some of the more notorious leaders in North Africa. Perhaps the most conspicuous omission from his letter was that his corporation clinched a €300 million deal with Muammar Gaddafi's regime in 2009; the deal provided for the installation of a surveillance system to thwart migrants from heading to Italy via Libya.[103] On second thoughts, the omission may make sense. The West was quite happy to hire Gaddafi as a subcontractor for Fortress Europe before our governments fell out with him again; in 2010, the EU even signed an agreement to formally give him that role.[104]

Cecilia Malmström, the EU's commissioner for home affairs at the time of writing, has overseen both the 'hiring' of Gaddafi and the operation of Frontex. I asked her why the arms industry is so heavily involved in the agency's activities. She responded by saying that manufacturers of border surveillance equipment have 'for decades been delivering products and services that can be used for civil and military purposes'. She added: 'This is a commercial reality and cannot be used as an argument to imply that the European Union would take a militaristic approach on asylum and migration. It is essential to remember that Frontex is exclusively interested in those technological applications that can be used for civil security purposes.'[105]

Her explanation shouldn't be taken at face value. Since 2005, the European Defence Agency has been coordinating a project aimed at linking up the national military networks of EU countries to improve maritime surveillance. This project (known as Marsur) is, in the agency's words, intended to 'enable early warning, identification and tracking of threats approaching the European homeland by sea'. Although the project clearly has a strong military nature, Frontex has been closely involved, just as it has participated in many of the EDA's other activities.[106] The EDA has always been a plaything of the arms industry. Frontex is at risk of becoming one, too.

Furthermore, if Malmström is sincere in thinking that Frontex has a purely civilian outlook, she needs to brush up on her knowledge of strategic discussions underway among that part of the EU bureaucracy she oversees. In 2011, Frontex was given an additional responsibility: to 'provide the necessary assistance' to developing a European border surveillance system (known, somewhat predictably, as Eurosur). Of course, this decision did not emerge from nowhere. It was preceded by two discussion papers from the European Commission urging that Eurosur be eventually integrated into a wider network that would be responsible for military matters, along with fisheries monitoring, pollution control and 'general law enforcement'.[107]

Let us be under no illusions about what is happening here. The European Union is becoming increasingly militarised and the same arms companies which are guiding this process are scooping up whatever contracts they can get their hands on.

4
How we live and diet

Monsanto is not a corporation deserving of trust. Between 1961 and 1971, the US sprayed more than 49 million litres of Agent Orange on South Vietnam.[1] The legacy of this highly toxic compound is still apparent today. UNICEF reported in 2008 that Vietnam has a 'disproportionately high number of disabled children, including many affected by exposure to chemicals left over from the spraying of Agent Orange. Estimates put the number at around 1.2 million.'[2] Although the US government continues to equivocate, it implicitly accepts that some congenital defects are attributable to the substance. The Department of Veteran Affairs 'presumes' that the exposure of soldiers to Agent Orange is relevant when their sons or daughters are born with spina bifida.[3]

Monsanto was one of the main companies directed by the US government to supply chemicals used in Agent Orange during the Vietnam War. Five decades on, the Missouri firm tries to absolve itself of any responsibility, insisting that the link between Agent Orange and high incidences of certain diseases has not been 'conclusively demonstrated'.[4] As well as hiding behind that pedantic fig-leaf, Monsanto has resorted to damage limitation by paying 'compensation' to some of its victims. In 2012, it agreed to finance the long-term medical monitoring of neighbours who complained of pollution from its plant in Nitro, West Virginia.[5] Nitro was a key site for the production of 2,4,5-T, one of the two potent weed-killers mixed together in Agent Orange.[6]

With that tarnished reputation, it is reasonable to expect that everything Monsanto says and does should be treated with suspicion. For one EU agency, however, Monsanto can do no wrong.

The honour of hosting the European Food Safety Authority (EFSA) was awarded to Parma, Italy, to appease Silvio Berlusconi in 2003. (As prime minister, Berlusconi insisted that a city synonymous with Parma ham and Parmesan cheese was the only plausible contender for the body's headquarters; he dismissed a rival bid by Helsinki on the grounds that Finns 'don't even know what *prosciutto* is').[7] Its establishment was presented as a response to a series of scandals, including the BSE ('mad cow disease') outbreak in Britain and a poultry contamination crisis that helped shape the outcome of the 1999 election in Belgium.[8] While those scandals might have prompted numerous parents to think more deeply about what they were putting in their children's mouths, EFSA has displayed an unwavering faith in industrial food production.

Between 2005 and 2012, Monsanto submitted about 80 requests for approval of genetically modified (GM) crops to the Parma authority.[9] By its own admission, EFSA has only issued favourable responses to such applications.[10] To see if the authority subjects these requests to rigorous scrutiny before rubber-stamping them, I studied a sheaf of documents relating to a GM soybean that received EFSA's blessing in 2012. EFSA originally received a copy of the application to sell this crop within the EU in August 2009.[11] According to Monsanto, the soybean (known by the codename MON 87701 x MON 89788) was initially developed for the Brazilian market. Intended for both human and animal consumption, it has been designed to resist insects and survive spraying with Roundup Ready, a herbicide also made by Monsanto.[12]

After reading the application, Per Bergman, head of EFSA's department for genetically modified organisms (GMOs), wrote to Monsanto in October 2009. Noting that Monsanto had conducted field trials on the soybean in the US during 2007, he recommended that the company provide some data on these trials in addition to that contained in its application. This extra data could be 'valuable for the risk assessment' of the soybean, he stated.[13] Monsanto responded by sending him a revised version of its application a month later.[14] Bergman then declared the application to be valid in December 2009.[15]

Over the next two years, EFSA forwarded Monsanto four sets of questions about the application. Each set of questions fitted on either one or two sides of an A4 sheet of paper. In most cases, the questions simply looked for further results of tests carried out by Monsanto. For example, one EFSA working group felt that Monsanto had submitted incomplete details about an experiment in which the soybean was fed to broiler chicken.[16] Monsanto's replies to these queries were deemed satisfactory; in January 2012, EFSA told the company that the scientific opinion on the request had been 'adopted' by the agency's GMO panel and that it would soon be published.[17] True to its word, EFSA published the opinion the following month; it concluded that Monsanto's soybean was 'as safe as its comparator with respect to potential effects on human and animal health and the environment, in the context of its intended uses'.[18] (As already mentioned, Monsanto has made clear that it wants humans to eat its soybean.) The 'comparator' in question was another GM soybean, this one developed by the German firm Bayer. The Bayer soybean had been deemed 'safe as its conventional counterpart' by EFSA in 2011.[19]

I was eager to learn more about the GMO panel which gave a thumbs-up to Monsanto's soybean based primarily on tests that Monsanto itself had carried out. So I consulted all the declarations of interests and biographical notes I could find for the 20 members of the panel at the time its opinion was finalised. I noticed that three of the panel had registered connections to the International Life Sciences Institute (ILSI), a food industry think tank with offices in Brussels and Washington. Jean-Michel Wal had participated in ILSI working groups and discussions organised by the institute on various topics, including GM foods, since 2002 and was still undertaking such work in 2012.[20] His colleague Harry Kuiper – who chaired the EFSA panel for almost a decade – stated that he had been an 'independent expert' with ILSI from 2000 to 2005.[21] And Gijs Kleter confessed he had belonged to an ILSI task force between 2002 and 2007; the 'force' was dedicated to the 'safety assessment of nutritionally improved crops derived through biotechnology'.[22]

ILSI's stated 'mission' is to 'provide science that improves public health and well-being and safeguards the environment'. Styling itself as a 'public-private partnership', ILSI is primarily financed by its corporate members.[23] As those members include Monsanto – which had a seat on ILSI's governing board in 2011 – it is hard to see how scientists contracted to work for the institute can be seen as impartial when they review applications from that firm.[24] Furthermore, ILSI promotes activities in which GM crops are defended with an evangelical fervour. In September 2012, it helped to organise an international symposium on 'biosafety of genetically modified organisms' in St Louis, which happens to be the same city where Monsanto is headquartered. The programme for that event asked if the 'slow approval process for GMOs in developing countries' was caused by a 'problem of weak regulatory capacity'.[25] Robert Paarlberg, a keynote speaker at the symposium, is a proponent of the theory that African farmers are poor because they are unable to access GM seeds.[26] I was less than surprised to learn that he has been an adviser to Monsanto.[27]

The EFSA panel handling Monsanto's soybean had some other links to big business. German biologist Christoph Tebbe's declaration of interests contained a hilarious qualification. Tebbe vowed to rule himself out of discussing approval bids for GM potatoes as he had worked on a tuber dossier financed by BASF between 2007 and 2009.[28] As far as I could ascertain, he was the only member of the panel who interpreted scientific ethics as a requirement to avoid showing favouritism towards a certain type of fruit or vegetable. Environmental consultant Jeremy Sweet, meanwhile, owned shares in the pharmaceutical giant GSK, as well as the oil firms Shell and BP.[29] And Huw Jones was a professor with Rothamsted, a research centre in Hertfordshire. Between 2007 and 2009, Rothamsted received a grant from Bayer 'to make transgenic wheat plants for a research project'.[30] Bayer, it should be recalled, had manufactured the 'comparator' for Monsanto's soybean.

In May 2012, EFSA belatedly took action against one corporate lobbyist who was masquerading as an independent scientist. The authority told Diána Bánáti that she could no longer remain as chairwoman of its management board because she had accepted a high-level post with ILSI.[31] Bánáti's resignation from the board followed criticism of EFSA in the European Parliament. Catherine Geslain-Lanéelle, director of EFSA at the time of writing, has insisted that the agency has 'full confidence in the impartiality of its scientific advice and integrity of the more than 1,500 experts' contributing to its activities.[32] And yet the EU's own financial watchdog, the European Court of Auditors, stated in October 2012 that at least six of EFSA's 'experts' retained links to a 'worldwide organisation' that was 'funded primarily' by the agri-food industry.[33]

I contacted Geslain-Lannéelle to ask if her agency was prepared to reassess the approval it had granted to the Monsanto soybean. In my query, I pointed out that some of the panel which had granted the approval were involved in ILSI and that Monsanto was a member of the group. The reply to my query came from James Ramsay, a 'media relations officer' with EFSA. He said that the members of the GMO panel had all given commitments to act independently and 'were considered by EFSA not to have any conflict of interest'.[34]

Assurances from EFSA do not alter the fact that the agency has facilitated and continues to facilitate discussions between scientists and industry, without inviting any critics of big business to attend. Unpublished documents that I have seen indicate that EFSA recognises that Monsanto and ILSI are effectively joined at the hip. In January 2012, for example, EFSA invited Monsanto to a workshop on food allergies. Antonio Dumont Fernandez, a scientific officer in Parma, informed Monsanto that the agenda for the meeting was 'confidential and for your internal use only!' (his exclamation mark). But he wrapped up his email message by noting that the 'participation of ILSI in the workshop will be very much welcomed'.[35] On other occasions, ILSI has contributed to conferences organised by the authority that were presented as being restricted to 'applicants' for GM crop approvals and the officials processing their files.[36]

EFSA relies on research conducted by the food industry when it is assessing whether or not new products should be placed on the market. Very often this research has been commissioned by the same companies that stand to gain from sales of these products. It hardly needs to be spelled out that this reliance is problematic. If I was eager to make millions from a particular invention, should you trust me to be totally upfront about flaws in that invention? Of course, you shouldn't.

Is it too much to ask that decisions about new food items that more than likely will be eaten by children are subject to independent analysis? EFSA appears to think that it is. In 2012, a team led by Gilles-Eric Séralini from the University of Caen in France, published the findings of a two-year study on the effects of two Monsanto products on rats. The two products were a GM maize and the herbicide Roundup and, according to the team, this was the first study of its kind that examined rats over their entire lives. (The standard feeding studies for GM soy and maize are limited to 90 days.)

The study found that the first large tumours were detected in male rats after four months and in females after seven months, indicating that the standard length of trials is, in Séralini's words, 'inadequate'. His team found that tumours observed in female rats were five times more frequent than in males after two years; most of the tumours affecting the females were in their breasts. It had previously been known that high quantities of glyphosate – the key ingredient in Roundup – can be hazardous to human health. But Séralini's team concluded that exposure to the substance 'at concentrations well below officially set safety limits induce severe hormone-dependent mammary, hepatic [liver] and kidney disturbances'.[37]

On 26 September 2012, EFSA was formally asked to review Séralini's paper by the European Commission.[38] By the standards of the EU bureaucracy, EFSA responded with an incredible haste. After little more than a week, it declared that the conclusions of the study could not be regarded as 'scientifically sound'. Among the reasons stated for the rejection were that a total of 100 rodents were used, rather than 500. More significantly, the authority stated it did not see a 'need to re-examine its previous safety evaluation' of NK603, the maize under scrutiny.[39]

It is, to put it mildly, intriguing that EFSA was so emphatic in rejecting a study that was not paid for by the food industry. Research funded by corporations, on the other hand, is generally embraced in Parma. Since the early 1960s, Monsanto executives have been hyping their potential to deliver a 'miracle' in the battle against hunger and malnutrition.[40] Some of its dealings with EU officials nonetheless hint at slightly more prosaic concerns. These concerns do not appear motivated by scientific rigour but by the desire to get products on the market at the earliest possible date. When Monsanto felt that EFSA was taking too much time over a soybean dossier in 2012, one of the corporation's representatives sought to know what was causing the delays. 'Sorry for the insistence but we are getting a lot of pressure to advance this particular application,' the representative wrote in an email message.[41]

WAITING FOR A MIRACLE?

Monsanto is active in the European Association for Bioindustries (EuropaBio), along with competitors such as Syngenta, Bayer, Dow and Eli Lilly.[42] Like the 'miracle' merchants of Missouri, EuropaBio has been swift to spread any good news to which it is alerted. In 2011, the *Guardian* reported that tests were being undertaken in Britain to see if medicines deriving from GM plants could be used to prevent HIV infection.[43] EuropaBio reacted as if AIDS had been definitively vanquished; in an email message sent to José Manuel Barroso and his fellow members of the European Commission, it gushed that 'these are the kind of things that make working in the biotechnology sector priceless'.[44] A separate letter from the association five days earlier presented genetic engineering as the cure to all of Europe's ills: 'No other industrial sector sits so comfortably at the intersection of enhancement of quality of life, knowledge, responsible innovation, productivity and environmental protection.'[45]

EuropaBio has been focused for some time on overcoming regulatory hurdles. In its contacts with EFSA, it has complained that questions asked by that agency during the 'completeness check' on applications are 'too prescriptive'. Requests to conduct additional field trials are especially irksome because such trials are 'really time-consuming', EuropaBio stated in 2007.[46] The whingeing had an effect: little over a year later, the association was commending EFSA for the 'important improvement in the duration of the completeness check', while noting that some 'bottlenecks' remained.[47]

So determined to have its way, EuropaBio has acted as a kind of a bulwark against any form of scientific enquiry that is not under its control. When seeking to have GM foods that are resistant to herbicides approved, it has 'questioned the need to re-assess the effects of the herbicide,' according to an EFSA note from 2009. EuropaBio felt that legislation pertaining to GM crops should not be invoked in order to enquire about the safety of chemical weed-killers often manufactured by the same companies that are heavily involved in biotechnology.[48] The association is adamant that herbicides are 'adequately covered' by other legislation.[49]

Perhaps the clearest manifestation of the harmonious relationship between EFSA and the agri-food industry relates to the case of Suzy Renckens. This Belgian engineer used to be the coordinator of the authority's GMO panel. In that role she acted as a go-between with corporations, by passing on their messages to the 'experts' sitting on the panel.[50] Renckens held that post from 2003 until 2008, when she was hired by the Swiss biotech firm Syngenta.[51] This was a clear case of 'revolving doors' or – more accurately – of swapping chairs. Whereas Renckens used to attend EFSA's workshops as a member of the agency's staff, her new capacity allowed her to attend them as part of a EuropaBio delegation.[52] In 2012, EFSA's chief Catherine Geslain-Lanéelle, stated that Renckens' Rubicon-crossing had been considered by EFSA in 2008 and it was decided that there was no 'conflict of interests' involved. Geslain-Lanéelle admitted that 'it failed to record the assessment of the move of Ms Renckens to a biotechnology company in a way as it would be done today'.[53]

For the 2011 financial year, EuropaBio stated that it employed 17 members of staff but that just two of them were lobbyists.[54] A 'tweet' by the Brussels office of Greenpeace poked fun at the inference that EuropaBio is not fundamentally a political outfit by noting it had 'a lot of people making tea'.[55] EuropaBio's aforementioned commitment to knowledge and 'responsible innovation' sits uncomfortably with efforts it has made to weaken new food safety initiatives. When the European Commission was preparing new guidelines for carrying out environmental risk assessments on GM foods in 2011, EuropaBio urged that they not be given a 'legally binding scope'. In making its case, the association said it 'wishes to underline the importance of a flexible case-by-case principle of risk assessment'.[56]

Speed is of the essence, too. EuropaBio has bemoaned how 'GM product approvals take longer in the EU than anywhere else'. According to its calculations, the 'average time it takes a GM import dossier to pass through the EU approval process is 47 months' – up to twice as long as in similar countries.[57] Any 'further escalation' in requests for information about GM foods by the EU authorities would be 'incompatible' with the 'better regulation objective' of the European Commission, the biotech industry feels.[58] Paraphrased crudely, this amounts to a plea that EU officials forget about how butterflies are affected by agricultural changes and concentrate on pleasing big business.

It is instructive that the Commission has become increasingly gung-ho in its support for GM food, despite how some of its own advisers have expressed serious reservations about their health and ecological effects. In 2002, the Commission's in-house research centre warned that the introduction of GM crops could have devastating consequences for organic and family farming.[59] Such concerns are not shared by their colleagues in other departments. Paola Testöri Coggi, the Commission's top food safety official at the time of writing, bragged in 2011 that she had overseen an acceleration in GM approvals. 'The Commission adopted 11 authorisation decisions on GMOs in 2010, including five files which, as you aware, had been pending for a long time,' she told EuropaBio. 'The average time taken by the Commission to approve GM products is decreasing year after year.'[60]

Her predecessor, Robert Madelin, had promoted 'loyal cooperation' between EU officials and the biotech industry, providing the latter with helpful advice about how to prepare applications. The cooperation was so loyal that the European Commission agreed to host secretive brainstorming sessions with EuropaBio and EFSA. Known as the 'tripartite meetings' – and still continuing today – these select gatherings were initiated after EuropaBio wrote to Barroso in 2006 to express fears that widespread public opposition to GM foods 'might greatly diminish' the opportunities to prove the association's theory that gobbling artificially manipulated sweet corn benefits our health.[61]

Steered by Barroso, the Commission has done what it can to shove unwanted foods down our throats. Soon after he began his second term in office, Barroso bestowed a dubious honour on a humble potato in March 2010. Known as Amflora, the potato became the first GM crop to be authorised for cultivation (as opposed simply to importation) by the EU executive in 12 years.[62]

Manufactured by BASF and intended initially for industrial uses, Amflora contains a gene making it resistant to two antibiotics, neomycin and katamycin, both treatments for tuberculosis. Right until he was forced to resign over a tobacco lobbying scandal in 2012, the EU's health commissioner John Dalli continued to insist that there is a 'low probability' of the potato undermining the effectiveness of these medicines.[63] His doggedness in standing by the spud was at variance with recommendations from the World Health Organisation, which advocates that biotechnology avoids using antibiotic-resistant genes.[64]

Mella Frewen has a largely unrivalled knowledge of how the food lobby works in Brussels. Having worked for the sugar and starch industry since 1989, she was hired by Monsanto, as its government affairs officer for Europe and Africa, a post she held from 2002 to 2007.[65] Her transition from Monsanto to FoodDrinkEurope, where she is the director general at the time of writing, appears to have been seamless. Under Frewen's leadership, this powerful trade association is trying to bring GM crops into Europe by whatever possible route.

In 2010, FoodDrinkEurope (then known by the French acronym CIAA) demanded an end to what it termed the 'zero tolerance policy' for GM crops then being followed in the EU. Its protest was prompted by the anti-GM stance of a number of EU governments. FoodDrinkEurope – and a few like-minded groups – blitzed high-ranking officials with pleas for 'urgent action' against restrictions on importing foods for human consumption and animal feeds containing GM ingredients. Continuing with 'zero tolerance' at a time when the quantity of GM crops being grown elsewhere in the world was increasing 'can only spell disaster for the economic sustainability of EU food and feed operators,' it warned. Arguing that the restraints hampered European companies from using imported material, FoodDrinkEurope stated the 'low level GM presence' in items required by farmers and industry was 'literally unavoidable'. A 'technical solution' to ensure that imports of GM products was allowed must be introduced 'as a first step', according to the call for action.[66]

The appeal was one of a series, some of which were prompted by events in the real world. A year earlier, for example, maize modified by Monsanto was detected in soybean meal from Germany. As both food and animal feed were deemed 'equally vulnerable' to this form of contamination, CIAA availed of the opportunity to seek that the presence of GM properties in food be accepted.[67] Frewen and her colleagues have been partially successful. A 'technical solution' of the kind FoodDrinkEurope has been seeking entered into force in 2011; it allowed animal feed to contain 0.1 per cent of GM material not yet authorised in the EU provided it met certain criteria (such as having been submitted for review to the European Food Safety Authority). FoodDrinkEurope regarded the move as being in a 'positive direction'. But FoodDrinkEurope also declared the move 'not sustainable' given that it didn't apply to ingredients directly consumed by humans.[68] And so the struggle to put more GM foods on Europe's dining tables continues.

The cordial relationship that Frewen enjoys with the EU hierarchy has survived despite the contempt she has displayed for the minimalist transparency rules introduced in recent times. Unlike its counterpart in Washington, the Brussels bureaucracy does not have a mandatory register for lobbyists trying to influence policy-makers. The European Commission has, however, made participation in some groups with which it consults on a periodic basis conditional on signing up to its voluntary register.

In 2009, CIAA was told that it would have to comply with this condition by the following year if it was to remain eligible for membership of the Commission's 'advisory groups' on agriculture.[69] For over a year, Frewen refused to comply with this demand, claiming that CIAA could not join the register until it had received clear information from the Belgian authorities about whether it would lose certain tax perks if it was regarded as a lobby group. Frewen told EU officials that it was proving difficult to obtain clarity on these matters, given a 'stand-still in Belgian politics' (talks on forming a government after a general election had proven inconclusive).[70] To its credit, the Commission did not buy her explanation and kept on threatening to exclude CIAA until the association eventually relented in November 2010.[71] The Commission's victory in this showdown led one EU official to send an amusing note to a colleague. 'Gerry, I know you hate transparency but even CIAA is learning,' the message read.[72] It is questionable, though, how much was really learned: less than a week after the issue was resolved, four EU commissioners took time out of their busy schedules to speak at the CIAA's 2010 congress.[73] Few other lobby groups can expect so many top-level members of the EU hierarchy to clear their diaries for the same event.

Far from scolding the CIAA over its lack of transparency, the commissioners spent most of their time fawning. John Dalli began his presentation by feigning concern over the 24 per cent of children in the EU who were overweight or obese. Rather than taking robust action to shield our young from ill-health, Dalli argued in favour of allowing industry to regulate itself over advertising and promotions directed at children.[74] The measured tone of his speech implied that with a little bit of encouragement, McDonald's and Coca-Cola will stop trying to tantalise our kids with cuddly mascots or colourful packaging.

The lax approach to oversight favoured by Dalli was in keeping with the way that the food industry has been operating for some time. In 2009, the European Commission published the findings of a 'high level group' it had assembled on guaranteeing the 'competitiveness' of food production. The group was dominated by corporate lobbyists, including representatives of Unilever, Cadbury, the CIAA, Pernod and Nestlé. Its report called for a reduction in the 'administrative burdens' faced by industry. While it acknowledged the importance of protecting health and the environment, it argued that 'consumer information and especially labelling provisions specific both to food and other issues of consumer concern should take competitiveness and the integrity of the internal market into account'.[75]

As a follow-up to that report, the food industry was given an even more direct input into policy-making. The 'European food sustainable consumption and production round table' set up in response was jointly chaired by industry and the European Commission. To signal who was really in the driving seat, the new forum's inaugural meeting was held in CIAA's Brussels headquarters, with Mella Frewen giving the introductory speech.[76] From the outset, it was stressed that its objective was to 'identify suitable means of voluntary communication to consumers'. The 'public relations' work on the initiative was handled by APCO, a corporate communications firm.[77]

Frewen also sits on the EU Platform on Diet, Physical Activity and Health at the time of writing.[78] Corporations have availed of this EU-sponsored grouping, which was formed in 2005, to parade their efforts to safeguard our health. One of its 'achievements' is a pledge, whereby fizzy drink and sweet makers undertake not to advertise on TV programmes with more than 50 per cent of viewers under the age of 12.[79] An audit found that signatories to the pledge had a 99 per cent compliance rate in 2011. The audit was described as independent but was partly financed by Unilever.[80]

It is somewhat ironic that Unilever has cast itself as a rescuer of children from marketing marauders. A few years earlier, this

Anglo-Dutch giant sought to win approval from the European Food Safety Authority for labels asserting that some of the vitamins and acids in its products provided 'important nutrients for the brain'. Unilever had to withdraw the application in 2008 because it was outside the scope of the EU's legislation on health claims. The company had planned to have images of children on the packaging and ads for these products.[81] Reading between the lines of its correspondence with EFSA, it becomes clear that Unilever is prone to viewing children as marketing tools, making it an implausible campaigner against child-targeted advertising.

A much more likely explanation for why corporations are offering to police themselves is that they are determined to avoid legislation. The European Consumers' Organisation – known by its French acronym BEUC – is seeking a ban on all TV ads for food products with a high sugar, fat or salt content between 6 a.m. and 9 p.m.[82] Such a measure would inevitably decrease the prospect of a seven-year-old boy nagging his parents for a packet of crisps or a brand of ice cream spotted while watching cartoons. As it could also have an impact on the profit margins of companies with a vested interest in padding our waistlines, it's not hard to see why they would be opposed to action of this nature.

BREAKING THE TRAFFIC LIGHTS

In 2012, the European Commission recommended that Mella Frewen should be appointed to EFSA's governing board. Fortunately, the nomination was rejected by EU governments.[83] Still, the willingness of the Brussels hierarchy to consider a private sector lobbyist for such an important role in regulating food speaks volumes about how things work in this city. The willingness is all the more disturbing when examined in the context of how Frewen and her cohorts torpedoed what was arguably the most important legislative initiative on nutrition in Europe's recent history.

Two years earlier, MEPs mulled the possibility of introducing a 'traffic light' system for labelling food products. The system had the beauty of simplicity. Each time we took a trip to our local supermarket, we would be able to identify which items could potentially send our cholesterol levels racing. Those packets would have information about the fat and sugar levels of their contents marked in red. Low calorie foods, on the other hand, would have green labels.

Its commitment to 'sustainable consumption' notwithstanding, CIAA waxed apoplectic at this move to give us clear indications of what was in our trolleys. Indeed, CIAA was even opposed to a proposal originally put forward by Markos Kyprianou, then the EU's health commissioner, in 2008, which was weaker than the traffic lights one. Kyprianou had advocated that 'mandatory food information shall be marked in a conspicuous place in such a way to be easily visible, clearly legible and, where appropriate, indelible' and that 'it shall not in any way be hidden, obscured, detracted from or interrupted by any other written or pictorial matter'.[84] In CIAA's assessment, this compulsory approach would be 'impractical' and impose a 'disproportionate burden on manufacturers'.[85]

The food industry undertook a massive offensive in order to break the traffic lights. MEPs were bombarded with email messages (as many as 150 per day as key votes neared), briefing papers and visits from lobbyists.[86] At one point, CIAA was quoted as saying that food companies had spent €1 billion promoting an alternative 'guideline daily amounts' scheme, under which nutritional details would be presented more subtly than under the red, green and amber scheme.[87] CIAA later issued a statement, claiming it would be 'factually false' to deduce that the one billion figure referred to its war chest for the campaign against the traffic lights. Rather, it said that the figure referred to voluntary efforts made over a period of four or five years.[88] It is significant that CIAA did not reveal how much it actually spent to defeat the traffic lights – a campaign that proved successful when a majority of MEPs killed off the plan in June 2010.[89]

As part of the final compromise, nutritional details can be shown on packages in the same colour, regardless of what a particular item is made of. There is nothing, therefore, to stop confectionery producers from trying to entice young girls by presenting information in a soft pink, rather than the more arresting and readily understandable traffic light system. Bizarrely, alcohol has won an exemption from nutritional labelling requirements despite how many types of booze brim with calories.[90] 'We have a peculiar situation where if you buy orange juice with alcohol in it, you don't get consumer information,' Mariann Skar, secretary-general with the European Alcohol Policy Alliance (Eurocare) told me. 'But if you buy orange juice with just orange juice in it, you do get that information. It's unbelievable.'[91]

A well-organised offensive was mounted by the alcohol industry in order to win the exemption. Renate Sommer, the German politician who oversaw the preparation of the European Parliament's response to the food labelling proposal, has admitted that she received delegations from the umbrella groups representing the wine and spirits industries at European level. She also consulted national drink industry associations from Germany, France, Spain and Ireland, as well as that behemoth of booze Diageo.[92]

UNDER THE INFLUENCE

The exemption for alcohol should be seen in the wider context of how the drinks industry is indulged by authority. Data cited by health professionals indicates that one out of seven deaths for men in the EU aged between 15 and 64 could be attributed to alcohol; the corresponding figure for women is one out of every 13. (It is telling that these estimates – branded 'conservative' by the World Health Organisation – relate to the year 2004; the unavailability of more recent statistics indicates that the problem isn't receiving sufficient attention.)[93]

The Brussels office of Eurocare has an impressive collection of containers for spirits. The most unnerving one I saw was shaped like a baby's bottle, complete with a rubber teat. The accompanying Spanish-language label on this *Batida de Coco* liqueur stated it was 'only for adults'. But surely that message was at odds with the underlying one. Because regulations are so lax, brewers and distillers can woo children and adolescents by giving the impression that potentially lethal concoctions are harmless.

I am not in a position to preach about the demon drink. In 2005, I stopped drinking alcohol completely, having consumed way too much of it over the preceding decade. My conversion to sobriety is one of the best things I have ever done – a life without hangovers is infinitely preferable to one plagued by sore heads and fuzzy recollections of what happened the night before. Yet switching from excess to abstention makes me a man of extremes (on this topic, at least). Today, I am horrified to see people knocking back beer and wine the way I used to. I don't, however, tend to register my disquiet, knowing from experience that alcohol abusers resent being lectured to.

It would be ludicrous to think that binge drinking will cease because politicians say it should. Nonetheless, there are things that can be done. Introducing minimum pricing for alcohol, for example, could be an important step in curbing the availability of cheap booze. And if a ban on tobacco advertising can be introduced across the EU, there is no reason that a similar one can't be introduced for alcohol. That way we wouldn't be confronted with billboards intimating that certain brands of rum or vodka enhance one's masculinity or sex appeal.

In order to have these kinds of measures put forward, policy-makers need to listen more to health professionals who deal with the consequences of alcohol abuse than to companies who profit from it. The European Union purports to treat both groups of 'stakeholders' equally but has effectively given industry the power of veto.

The European Commission recommended a strategy to reduce alcohol-related harm in 2006. Rather than concrete proposals, it offered ideas about 'good practice'. One of its most telling lines was: 'The alcohol beverage industry and retailers can play an important role to ensure that alcohol is consumed responsibly.'[94] This can either be interpreted as a manifestation of ignorance or as a cop-out: in a capitalist economy, private corporations have no mandate to behave 'responsibly'; their only role is to make money. The strategy led to the establishment of the European Alcohol and Health Forum (EAHF) a year later. Set up under the auspices of the European Commission, it was comprised of 27 associations at its inception. Eighteen of these organisations represented producers or retailers of alcohol or publishers and communications firms that made or carried ads for alcohol. The 18 included two institutes dedicated to alcohol research that relied on funding from the drinks industry and, therefore, could not be viewed as impartial. While doctors and public health campaigners were part of the forum, they were clearly outnumbered by private interest groups.[95]

One of the groups involved – the European Forum for Responsible Drinking (EFRD) – contends that alcohol companies should be allowed to regulate themselves. Binding together Diageo, Bacardi-Martini, Pernod Ricard and Moët Hennessy, it publishes glossy brochures and hosts a number of slick websites to underscore its core message: that there is a 'cultural complexity' to the way people drink, so no 'single approach to alcohol policy is likely to succeed uniformly across Europe'.[96] Hoping to find out more about the flexibility it recommends, I approached EFRD spokesman Alan Butler, who also heads Diageo's Brussels office at the time of writing. Butler refused to be interviewed, saying: 'I don't think we can be of much help as for some time now EFRD has not been involved in advocacy'.[97] His excuse was misleading: an organisation that tells legislators to back off is, by definition, involved in advocacy.

Then again, it is not surprising that an industry which benefits from human misery would be in denial about what is really going on.

The European Alcohol and Health Forum has struggled to come to terms with new marketing opportunities for the drinks industry. In April 2012, it discussed with Facebook the possibility of ensuring that ads on social media websites do not tempt children or teenagers to drink alcohol.[98] Barely two months earlier, Erika Mann, a former MEP who went on to become Facebook's head of EU affairs, spoke at a reception hosted by Brewers of Europe. 'We are delighted to be able to show our support for the work that the Brewers of Europe are undertaking in their pledge to improve consumer information, ensure responsible advertising and address alcohol misuse,' she said.[99] Her vote of confidence in her hosts must surely be called into question. It has subsequently been revealed that the Alcohol Beverage Federation of Ireland – a fully paid-up member of the Brewers of Europe – sought to delete key paragraphs from a report commissioned by the Dublin government which addressed the connections between alcohol abuse and rape. Among the statistics that the Irish association wanted to have erased were that 41 per cent of suspected rapists were severely intoxicated when the rape occurred and that alcohol was a potential trigger in one-third of domestic violence incidents.[100] Can an industry that tries to suppress facts it does not like be expected to act 'responsibly'?

One measure of the Brewers of Europe's strength is that it runs a 'beer club' for MEPs. The latest membership list I have seen contains 76 names – more than one-tenth of the entire Parliament. The members include Renate Sommer, the woman who shepherded the food labelling law through the assembly.[101] The club regularly organises beer tasting parties, which have been known to attract powerful figures. Anders Fogh Rasmussen, the NATO secretary-general, turned up to toast Danish brewers at a gig marking Denmark's presidency of the EU in May 2012.[102]

The brewers are not alone in throwing such parties. I remember once attending a reception sponsored by the European spirits industry, to which staff of all the main EU institutions had been invited. The quantity and variety of complimentary alcohol on offer that evening was stupendous and I have to confess that I lost count of how many glasses I quaffed. I'm not suggesting that all such events are quite so Bacchanalian – the wine companies' association CEEV (another French acronym) has been organising a 'wine in moderation' programme to press the case for 'self-regulation'.[103] Although I haven't been invited to its soirées, I can imagine that they are restrained and cerebral. Of course, though, there is a purpose to all the networking here. The politicians and civil servants enjoying this hospitality can be asked to return favours when dossiers of relevance to the drinks industry pop up on their agenda. In that sense, the drink on offer is not really free.

HARMLESS TO HONEY BEES?

One thing that used to puzzle me about firms like Monsanto was how they manufactured weed-killers and then produced GM crops that were resistant to those same weed-killers. Eventually, it dawned on me that just a handful of corporations – Monsanto among them – crave dominance over every aspect of food production. By 2004, just ten companies controlled half of the world's commercial seed sales, Monsanto being the largest.[104] There was a huge overlap between those firms and the ten controlling 84 per cent of the world's market for pesticides.[105] Five years later, the top ten companies controlled 73 per cent of commercial seed sales, Monsanto remaining at the number one spot, followed by DuPont and Syngenta.[106] All bar one of the six leading agrochemical companies also feature on the list of leading seed companies.[107]

The number of pesticides approved for use in the EU has risen considerably in recent years. By 2012, some 350 pesticides had been approved for use. This means that about 100 fresh approvals have been issued by the Union's authorities since 2008.[108] Environmentalists have calculated that about 40 of these pesticides contain endocrine disrupting substances, which mimic the hormonal systems in humans and animals and have been linked to such problems as lower fertility and breast and testicular cancer.[109]

A number of key individuals in the EU bureaucracy are known to be favourably disposed towards the pesticides industry. Before becoming head of EFSA, Catherine Geslain-Lannéelle ran the French national food authority from 2000 to 2003. In that post she stoutly defended the placing on the market of Gaucho – an insecticide suspected of causing widespread damage to bees.[110]

Just as it has an 'expert' panel on GM foods, EFSA has one on pesticides, too. During 2011, a scientist on the pesticides panel resigned, reportedly because he had not declared his shareholding in a consultancy firm specialising in chemicals.[111] Had the scientist been more upfront, he would probably have kept his seat. For a number of those appointed to the 19-strong panel for its 2012 to 2015 term have clear ties to companies who make the products that they assess. Theodorus Brock, the panel's vice-chairman, had undertaken research funded by BASF in 2010 and was still involved in a fungicide project financed by the chemical industry association CEFIC in 2012.[112] Michael Klein continued to have a contract with the German firm Fraunhofer, with whom he had worked on pesticides and other 'environmental fate' issues (his words) since 1987.[113] Daniel Pickford had taken part in a North Carolina project funded by Syngenta between 2006 and 2009.[114] And Robert Smith was a member and former chairman of the Rodenticide Resistance Action Group in Britain.[115] The biologist's 2012 declaration of interests failed to explicitly acknowledge that BASF is one of the companies in that group.[116]

The role of Italian chemist Ettore Capri in the panel appeared especially problematic. At the same time as he was assessing pesticide applications for EFSA, he was working on a project run by the European Crop Protection Association, a lobby outfit for the pesticides industry. He also remained the director of the European Observatory for Sustainable Agriculture (known as OPERA) in the Catholic University in Piacenza.[117] Despite being attached to a university, this outfit behaves like a think tank. One of its 2011 publications attempted to dismiss mounting evidence indicating that the use of chemicals is a cause of or a major contributory factor to the decline of bees. The paper's main finding was that the 'honey bee can cohabitate with modern agricultural practices provided that necessary precautions are taken to maintain viable food resources for bees'. I checked the acknowledgements on the paper; it named Capri as a member of the team which prepared it but also gave a list of 'technical contributors'. Most of them belonged to chemical and biotechnology companies such as Dow, Syngenta and Bayer.[118]

It is perhaps superfluous to add that those companies are more concerned with increasing sales than in preserving fragile ecosystems. A leaked 2010 memo from the Environmental Protection Agency in the US found that clothianidin – a pesticide manufactured by Bayer – was 'highly toxic' to bees.[119] Several subsequent papers have drawn similar conclusions.[120] With the case against it becoming stronger, Bayer is unlikely to be providing 'technical' contributions to think tanks for purely altruistic reasons. But why is an Italian professor allowed both to help Bayer get its message across and to sit on an EFSA panel? This question is all the more pertinent considering that EFSA has asserted that it has 'an important role to play in ensuring that healthy bee stocks are maintained in Europe'.[121]

OPERA's website says its 'vision is to be transparent to all the relevant stakeholders and the public'.[122] Unfortunately, that vision has not been realised. It took me a total of five months to get a response to a simple query that I put to Alexandru Marchis, head of OPERA's Brussels office. When I finally spoke to him after repeated requests for information, I asked him which companies help finance the think tank's activities. 'It is very difficult to provide a comprehensive list of our partners,' he replied, promising to come back to me with more concrete details. I am still waiting.

Marchis insisted that he is objective. 'At most we are acting as a facilitator, bringing together different stakeholder groups to discuss issues relating to sustainable agriculture,' he told me. 'We do not lobby. We do not have our own agenda.'[123]

I don't buy that explanation. The reason why I do not buy it is that it fits a pattern. OPERA bears many traits in common with the European Food Information Council (EUFIC), an outfit that pumps out 'fact sheets' about how food additives 'can be considered safe components of our diet' and how biotechnology enables 'quicker diagnosis of diseases in plants and animals'.[124] EUFIC has all the outward appearances of independence and it, too, has a stated policy of transparency. Sadly, the details of the policy are very easy to miss. To find them, you first have to study small text at the bottom of its homepage. By accepting the invitation to 'read more', you might learn that EUFIC is sponsored by Coca-Cola, Kraft, McDonald's, Nestlé, Pepsi and Unilever. With an annual budget of €2 million, it's no wonder that it has such a professional website.[125]

John Stauber, a pioneering investigator of 'public relations' in the US, once marvelled at how there really was a campaign saying that 'toxic sludge is good for you'.[126] An attempt to surpass that fallacy is now being made on this side of the Atlantic. There really is a think tank telling us that toxic chemicals are harmless for honey bees.

5
Smoke and mirrors

Political controversies are a bit like sunny days in Brussels: rare enough that it's a shame not to enjoy them wholeheartedly. To my delight, the European Commission found itself embroiled in a scandal during October 2012. Even if it wasn't quite the stuff of a thriller novel, there was a whiff of skulduggery about the whole affair.

First, it was announced that John Dalli, the EU's health commissioner, had resigned when it emerged that he was under investigation by the Union's anti-fraud department over dealings with a Maltese compatriot who was working for the tobacco industry. The Maltese lobbyist was alleged to have used his contacts with Dalli to gain 'financial advantages' from the company Swedish Match, which was seeking to overturn an export ban on snus, a chewable tobacco product.[1] Next, Dalli protested his innocence, suggested that he was sacked by the Commission's hierarchy and contended – not unreasonably – that he should be allowed see the full evidence against him.[2] Then came the tantalising twist: less than 48 hours after Dalli's resignation, the offices of two anti-smoking groups in Brussels were burgled. The laptops stolen in the raid belonged to campaigners pushing for new rules on increasing the size of health warnings on cigarette packets.[3]

At the time of writing (late 2012), many aspects of the affair remain fuzzy. The European Commission has not published the report from its anti-fraud department so it is impossible to know if the evidence against Dalli is strong. What can be said with certainty, however, is that there is more contact between the tobacco lobby and EU officials than there should be.

Data collated by the World Health Organisation (WHO) indicates that smoking kills six million people globally each year, with that figure projected to reach eight million by 2030.[4] Smoking is the leading cause of early death, claiming more than 100 million lives in the twentieth century.[5] It is also big business: Europe's largest cigarette-maker British American Tobacco (BAT) amassed profits of $4.4 billion for the first half of 2012.[6] Because the tobacco industry inflicts enormous suffering, it follows that it should not be allowed to influence health policies in any way. Indeed, this principle is contained in the WHO's convention on tobacco control, which entered into force in 2005. Article 5.3 of that convention obliges public authorities to ensure that their health policies are not diluted to protect the commercial interests of any firm.[7]

Frédéric Vincent, a European Commission spokesman, told me that its health officials have 'always fully respected' the WHO's guidelines on implementing that clause.[8] To test out his assurance, I consulted those guidelines. They recommend regulators to limit their contact with the tobacco industry to interactions that are 'strictly necessary' for the control of tobacco products. Such interactions should be conducted in public 'whenever possible', the guidelines add. They also encourage policy-makers to raise awareness about any 'front groups' that act 'openly or covertly' in the interests of Big Tobacco and to ensure that no tobacco lobbyist sits on an advisory group involved in formulating health-related policies. They urge politicians and civil servants not to participate in 'activities of the tobacco industry described as socially responsible'. And they state that independent organisations can play an 'essential role' in monitoring what cigarette-makers get up to.[9]

Are these guidelines fully respected by the Brussels institutions? The short answer is 'no'.

In 2011 and 2012, the European Commission's health department had at least three meetings with the tobacco industry. The meetings cannot be described as 'strictly necessary' for the control of tobacco products. Instead, because they dealt with planned legislation, they were useful for the industry as it could gain an insight into the Commission's thinking and prepare a strategy to counter the laws before they were formally proposed. And instead of respecting the recommendation that interactions take place in public 'whenever possible', the Commission allowed these talks to take place behind closed doors, with only industry representatives and EU officials present. No recordings of the meetings have been posted on the Commission's website. The only published accounts of these meetings were summaries of the main items discussed. An account of a December 2011 encounter was limited to one and a half pages.[10] Neither of the other two published summaries exceeded three pages.[11] No transcripts outlining precisely who said what have been made available.

Robert Madelin, the top official in the Commission's health department (directorate-general in Brussels parlance) from 2004 to 2010, admitted that he was in contact with tobacco lobbyists. 'It was policy throughout that period that the directorate-general received all stakeholders,' he said. 'A stakeholder was anyone sharing our goals or affected by our rule-making. This definition included the tobacco products sector. I engaged equally, of course, with all stakeholders – the WHO, health professionals and civil society – around the tobacco file.'[12] Madelin might think he was being fair-minded by engaging equally with 'stakeholders'. Yet the aforementioned WHO guidelines implicitly warn against creating a parity between the tobacco industry and public health campaigners. As the latter are presented as useful allies for regulators in monitoring the tobacco industry he should, by definition, have given them more of his time than he did the peddlers of cancer. Madelin was known to provide helpful tips to BAT about how it could develop a relationship with the Commission. In 2005, for example, he told Ben Stevens, then BAT's director for Europe, there would 'at least be a basis for open discussions' if it developed a position whereby 'smoke-free environments are favoured by some of your interlocutors on grounds of health'. Madelin expressed no more than 'mild disappointment' about hints that BAT was touting improved ventilation as a substitute to banning smoking in cafés and bars.[13]

The continued dialogue with the tobacco industry represents a reversal of the Commission's previously stated policy. By claiming that the Commission had a policy to receive all 'stakeholders', Madelin was directly contradicting an unambiguous pledge made by his boss at the time. In 2008, Androulla Vassiliou said: 'I am ready to commit today to not accept any invitation coming from the tobacco industry or those working in its interests so long as I hold office.'[14] This commitment evidently was not heeded for long. In February 2010, Vassiliou was given responsibility for a different portfolio (education). A few weeks before she took up her new post, Madelin – the highest-ranking civil servant working under her tutelage – met a delegation from the Confederation of European Community Cigarette Manufacturers (CECCM). In a follow-up letter, the CECCM's Jacek Siwek inferred that tobacco should be treated as any other business. He reminded Madelin that the Commission was required to undertake impact assessments of any 'policy option' that was likely to affect the bottom line of corporations. Tobacco firms 'are part of the stakeholder community and participate in the democratic debate regarding the evolution of the EU and its regulations and processes,' Siwek added. 'As you are aware, we do so in a fully transparent manner, fully respecting relevant laws, regulations and codes of conduct.'[15]

In January 2010, the Commission was also invited by BAT to attend a 'stakeholder dialogue' in Brussels during March that year.[16] A senior EU health official, Antti Maunu accepted the invitation and attended the event. In a 'thank you' letter that BAT sent him afterwards, the company's representative Jack Bowles said that the discussion provided an 'important opportunity to communicate the steps we have taken to deliver on our commitments'.[17] By going to that meeting, Maunu defied the WHO's recommendations in two ways, if not more. Clearly, it was not 'strictly necessary' for him to attend an event initiated by a cigarette maker in order to regulate tobacco products. And he allowed himself be used as a pawn for a propaganda exercise by taking part in something billed as 'socially responsible'. A report of the conference drawn up at BAT's request stated that it was held in order to help 'shape the company's approach to sustainability' when reporting on its 'social, environmental and economic performance'. The report then stated that BAT wished to have exemptions to bans on smoking in enclosed indoor places. Opposing outright bans such as those introduced in Ireland and Britain, BAT called for smoking to remain permitted in designated rooms that would be 'appropriately ventilated and separated from areas frequented by non-smokers'.[18] This demonstrates that BAT was still professing its faith in ventilation almost five years after Madelin had expressed 'mild disappointment' in its stance. Despite how there had been no fundamental shift in BAT's stance, the Commission has remained willing to lend credibility to the firm's efforts to improve its image.

POACHING THE POWERFUL

BAT's 'social reporting' unit in Brussels has been headed by Pavel Telicka, an inscrutable Czech who was both his country's chief negotiator when it was seeking to join the EU and later its first member of the European Commission.[19] There is a rich irony behind how Telicka made a rapid transition from being a political figure to being a lobbyist. During his brief stint in the Commission in 2004, he was given partial responsibility for the public health dossier. In that capacity, he penned a tract about how 'sadly, alcohol-related harm comes directly after tobacco and high blood pressure as a cause of ill-health'.[20] His anguish about that massive disease burden did not deter him from signing a contract with the industry that

– according to his own assessment – was the number one cause of needless death. Telicka's hypocrisy is compounded by the fact that he is an avid sportsman, with rugby and squash topping the list of his hobbies.[21] I have borne witness to his desire to keep fit and healthy: we both used to work out in the same gym.

Telicka does not appear to have been chastised in any way by the European Commission for being hired by a company he was tasked with regulating. On the contrary, his knowledge has remained sought after. Telicka has been an active member of a 'high level group' on 'reducing administrative burdens' established by the Commission in 2007 and chaired by Edmund Stoiber, a grandee of Bavarian politics.[22] The group became embroiled in a mini-controversy during 2012 when it emerged that Stoiber had expressed concerns – in correspondence with John Dalli – about the impact that a planned EU anti-smoking law would have on Germany's tobacco industry.[23] Most of the group's deliberations, however, do not attract publicity. And Telicka has been clever enough to keep mum about his links to BAT. Another member of the group, speaking on condition of anonymity, was unaware that Telicka had been working for the tobacco industry. The source confirmed that Telicka had not referred to his relationship with the tobacco industry during the group's meetings.[24] Nonetheless, official records show that Telicka has been raising issues relevant to BAT in discussions with the EU institutions. In particular, he has shown a keen interest in the whole concept of performing 'impact assessments' on EU regulations.[25]

It is significant that Telicka was nominated to the group by the European Policy Centre (EPC), a prominent think tank. Telicka is described as a 'senior adviser' to the EPC on its 2011 annual report; the same document names two cigarette makers – BAT and Philip Morris – as 'gold members' of the centre.[26] The fee for each 'gold member' – a category of belonging open to 'large/multinational companies', according to the EPC's website – comes to €10,000 per year. In return for that sum, the centre promises 'unparalleled networking opportunities'.[27] The EPC was set up in 1996 by Stanley Crossick, a lawyer who began consultancy work for BAT in the 1980s and continued working as a 'policy analyst' (frequently a byword for corporate lobbyist) until his death in 2010.[28] A paper that Crossick wrote for the centre around the time of its inception stated that his law firm Belmont had been asked by 'a number of companies to produce a brief report on the need for rigorous cost-benefit analysis'.[29] Documents made public as a result of litigation against the tobacco industry have shown that Crossick counselled BAT on how to make the British government more aware of this 'need' after Tony Blair became prime minister. When Britain held the EU's rotating presidency in 1998, Crossick recommended that Blair seek a formal commitment from other European leaders to minimise 'any burden, whether financial or administrative' falling on corporations.[30]

Wisely, Crossick and his consorts did not present their initiative as entirely tobacco-driven. Although a 'risk forum' set up by the EPC was chaired by Chris Proctor of BAT, it attracted support from a range of firms, including Coca-Cola, Shell, Mars, Dow and Tesco. By presenting a united front, the forum was able to persuade the European Commission to devise guidelines stating that firms must be consulted about any rules which would have an impact on their business. The EPC was the sole think tank that took part in a group helping the Commission draft these guidelines, which have been followed since December 2002.[31] Having these guidelines introduced was a masterstroke by Big Tobacco. The practical effect of them has been that even when EU commissioners have fulminated against cigarette makers, the officials working for them have continued to treat the same companies as legitimate 'stakeholders'. This double standard can be found in a reply that Androulla Vassiliou gave to Godfrey Bloom, an MEP from the United Kingdom Independence Party who – bizarrely – depicted her stated refusal to meet tobacco companies as tantamount to an abuse of human rights. (That Bloom was more concerned about the rights of people who cause cancer than those afflicted by it speaks volumes about UKIP's priorities.) Vassiliou stressed that her own commitment to the World Health Organisation rules and policies 'does not prevent the tobacco industry from expressing its views freely and openly in the context of stakeholder consultation processes'.[32]

NICOTINE-STAINED NITPICKING

As tobacco firms were instrumental in writing these guidelines, it is only logical that they are invoking them to try and block – or, failing that, delay – anti-smoking initiatives. In 2010, the Confederation of European Community Cigarette Manufacturers sent a detailed 44-page submission to EU officials who were studying ways of toughening a 2001 law covering the ingredients and packaging of tobacco products. The CECCM reminded these officials that under the 2002 guidelines it was mandatory to 'assess the impact of each of the identified policy options on all potentially affected stakeholders in qualitative, quantitative and monetary terms'. With typical insolence, the CECCM objected to how a document drawn up as part of plans to strengthen the law had referred to a 'tobacco epidemic'. According to CECCM, the term was 'clearly pejorative'. The CECCM also described an analysis about the health effects of smoking as 'irrelevant', implying that all measures must be dictated by hard-headed business considerations.[33]

The document provoking Big Tobacco's ire was prepared by the consultancy RAND. It was asked by the European Commission to analyse various options for what to do with the 2001 law. Both RAND's interim and final reports were dissected in minute detail by individual tobacco firms, as well as by their umbrella groups. RAND examined five possibilities, ranging from maintaining the status quo to making cigarette companies foot some of the medical bills for treatment of lung cancer (under a principle – nominally supported by the EU – known as 'the polluter pays'). Instead of making firm recommendations, the consultancy gave estimates for the cost and effects of different courses of action. Among its conclusions were that a ban on all forms of tobacco promotion in shops would save 200 lives per year by 2027 and that a coordinated EU move to put images of disease on cigarette boxes would pack a stronger punch than leaving the introduction of such measures to the discretion of individual governments.[34]

Despite the non-prescriptive nature of the RAND study, the tobacco industry subjected it to exhaustive nitpicking. BAT recruited Jonathan Klick, a law professor in the University of Pennsylvania, to attempt a hatchet job. Boasting that he held a doctorate in economics, as well as his legal qualifications, Klick aggressively dismissed the report. Taking issue with projections contained in it, he accused the RAND team of displaying 'either a lack of the elementary grasp of microeconomics or a deliberate intent to inflate the benefits of additional regulation'. Klick argued that the study suffered from 'fatal problems' and therefore 'the European Commission should ignore the RAND report in its entirety'.[35] BAT resorted to especially spurious reasoning in seeking to rubbish the idea that health warnings should be enlarged or made more graphic. Citing a Spanish survey in which most respondents estimated that half of all smokers contract lung cancer, BAT contended that the public tends to 'overestimate' the risk from tobacco, so there are no grounds to justify further regulation of packaging.[36] BAT was clearly hiding behind semantics. The truth is that tobacco kills about half of all its long-term users by inducing a number of diseases, not just lung cancer.[37] There are good reasons to believe, then, that by primarily associating tobacco with one ailment, the public is underestimating its effects, not overestimating them.

As well as hunting for flaws in the RAND report, cigarette firms have tried to put technical obstacles in the way of bigger and more explicit warnings. In one of several detailed submissions that the CECCM made to the European Commission, it argued that there are 'severe limitations available to the space available on tobacco packaging'. After implying that there was no room for phone numbers or website addresses for 'quit smoking' services, the organisation contended that if such information must be included it should be squeezed into that part of the box already reserved for health warnings.[38] Imperial Tobacco resorted to similar tactics when dealing with the idea that cigarette boxes should contain an insert that expands on the main points made in the warnings on the main packaging. While lots of industries have decided to include paraphernalia – collectable cards or discount coupons – inside their products, Imperial gave the impression that putting an extra bit of paper into a cigarette box would involve a reinvention of the wheel. 'We have serious doubts that suitable technology exists' for the necessary procedure, it said. 'Inserts would slow down the speed of packaging machines significantly, which also leads to higher costs.'[39]

Even though a handful of firms dominate cigarette manufacturing in the EU, the tobacco industry has tried to present itself as a friend of the little people. In Poland, Philip Morris teamed up with Solidarity – a trade union federation historically associated with Lech Walesa and the Gdansk shipyard strikes of the 1980s – to oppose stricter regulation. Although trade unions are supposed to defend health and safety measures against the rapacious agenda of bosses, Solidarity's leaders at a Philip Morris plant in Krakow put forward identical arguments to those of the tobacco industry's masters. Predicting that new rules on cigarette packaging would encourage the illicit tobacco trade, Solidarity argued they 'would directly put at risk' current jobs 'and the creation of jobs in the future'.[40]

The tobacco retailers association CEDT (a French acronym) has echoed almost verbatim the main points against stronger regulation made by cigarette makers. The only substantial difference between its case and that of the manufacturers is that CEDT professes a concern for the future of family-run businesses and – perhaps less convincingly – for aesthetics. Stating that it represented half a million 'independent convenience and tobacconist stores', CEDT expressed certainty that 'consumers in the EU are fully aware' of the harm caused by smoking. 'There is nothing to be gained in turning retailers' tobacco shelves into a montage of repulsive images,' it added.[41]

DOWNPLAYING THE DANGERS

Shielding children and adolescents from 'repulsive images' may sound admirable on the surface. It sounds less admirable when you realise that Big Tobacco has a history of courting the impressionable. Philip Morris, for example, is known to have sponsored professional soccer players on the grounds that they would appeal to young adult male smokers (inevitably abbreviated to YAMS), while some of its marketing plans for Europe have identified 'starting smokers' as prime target groups.[42] The same firm has the gall to blame the poor example set by puffing parents for how teenagers become hooked on nicotine. In a letter to the European Commission, Kristof Doms from Philip Morris' Brussels office, argued that there is a 'broad scientific consensus' that kids' behaviour is determined by their families and that 'nothing points' to corporate marketing as a 'determining factor' behind anyone's decision to smoke. In the next paragraph, Doms asserted that 'smokers in the EU should have the choice to use snus instead of cigarettes'. According to him, there is 'substantial epidemiological data, including data from Sweden' that it is less harmful to chew on little pouches of tobacco than to suck on a cigarette and 'available studies' suggest that snus helps smokers to kick their habit.[43]

Snus is currently banned in EU countries, with the exception of Sweden. But the Stockholm government has been campaigning for the ban to be lifted, with the help of major tobacco companies.[44] Philip Morris, for example, has been examining if it could be sold in other countries as an alternative to cigarettes. In 2007, for example, it announced plans to test market a few flavours of snus under the Marlboro brand name in Texas.[45] The company, therefore, has a vested interest in downplaying any dangers posed by snus. So it comes as little surprise that Doms' effort to present snus as akin to an anti-smoking aid was misleading. In 2009, Sweden's National Institute of Public Health cited estimates that four out of every ten men in the country who used snus also smoked cigarettes. Snus, it added, 'contributes to a high likelihood that one does not quit smoking but acquires a new form of addiction'. Furthermore, it stated that snus contains around 2,600 substances which can damage a user's health, 20 of which are carcinogenic.[46]

With indoor smoking bans becoming increasingly commonplace in Europe, it is logical that industry is thinking outside the cigarette box. The idea of consuming tobacco by chewing it or putting it up your nose is hardly novel, yet there are strong indications that tobacco strategists wish to promote new brands of snus and nasal snuff. The strategy could, however, be undermined by policy-makers conscientious or well-informed enough to say that because tobacco has caused enough pain, the last thing the world needs is fresh tobacco products. In a desperate bid to stave off regulation, corporate lobbyists have misrepresented what public health authorities have to say.

The European Smokeless Tobacco Council (ESTOC) has been eager to portray itself as part of the solution to smoking. This is a little odd as many of its members – BAT, Philip Morris, Imperial Tobacco – benefit from the problem.[47] ESTOC has been seeking that smokeless tobacco should be regulated according to food safety standards which set 'maximum permissible limits for certain compounds that are viewed as undesirable'. In its correspondence with EU officials, the association has claimed that voluntary efforts by the industry have already led to robust standards. To support that claim, it has referred to findings by the World Health Organisation, implying that snus has a 'lower nitrosamine content' than cigarettes.[48] In conveying the impression that it has the blessing of a respected international body, the snus lobby neglected to mention that the WHO has stated unequivocally that no form of tobacco is safe. Far from endorsing smokeless tobacco, the WHO has expressed concern that its greater use (especially among girls and young women) may mean that its forecast of tobacco killing ten million people across the planet by 2020 will turn out to have been too conservative.[49]

In another submission, ESTOC contended that it was unfair to 'deny 107 million smokers in the EU access to a traditional non-combustible tobacco alternative to their cigarette'. To support its case, ESTOC referred to a report approved in 2008 by the Commission's own scientific committee on emerging and newly identified health risks (SCENIHR). According to ESTOC, the report in question concluded that 'snus use is not a risk factor for oral cancer' and 'smokeless tobacco is around 90 per cent less harmful' than cigarettes.[50] As it happened, the report was considerably more nuanced. It explicitly stated that there was 'sufficient evidence that the use of a wide variety of STP [smokeless tobacco products] causes cancer in humans'. SCENIHR acknowledged that some studies were inconclusive on the suspected links between mouth cancer and snus. Yet it mentioned that one Swedish study and 'several studies from the US' reported 'an increased risk of oral cancer' among snus users. The suggestion that smokeless tobacco was 90 per cent less harmful than cigarettes was incorrectly attributed to SCENIHR. The claim, in fact, came from another paper that was merely cited by the committee during a literature review.[51]

Perhaps the single biggest worry of cigarette makers lately is that they would be forced to sell their products in plain packaging. This idea clearly has merits: making all cigarette boxes identical would deal a blow to tobacco firms. They would no longer be able to design their packaging in such a way as to appeal to first-time smokers or to a particular group in society. It is easy to understand why Imperial Tobacco is upset about the prospect of having the identity of its brands eroded. Imperial's top seller is Gauloises Blondes, which it describes as an 'iconic French heritage brand'. By putting the slogan '*liberté toujours*' on its packets, Gauloises is marketed as a byword for sophistication and freedom.[52] As part of its efforts to convince the European Commission not to make plain packing compulsory, Imperial has posed as a child protection advocate. Predicting that the measure would be a godsend for counterfeiters and tobacco smugglers, Imperial has argued that its net effect will be children having readier access to cigarettes.[53]

FRONT GROUPS AND FILIBUSTERING

The International Chamber of Commerce (ICC) in Paris has been beating the same drum. In a 2010 letter to the European Commission, the ICC's Jeremy Hardy expressed fears that 'plain packaging would increase the prevalence of counterfeit goods in the market and reduce brand owners' ability to take action against such activity, besides undermining the ability of consumers to make informed purchasing decisions'.[54] Hardy stressed that because plain packaging was perceived as an affront on 'intellectual property', corporations from many sectors were perturbed by this issue. Although it's certainly true that corporations club together when their collective interests appear threatened, there was a strong presence of cigarette makers in the Business Alliance to Stop Counterfeiting and Piracy (BASCAP), which Hardy has been coordinating. BAT, Philip Morris and Japan Tobacco all belong to this coalition of 22 chief executives.[55]

BASCAP is one of several front groups for the tobacco industry seeking to influence the EU. Another such group, the Trans Atlantic

Business Dialogue (TABD), enjoys the status of being recognised as the 'voice of enterprise' on both sides of the Atlantic. This forum was set up at the behest of the US Department of Commerce and the European Commission in 1995 and regularly meets high-level politicians in Washington and Brussels.[56] BAT and Philip Morris are heavily involved in this 'dialogue'.[57] From 2007 to 2012, the group's Brussels office was headed by Jeffries Briginshaw.[58] He had spent the previous 14 years working directly for BAT, rising from its trademark counsel to head of political and regulatory affairs.[59]

Briginshaw, too, is horrified by the prospect that cigarette branding could be outlawed. When Australia moved to introduce a plain packaging law, he made an appeal to the EU and US trade policy chiefs. Craftily, he argued that this wasn't only about tobacco but about defending intellectual property. The Canberra initiative 'opens a Pandora's Box of unintended consequences which the business community finds most troubling,' he wrote.[60] Briginshaw similarly objected to plain packaging when the idea cropped up on Britain's political agenda; in a submission to the Department of Health in London he suggested that brands had to be respected under EU law.[61] Briginshaw is unwilling to address criticisms of his activities. When I asked him for an interview, he originally agreed. He, then, emailed me to say: 'Sorry to disappoint you, but having run a few Google searches online into your work I rather feel you have a predetermined perspective and agenda, which leads me to conclude that I don't think I could be very helpful to your line of enquiry.'[62]

The European Risk Forum (ERF) is even less open about its links to Big Tobacco. This outfit's website says it is 'an expert-led not-for-profit think tank' which addresses the 'risks and benefits of new and emerging technologies, climate change and lifestyle choices'. A short biographical note on its chairman, Dirk Hudig, tells the reader that he used to be the chief administrator in the employers' federation UNICE (now BusinessEurope).[63] There is no mention of how Hudig – along with the late Stanley Crossick – set up the European Policy Centre's risk forum in the 1990s. Although that forum was largely financed by BAT, Hudig was instrumental in seeking to broaden its membership, according to documents released due to litigation against tobacco companies.[64] Nor is it mentioned that the European Risk Forum boasted BAT and Philip Morris among its 15 members in 2012.[65] When I asked Hudig how much each of these corporations contribute to the forum, he would not divulge any details. 'The ERF does not promote the views of any single company or industry or the narrow interests of any of its members,' he said. Yet he implicitly acknowledged that it obstructs proper scrutiny of its activities: the ERF's debates, he added, are held under 'Chatham House rules', whereby anyone who reports about them gives an undertaking not to attribute quotes to particular speakers.[66]

There are strong indications that the forum does not disclose its tobacco connections when inviting senior officials to its events. During 2012, I spotted that Henning Klaus, an adviser to the European Commission's president José Manuel Barroso, and Klaus Welle, chief administrator in the European Parliament, were named as participants in discussions that the forum was organising that year. I contacted the two men, asking them if they were aware that the forum's members included tobacco companies and that, under World Health Organisation guidelines, front groups for the tobacco industry should be shunned by politicians and civil servants. Both replied to say that their names had been added to the forum's website without their permission, that they had never accepted invitations to attend the events in question and that they had instructed the forum to remove their names after I had brought the matter to their attention.[67] It felt satisfying to have caused a little embarrassment for a tobacco-funded think tank. But there is still too much secrecy about what cigarette makers are up to.

As it has been proven beyond any reasonable doubt that smoking kills, cigarette makers know they can't completely duck the fact that their products are unhealthy. What they can do instead is use all kinds of tactics to block and filibuster. Unfortunately, these tactics can be successful. In late 2012, the European Commission published new proposals on regulating tobacco. Capitulating to pressure from Big Tobacco, the Commission abandoned the idea of requiring that cigarettes be sold in plain packaging. While it recommended the introduction of compulsory pictorial warnings, it advocated that 30 per cent of a cigarette box should be reserved for branding.[68]

Forced or not, the resignation of John Dalli helped draw attention to the sleazy world of tobacco lobbying. Yet it doesn't seem to have convinced the Commission that it should be more transparent about its dealings with the cigarette industry. In November 2012 – one month after Dalli stepped down – the Commission's in-house legal service held a discussion with Michel Petite, a former EU official who went on to work for Clifford Chance, a law firm that includes Philip Morris on its roster of clients. Petite is known to have been pressing his erstwhile colleagues to go easy on the tobacco industry. But this didn't stop the Commission from re-appointing him to a three-person ethics advisory group in December 2012. Comically, the ethics group has been tasked with helping the Commission avoid conflict of interest issues when its top representatives leave to join the private sector.[69]

It is estimated that there are about 100 full-time tobacco lobbyists in Brussels.[70] Raising the spectre of organised crime is one of their favourite ploys. It is both dishonest and dishonourable: any industry that causes addiction and disease is, in my view, criminal. So the distinction drawn between the 'legitimate' and 'illicit' cigarette trade is nebulous.

The ultimate goal of any responsible policy-maker dealing with health issues should be to put the tobacco industry out of business. The proliferation of smoking bans in Europe is an important step in that direction but tobacco firms are clever enough to find new ways of remaining profitable. To have any hope of a tobacco-free future, it is surely vital that the tobacco industry be treated as a pariah.

6
Cheating on climate

Angela Merkel makes an improbable superhero. And yet she has been known to pose as a saviour of the earth. In 2007, Merkel put climate change high on the priority list for Germany as it took over the EU's rotating presidency. 'It is not five minutes to midnight,' the chancellor said. 'It's five past midnight.'[1]

At a time of great unease with the isolationism of George W. Bush – particularly his rejection of the Kyoto protocol on global warming – it was politically astute for Merkel to assert her green credentials and demand that Europe act as a role model. At an annual Spring summit, she persuaded other EU prime ministers and presidents to approve what looked like an ambitious set of targets. Under this plan, the Union would achieve a minimum of a 20 per cent reduction of its greenhouse gas emissions by 2020, compared to 1990 levels. This target would be increased to 30 per cent if other industrialised countries agreed to follow suit.

Certainly, the '20 per cent by 2020' goal sounded catchy. But the means through which it was to be achieved raised questions about whether the EU was really determined to solve the biggest problem facing humanity. Two clauses in the plan indicated that the EU leaders had no interest in dealing with the roots of climate change. These stated that 'absolute emission reductions are the backbone of a global carbon market' and that 'emissions trading' would have a 'central role' in the Union's strategy.[2]

Rather than recognising that climate change was a consequence of an economic system that relies on the voracious exploitation of natural resources, the EU has decided that the 'right' to pollute should be treated as a good to be bought and sold – or, in many cases, given away for free.

The theory behind emissions trading is simple. A limit is placed on the amount of carbon dioxide (CO_2) that any given country may release into the atmosphere. The amount is divided up between the most polluting firms operating in that country. Firms which emit more CO_2 than their quota allows must buy extra licences; firms that emit less than their allocation may sell their unused permits.

In practice, the EU's emissions trading system (ETS) has proven to be an abject failure for two main reasons. First, protecting the environment requires big government, not market-based mechanisms. And second, the way the system functions has been dictated by some of the worst polluters. The writer and campaigner Raj Patel has observed that this is 'as good an idea as letting the iceberg fix the *Titanic*'.[3]

The EU's system went into operation in 2005. Three years earlier, the European Petroleum Industry Association (EUROPIA) made detailed recommendations about how it should function. EUROPIA bands together Shell, BP, Statoil, Total and ExxonMobil and other companies that traditionally profit from the burning of fossil fuels, a central cause of global warming.[4]

The EUROPIA paper advocated a 'learning by doing' approach towards emissions trading. Though broadly supportive of the basic concept, it argued that penalties for exceeding emission thresholds should be 'moderate' and that permits to emit should be given to participants in the scheme free of charge. 'Auctioning of allowances should be avoided by all means,' the paper contended. Having to pay for permits would put European industry at a 'competitive disadvantage', it added.[5]

Most of EUROPIA's wishes were granted. Later in 2003, the EU's governments agreed the contours of the system. All permits to pollute would initially be offered free of charge, they decided, albeit with the possibility of auctioning 10 per cent of these permits from 2008. The penalty for exceeding the emissions limit was set at €40 for every tonne of carbon dioxide equivalent above the limit that is released. This was lower than the €50 penalty proposed by the European Commission when it was mulling over how the system should work.[6] (Carbon dioxide equivalent is a measure designed to compare different heat-trapping gases, based on their contribution to global warming.)[7]

Oil giants have also monitored the evolution of the system on an individual basis. BP has something of a proprietary interest in the ETS because it claims to have set up the prototype. Formed in 1999, the internal BP system involved giving each of the company's 120 units an emissions quota. Units that could not keep within their quota had to buy permits from units with a better environmental record. Charles Nicholson, a senior adviser to BP, claimed that the firm showed emissions trading was possible and bragged at how a target of pushing down emission levels 10 per cent below a 1990 baseline by 2007 was in fact reached by 2000.[8]

This attempt to assert BP's green credentials was premature. Citing BP's own data, the book *Eminent Corporations* by Andrew Simms and David Boyle states that this single firm was responsible for 6 per cent of the entire world's greenhouse gas emissions from fossil fuel use in 2004.[9] And, of course, BP would later become synonymous with a disaster in the Gulf of Mexico.

It is no surprise that a system heavily influenced by the oil industry has brought no benefit to the environment. Leaving aside the fact that it was no substitute for stringent anti-pollution laws, the core deficiency in the ETS was that it was too generous towards energy guzzlers during its trial phrase between 2005 and 2007. The overall cap of 2,298 million tonnes of CO_2 set for 2007 was actually more than 8 per cent above known emissions in 2005. An analysis by Friends of the Earth concluded that the surfeit of unused permits meant that most industries covered by the scheme were not required to slash their emissions before 2016.[10]

Despite being aware that their generosity has been ruinous, EU officials have continuously succumbed to pressure from polluters. Faced with the prospect that oil refineries might have to pay for emission permits in the second phase of the system – which began in 2008 – EUROPIA undertook a strenuous lobbying campaign to maintain the free allowances. The campaign was successful. Isabelle Muller, a representative of the French energy firm Total and then secretary-general of EUROPIA, has credited Günter Verheugen, the EU's enterprise commissioner at the time, with thwarting efforts by some Brussels officials to make refineries pay.[11]

ADDICTED TO OIL

Muller has forecast that oil will remain of critical importance to the European economy for another few decades 'so it is not so easy to get rid of us'.[12] Her deputy, Chris Beddoes, displayed even greater gall by presenting fossil fuels as part of the solution to climate change. In 2010, Beddoes held talks with advisers to Günther Oettinger, then the EU's energy commissioner. Email messages that he sent to the advisers focused on a €9.1 billion plan to upgrade energy infrastructure. Beddoes urged that the plan underscore how Europe hasn't yet abandoned oil. His key message read: 'The transition to a lower carbon economy will become more difficult and carry greater risk if the existing supply chain assets become uncompetitive.'[13]

That the oil industry enjoys privileged access to the EU institutions is not in doubt. In 2009, for example, the Commission organised a seminar on future oil demand. The discussion was largely sparked by fears that Russia could disrupt supplies of energy to other parts of Europe, as it had previously done with gas.[14] After a room with a capacity for 50 people was booked for the event, EUROPIA was asked to submit a list of industry representatives to attend. A briefing paper intended to form the basis of the meeting was drawn up 'in close cooperation' between a few officials and EUROPIA.[15] All of the speakers named on the agenda were either directly employed by the oil industry or worked as 'consultants' on energy issues; voices calling for Europe to kick its oil habit were absent.

Fear of Russia pops up frequently in the EU's energy debate. While it is entirely legitimate to argue that – as part of a shift from fossil fuels to renewable energy – the EU should lower its imports from Russia and aim for self-sufficiency, the oil lobby wields the weapon of fear in a more simplistic manner. This can be seen from how it mobilised against a revised fuel quality law with the objective of making cars run on less polluting forms of petrol and diesel. EUROPIA was especially aggrieved by drafts of the proposal, which suggested a 'batch-by-batch' reporting system on the contribution that transport fuels make to climate change. According to Muller, the reporting system would be too onerous for her industry. She argued that it would 'significantly penalize' the 'complex refineries' on which Europe depends to process crude oil into 'useful clean products such as diesel and gasoline'. Unless the system was abandoned, oil firms would move out of Europe and invest in 'simple refineries' in places like Russia, she warned in a March 2010 letter to Connie Hedegaard, the EU's first 'climate action' commissioner.[16]

Muller did not elaborate on what she meant by 'simple refineries', apart from saying that they failed to provide 'useful clean products'. Her risible lack of precision – not to mention the novel idea that petrol is 'clean' – did not seem to bother the European Commission's staff. By the end of 2010, she was expressing her appreciation to EU officials for how they had dropped the dreaded 'batch-by-batch' system.[17]

CHEMICAL BROTHERS CRY WOLF

There is a considerable overlap between the membership of EUROPIA and that of the European Chemical Industry Council (CEFIC). Shell, BP, Total and ExxonMobil belong to both groups.[18] CEFIC has been at the forefront of efforts to remove any muscle from the EU's environmental initiatives. It has gone so far as to encourage a turf war between different departments of the European Commission. When the Commission's 'climate action' department won responsibility for handling dossiers relating to energy-intensive industries, CEFIC objected, arguing that such matters should remain the preserve of the enterprise department as it was considered friendlier to big business.[19]

By their own calculation, chemical producers use 30 per cent of all energy gobbled up by the world's industries.[20] Showing little desire to mend their industry's ways, their work has focused on opposing the 'avalanche of simultaneous requests' they claim to receive from bureaucrats by warning that too much regulation harms energy-intensive manufacturers.[21]

Giorgio Squinzi, who was appointed CEFIC president in 2010, is treated with deference by the European Commission. In 2007 the Commission selected Squinzi – head of the Italian company Mapei – for a 'high level' team of advisers to recommend a strategy guaranteeing that the chemical industry would remain 'competitive'. Dominated by business representatives – though including a token environmentalist from Sweden – the team warned that chemical companies would relocate to China and India if the EU introduced tougher climate legislation than Asia.[22]

Squinzi has a sense of entitlement. When he pops in to see Hedegaard, his staff ask that a parking spot be reserved for his chauffeur-driven Lancia Thesis.[23] His correspondence with the 'climate action' chief indicates that he regards himself as the boss and that Hedegaard had better do what he tells her. Squinzi has strongly opposed the very idea that the Union could unilaterally decide to set more ambitious emissions reduction targets than 20 per cent by 2020. Higher targets would 'adversely affect EU industry competitiveness,' he believes. He 'especially insists' that the Union safeguard the allocation of free pollution permits to chemical plants. Any delay in doing so would 'handcuff domestic EU manufacturers from pursuing future investment and planning,' he told Hedegaard during 2011.[24]

CEFIC is part of a wider web of corporate power. Nick Campbell, a representative of the French chemical firm Arkema, has been dexterous enough in recent times to act as a lobbyist for CEFIC and the employers' coalition BusinessEurope, as well as chairing a 'climate change taskforce' for the International Chamber of Commerce. Campbell was instrumental in having a planned modification to the emissions trading system removed. In March

2011, EU officials toyed with the idea of 'setting aside' 500 to 800 million emissions allowances in the third phase of the system (running from 2013 and 2020). The rationale behind this idea was that it was needed to address the large surplus of free pollution licences granted to the chemical industry and its fellow energy gluttons at earlier stages of the system's operation.[25]

Campbell followed a kind of 'divide and rule' strategy in order to defeat the plan. Documents obtained by green campaigners show that he coordinated his arm-twisting of Hedegaard, who backed the set-aside rule, with officials from the Commission's enterprise department. His tactics worked: the 500 to 800 million figure was erased from the final version of a 'roadmap' for the ETS published by the Commission in March 2011. It was replaced with some fuzzy language about 'appropriate measures' being considered at a later point.[26]

Campbell is nonetheless astute. In April 2012, he shared a podium with Hedegaard at the European Business Summit. Although that annual event is essentially a naked display of capitalist triumphalism, Campbell used his presentation to speak about the need for a clear definition of 'green jobs' and to applaud his own industry for trying to reduce pollution. Afterwards, I put it to him that his presentation amounted to a deceptive public relations exercise, considering his efforts to weaken the EU's climate change initiatives. 'Of course, the chemical industry has a severe [emissions reduction] target under the ETS,' he replied. 'Our companies are striving to meet that target of 21 per cent. We're striving to do it.'[27]

The 'severe target' he complained of was for a 21 per cent cut in greenhouse gas emissions between 2005 and 2020.[28] And yet CEFIC has previously stated that while production levels for the EU's chemical industry rose by 60 per cent between 1990 and 2009, the quantity of greenhouse gases discharged fell by 49 per cent over the same period.[29] If the industry was already capable of chopping its emissions in half, why should it fret over a less taxing reduction target? Maybe the chemical brothers are crying wolf.

The oil industry's aforementioned threat to decamp to Russia invoked the spectre of 'carbon leakage'. When I first heard of this 'leakage', I assumed that it was a type of pollution. Instead, it is a type of jargon invented to describe an imaginary phenomenon whereby firms aggrieved by high environmental standards in one part of the world relocate to another part of the world, where they can merrily belch out whatever substance they want.

There is no strong – or even weak – evidence that executives chose if they should invest in a particular country or region based on its environmental laws. The notion that manufacturers would quit Europe in droves if our policy-makers try to save the planet is ludicrous. A study by the Carbon Trust concluded that less than 2 per cent of polluting industries would be driven outside the EU if they were required to pay for emissions permits under the ETS.[30] The Carbon Trust is not a bunch of Bolsheviks: among the clients it has advised on adjusting to a low-carbon economy are Coca-Cola, Tesco, GE and Heinz.[31]

Still, the hyperbole has been effective. A total of 169 sectors have been recognised as vulnerable to carbon leakage by the EU. Some EU officials have given up trying to defend the rationale by which sectors such as bicycle and wine-making were added to the list. Damien Meadows, an official in the European Commission's 'climate action' department, told a conference in November 2011 that the list had 'at least provoked some humour'.[32]

One less amusing effect of treating carbon dioxide as a tradable good is that financial alchemists have 'derived' other 'products' from selling the 'right' to pollute on the assumption that the money generated will help realise 'clean development' projects at some point in the future.[33] Data cited by the European Commission in 2011 indicates that 90 per cent of the carbon market consists of derivatives. The notion that these opaque 'products' could help stop the planet from burning should always have been regarded as foolish. Now that the financial crisis has erupted, continuing to believe that derivatives can magically arrest ecological damage is patently irresponsible. Blinkered by ideology, EU officials continue to place their faith in a 'healthy future development' of the carbon market, in the words of Connie Hedegaard.[34]

The International Emissions Trading Association (IETA) is arguably the most influential group in dictating how the ETS functions. Founded in 1999, its 155-strong membership list reeks of oil and opulence. BP, Shell and Total are on it (of course). So, too, are Goldman Sachs, Dow Chemicals, Morgan Stanley, Deutsche Bank and Toyota.[35]

IETA has deep pockets and strong political connections. Its chief executive in recent years, Henry Derwent, worked as a climate adviser to Tony Blair when he was prime minister.[36] Although it also has offices in Geneva, London, Toronto, San Francisco and Washington, much of its work is focused on Brussels, given that the

EU operates the world's largest emissions trading scheme (worth €89 billion in 2009).[37]

Derwent is continuing to preach the gospel of lax regulation that New Labour followed. In September 2011, he reacted with horror upon learning that EU officials were considering categorising emissions allowances as 'financial instruments' as part of a revamp of core legislation for the Union's single market. Derwent complained that his association had not been kept abreast of this move, which – he predicted – would 'place the carbon market under the full suite of financial market rules, on a par with far more developed, active and mature markets such as stocks and bonds'. Derwent resorted to classic lobbying tactics: he warned of dire economic consequences if his demands were not met. As a 'number of market participants are contemplating leaving the market or reducing their level of involvement', it was of the 'utmost importance to ensure that regulatory measures are appropriate and proportionate'. Arguing that 'such is not the case with the classification of emissions allowances as financial instruments', he urged that the plan to do so be deleted.[38]

Derwent did not have a terribly strong hand to play at the time. As the ETS had been beset by a series of fraud and hacking scandals – one costing governments €5 billion – the Commission felt compelled to be seen regulating the system.[39] Yet Derwent's threatening noises were taken seriously and helped him win pledges from Hedegaard that there would be 'justified adaptations to the specificities of the carbon market' and that IETA would be consulted about the practical issues involved.[40]

WHY OFFSETTING IS A SCAM

Simone Ruiz, head of IETA's Brussels office at the time of writing, told me that her association initially perceived the Commission's proposal as a 'hammer that would destroy the market'. She added: 'It was a very heavy instrument to apply to the market in its infant stages. We are a bit more relaxed now. We can live with it.' Sitting in her spacious office beside Rond-point Schuman, the centre of Brussels' European quarter, Ruiz tried to downplay her clout. 'You don't see organisations like us steering the agenda too much,' she said. 'I wish we were more successful. But once the Commission sets the agenda, there is very little we can change.'[41]

Internal documents that I have seen tell a different story: they attest to how Ruiz has made sure she is consulted on virtually every detail of policy relating to emissions trading. When she felt that the consultation did not go far enough on one occasion, she complained that the Commission would 'create some bad blood among our members'.[42]

Her complaint related to a study being prepared on 'offsetting' – the idea that it is acceptable for rich people to drive and fly as much as they wish, provided they pay to have a few trees planted in Africa. And it appears that her protest was misplaced: EU officials swore to her that data supplied by IETA was used 'extensively' in the study.[43]

The European Commission had requested the study in question from AEA, a consultancy formed as an offshoot of Britain's Atomic Energy Authority, when it was privatised in the 1990s. AEA's credibility as a source of environmental advice is less than pristine: as a provider of transport services to Britain's nuclear industry, it was fined £250,000 in 2006 over a radioactive leak that occurred when one of its lorries was bringing material to Sellafield, the infamous nuclear reprocessing complex, four years earlier.[44] Yet even though AEA had a sullied reputation, it was deemed to have the requisite expertise to assess the 'integrity' of the clean development mechanism (CDM), the main international scheme for offsetting. AEA concluded that the CDM's operations had been a 'resounding success' but that it could benefit from some tweaks. This message must have been comforting to 'climate action' mandarins as the European Union is the CDM's most active participant.[45]

Cynical – or realistic – observers could surmise that AEA was telling the Commission exactly what it wished to hear. Offsetting is an integral part of the emissions trading system. Instead of requiring that pollution be reduced in Europe, the laws covering the ETS allows industries to buy 'credits' so that the reductions can – theoretically – occur by financing ecologically sound projects in Africa, Asia and Latin America.[46]

As a method of stopping the planet from burning, offsetting is morally dubious. The best analogy I have seen is of paying someone else to be faithful to his or her spouse, so that you can have an affair (a satirical website, cheatneutral.com, has been set up based on this analogy).

Not only is it unethical, offsetting is a scam. Stopping electricity generation by coal is not comparable to planting a row of trees, which can be felled or damaged at any time. As it replaces the obligation to verify emission cuts from one part of the world with guesswork about what might happen in another, offsetting often leads to a net increase in pollution.[47] This was illustrated by how 59 per cent of CDM offsets used by European companies in 2009 related to projects supposedly designed to destroy HFC-23. Also known as trifluoromethane, HFC-23 has a 'global warming potential' 11,700 times higher than carbon dioxide and is a by-product of HFC-22, a gas used in refrigeration. Evidence gathered by environmental watchdogs indicated that because the system was market-based, companies were deliberately producing HFC-22 so that they could be paid to destroy its by-product. The picture looks even more obscene, when one considers that an international agreement (the Montreal protocol) to phase out the use of HFC-22 – because of the damage it causes to the ozone layer – had entered into force back in 1989.[48]

India and China have the highest concentration of CDM projects in the world. A thorough analysis of the CDM in India in 2011 published by the National Forum of Forest People and Forest Workers cited a number of cases where fossil fuel projects were being financed. A coal-fired thermal power plant at Ucchpinda-Band-hapalli in the state of Chattisgarh will require the transportation of 1,200 trucks through the surrounding villages, according to the report. Another plant – at Tirora in the state of Maharashtra – has been selected as the first 'clean coal' project financed by the CDM. Locals have been kept in the dark about the project, even though it will encroach onto their land. No information has been provided to them about the effects on forests and biodiversity.[49]

CORPORATE CAPTURE AND STORAGE

The phrase 'clean coal' is an oxymoron, albeit a seductive one. Policy-makers and the fossil fuel industry have been in cahoots for some time to promote the idea that the noxious properties of coal can be removed and buried underground through a process known as carbon capture and storage (CCS).

Soon after she was appointed the EU's 'climate action' chief in 2010, Hedegaard invited a few big business representatives to a 'roundtable' discussion. Her aides' written account of the meeting gives the impression it was intended to allay fears she was an eco-warrior disguised as a Danish liberal. Hedegaard opened the proceedings by insisted that the department she headed did not have an 'anti-growth agenda'. As the 'competitiveness of our economies must not be hurt,' she added, advice from big business was required on how to move towards a 'low-carbon economy'.

Shell responded by claiming that electricity could be produced with 'almost zero emissions' of greenhouse gases. Rather than advocating proven methods – such as wind or solar energy – of attaining this objective, Shell proposed a combination of natural gas and CCS. When Hedegaard enquired what the 'realistic timeline' was for deploying this techno-fix, Shell assured her that 'we should have demonstration projects running' by 2020.[50]

Well-informed adults would be justified in treating Shell's recommendations sceptically. Even if it has not been subject to the same level of unfavourable coverage as BP in recent times, Shell's credibility as a source of environmental advice falls to pieces when one examines its record in the Niger Delta. Shell has not complied with a Nigerian court order to desist from gas-flaring in the Delta by an April 2007 deadline. The quantity of CO_2 released by Shell from that single activity per year has been estimated as similar to that released by all of Sweden.[51] The United Nations Environment Programme, meanwhile, estimated in 2011 that the damage caused by Shell in Nigeria's Ogoniland is so widespread that the process of cleaning it up could take 30 years.[52]

Shell's abysmal record in West Africa has been airbrushed out of the corporate image it presents to EU officials. As well as directly trying to mould policy, Shell has worked hard at convincing the European Commission to endorse sporting competitions that it sponsors. An 'eco-marathon' in which the winning vehicle travels the farthest on the least amount of fuel was promoted as 'a kind of Olympic Games of energy efficiency' by Hans van der Loo, then director of Shell's Brussels office, in a 2011 letter to Hedegaard's office.[53]

Shell has been assisted in its 'green-washing' by *European Voice*, a newspaper widely read by Brussels officials and lobbyists, and the TV channel Euronews. The troika are involved in the Comment:Visions project, which presents itself as a platform for debating energy issues. At one corporate event, I picked up a leaflet for Comment:Visions. According to the leaflet a journalist involved in the 'unique partnership' travels 'throughout the world each month to interview a visionary. Whether he's at a solar panel field in Spain, a nuclear plant in Sweden, or the world climate talks in Copenhagen, he always gets to the heart of the story.' The leaflet also made clear that its events reach key decision-makers as 'throughout the year, Comment:Visions hosts live debates, usually inside the European Parliament'.[54]

When I contacted the Comment:Visions team, I was told that Euronews has 'full ownership' of the project, although there is a 'partnership' with *European Voice* for the organisation of events. Martin Deloche, the account manager for the project at Euronews, would not say how much finance Shell provides on the grounds that 'this is commercial information, which I can't disclose'. He then contradicted himself by adding 'we are completely transparent' about Shell's support.[55]

From 2001 to 2006, I worked for *European Voice* (then part of The Economist Group). Whenever I and other journalists expressed concerns to management about commercial considerations influencing editorial matters, we were told that the paper's content would never be dictated by advisers. Not only does Comment:Visions blur the distinction between advertising and journalism, that seems to be its selling point. Tim King, editor of *European Voice* at the time of writing, told me that 'of course, the Comment:Visions project raises ethical issues'. Although he stated that 'the important aim is to keep separate the editorial mission and advertising', King argued that 'journalism has involved commerce since the days when the front page of the *Daily Universal Register* was made up of classified advertisements'.[56]

During a 2009 Comment:Visions 'debate', Shell's Graeme Sweeney predicted that carbon capture and storage could be responsible for 'a quarter to a third of the total mitigation [of climate change] required between now and 2050'.[57] Far from being a neutral pundit, Sweeney has a vested interest in CCS. Not long before he gazed into his crystal ball at that 'debate', Sweeney was appointed chairman of the advisory council for the Zero Emissions Platform (ZEP).

The ZEP is essentially a cash cow for the fossil fuels industry. The presence of two environment groups – neither of which could be considered radical – on the platform is a feeble attempt to provide some sort of counterbalance to how the 27 corporations taking part include the usual suspects (Shell, BP, Total).[58] Although those corporations have ample funds at their disposal, nearly half of the platform's €1 million administrative costs between 2009 and 2011 were paid by the European taxpayer.[59]

Moreover, the ZEP epitomises how the 'public-private partnership' model favoured by the European Commission is fundamentally anti-democratic. This model was first put into effect through the Private Finance Initiative launched by John Major's Conservative government in 1992: a systematic attempt to put the running of essential services in the hands of for-profit corporations. Applied at EU level, the model has meant that the same firms are invited to draw up the agenda for how the Union should allocate subsidies and then to apply for those subsidies. It would be more honest, then, if CCS stood for corporate capture and storage.

It is significant that estimates made by the ZEP for the amount of pollution abatement it can achieve have changed dramatically. Sweeney's aforementioned forecasts are far lower than those contained in a 2006 'strategic deployment document' issued by the platform in 2006, one year after its inception. That blueprint foresaw CCS driving down emissions by 56 per cent between then and 2050. Despite this uncertainty, the EU's institutions have accepted the ZEP's main calls: that carbon capture and storage should benefit from both the emissions trading system and the Union's scientific research programme.[60]

In July 2012, the European Commission rubberstamped a shortlist of the first eight CCS projects declared eligible for funding with revenue accruing from the emissions trading system. The Commission stated that two or three of the projects should eventually receive a combined total of up to €1.5 billion. It is hardly a coincidence that Alstom, one of the probable beneficiaries of the largesse, is active in the Zero Emissions Platform.[61] Alstom, a French energy and transport giant, is prominent in a consortium attempting to bring carbon dioxide produced by a power plant in Yorkshire out into the North Sea where the gas would be 'permanently stored'.[62] Alstom is also hoping to build a CCS facility at the lignite-fired Belchatow plant in Poland.[63] Both of these projects featured on the Commission's shortlist.

Advocates of CCS have done well out of the financial crisis. In 2009, the Commission announced a 'European recovery package', under which six CCS projects were granted a total of €1 billion. This handsome sum was in addition to the €282 million reserved for CCS as part of the EU's scientific research programme between 2007 and 2013.[64]

Chris Davies, a British Liberal Democrat MEP, has been instrumental in securing large-scale funding for CCS. When a 'package' of laws on energy and climate change was proposed by EU officials in 2008, Davies was tasked with drawing up the European Parliament's official response. On his personal website he describes the money pledged for CCS at his behest as 'Davies's billions'.[65]

To secure this cash, Davies resorted to 'blackmailing' (his word) EU officials. Parts of the package would be blocked by the Parliament unless the EU's other key institutions gave a clear undertaking to use revenue from the emissions trading system for CCS experiments, he warned in an email message to other MEPs (which he later released to transparency campaigners).[66] Davies overcame objections from Climate Action Network, a reputable green organisation, which argued that as the ETS was market-based it was not supposed to favour one type of organisation. He was assisted in doing so by BP, which drafted amendments to the package that Davies signed. BP's winning formula promoted carbon capture and storage as 'novel, low carbon technologies that did not already receive material public funding'. After a long battle, the Commission and EU governments accepted Davies's core demands. In 2010, they agreed that more than €4 billion would go to CCS projects when money resulting from the emissions trading system was being divvied up. A cock-a-hoop Davies proclaimed the breakthrough as 'the most important achievement' of his life.[67]

The London-based Carbon Capture and Storage Association (CCSA) remains at the forefront of efforts to wheedle funds for CCS from custodians of the public purse. Supposedly distinct from the Zero Emissions Platform, the membership of the two organisations is nonetheless largely the same (as may be surmised, Shell, BP and Total belong to both groupings).[68] For help navigating its way in Brussels, the CCSA has hired The Centre, reputedly the city's first 'think-do tank' (bubblier than the bog-standard think tanks, which have proliferated in recent times, it would have us believe). The Centre was formed by the flamboyant lobbyist Paul Adamson – a donor to the British Labour Party when Tony Blair was prime minister – in 2003.[69] Seven years later, it was bought by the American 'public affairs' firm Edelman.[70]

Martin Porter, general manager of Edelman:The Centre at the time of writing, told me that he worked with the CCSA in 2010 and 2011. This work included 'periodic support with meetings with policy-makers and other EU stakeholders in Brussels'. Among those lobbied were 'MEPs working closely on the subject, notably Chris Davies'. I asked Porter if his firm was trying to give an image makeover to Shell and BP so that they could appear more ecologically responsible than they are widely perceived to be. 'No, but the question of how public acceptance of CCS technology could be developed was a question that the association was addressing,' he said.[71]

Big Oil does not do humility well. While only the terminally naive could expect Shell or BP to atone for their sins, the way they try to pose as protectors of polar bears is always hard to stomach. When

I once put it to Hans van der Loo of Shell that the case for carbon capture and storage was unproven, the most he would concede was: 'CCS is not a silver bullet'. He added: 'It will not save the world. But without it the world will not be saved.'[72]

Showering subsidies on CCS projects is a dangerous distraction from the need to invest in renewable energy and power conservation projects that – unlike CCS – have already been shown to have environmental benefits. Pressure from the fossil fuels industry has meant that scarce financial resources are being diverted from renewables into CCS. The €1 billion awarded to CCS by the 2009 European economic recovery plan was nearly twice as much as the amount reserved for offshore wind energy projects in the same plan.[73]

Furthermore, the argument that industrialised countries can apply a 'techno-fix' to climate change appears hypocritical when you realise that corporations are seeking to prevent poorer countries from having access to renewable energy technology at affordable prices.

Applications for and the granting of patents on 'clean energy technologies' have risen by 20 per cent since 1997, according to a 2010 study financed by the United Nations Environment Programme. The choice of 'clean energy technologies' by the study is debatable: it lumps wind and solar power (verifiably clean) with CCS (cleanliness unproven) and biofuels (often dirty). It is noteworthy, though, that photovoltaic technology – required to harness the power of the sun – accounts for the bulk of the patenting. Three members of the EU – Britain, Germany and France – are among the six countries with the highest rate of 'patenting activity' relating to 'clean energy' worldwide. Denmark, also in the EU, tops the league for wind power patents. Wind energy is described as 'now a mainstream technology' in the study.[74]

During the apparently never-ending 'Doha round' of world trade talks, the idea has been floated that patents on technology required for mitigating or adapting to climate change could be revoked for countries with limited means. The suggestion that a gesture of solidarity should be displayed towards nations and people most vulnerable to the effects of global warming should be 'vigorously and immediately rejected', according to BusinessEurope. Philippe de Buck, its then president, pointed out in April 2011 that 'developing countries' (his quotation marks) which might be allowed override patents 'would include successful emerging economies such as China, India and most Latin American nations'.[75]

Later that year, de Buck urged the European Commission to resist any attempts by China and India to have intellectual property issues placed on the agenda of international climate change talks, then chaired by South Africa. Patents 'are not the problem and weakening them is not the solution,' de Buck insisted. 'Instead a real commitment to development and climate financing is needed.'[76] I was struck by how his reasoning – even his choice of words – mirrors that used by big pharmaceutical firms when opposing any effort to waive patents on life-saving medicines.

THE WRONG ROAD

I began this chapter by referring to a 2007 EU agreement trumpeted by Angela Merkel. The commitment to put the future of the atmosphere at the mercy of financial markets wasn't the only dodgy aspect of that accord. It also contained the goal of ensuring that drivers used biofuels for one-tenth of all road journeys in the EU by 2020.

It's easy to see the goal's attraction. At the time it was drawn up, 90 per cent of all greenhouse gas emissions resulting from transport came from road vehicles.[77] Genuinely grappling with this problem would require taking on powerful vested interests – especially the car lobby – and investing massively in public transport. Banning or restricting cars in large parts of our towns and cities would also be required, a move that would bring many benefits to the air we breathe, our health and the quality of our lives. None of this would necessitate reinventing the wheel (pun intended): the residents of Amsterdam have proven that it is possible to have a vibrant and pleasant city, where cycling is the most common means of getting around.[78]

Rather than taking the bold initiative of replacing traffic jams with tramways and cycle lanes, our politicians have opted not to curb the congestion. They prefer to pretend that filling up petrol tanks with agricultural crops is a substitute for decisive action. (I fully accept that the term 'agrofuels' is more accurate than 'biofuels', with its connotations of being organic and wholesome. Nonetheless, I will stick with writing 'biofuels' because the term is more widely known).

Of course, the 10 per cent biofuels target was not a result of happenstance. It was formulated partly in response to a 2006 report by the corporate-dominated Biofuels Research Advisory Council (BIOFRAC). Set up by the European Commission, that body advocated a series of measures aimed at ensuring that biofuels would power up to one quarter of car and truck journeys in the EU by 2030. While BP was conspicuous by its absence on BIOFRAC, Shell and Total were very much present. Many other companies and associations that stood to gain from shaping transport and energy policy – Volvo, Volkswagen, the European Biodiesel Board, EuropaBio (the umbrella group for the biotechnology industry), Abengoa Bioenergy and British Sugar – were there too.[79]

To outsiders, the EU bureaucracy appears to move at a snail's pace. The proverbial snail has been pumped with performance-enhancing drugs in the case of biofuels promotion. Once BIOFRAC had completed its deliberations, it morphed into the European Biofuels Technology Platform. Not only had BIOFRAC advocated the establishment of the platform, the membership list of the two bodies is largely identical.[80]

The platform's work offers a riposte to all those in denial about how corporations often set the EU's agenda. Its first major publication was even called the 'strategic research agenda'. That January 2008 document advocated joint funding for biofuels (the platform is itself partly financed by the European Commission) and that any 'quality standards' introduced should not create 'unnecessary barriers for biofuels deployment'.[81]

To help decode what the platform meant, I read Jean Ziegler's book *Destruction Massive* (its English-language translation is titled *Betting on Famine*). As the UN's special *rapporteur* on the right to food, Ziegler stated in 2007 that 'producing biofuels with food is criminal'. The European Bioethanol Fuel Association (a member of the EU's technology platform) was so furious that it complained to Kofi Annan, then the UN's secretary-general about Ziegler's 'apocalyptic' remarks.[82]

Ziegler is not alone in expressing concern about how food crops that should be filling the bellies of the world's poor are instead filling petrol tanks. The World Bank (an organisation largely controlled by the US) has cited estimates that biofuel feed-stocks may account for 52 per cent of increased demand for maize and wheat over the 2008–18 period if targets for greater biofuel use in industrialised countries remained in place.[83] A 2012 study by the Institute for European Environmental Policy in London found 'it is clear' that rising demand for biofuels will drive up food prices, although there is 'continued debate' about how much inflation will occur.[84] ActionAid has highlighted how the poor will inevitably suffer the most from higher grocery bills: in Ghana, for example, three-quarters of household income is spent on food, making a family in Accra far more vulnerable to price volatility than one in Aachen.[85]

Europe's biofuels bonanza is an important factor behind the large-scale acquisition of arable land in poorer countries. By some estimates, more than 200 million hectares – an area eight times the size of the United Kingdom – was snatched up in speculative deals between governments (mostly in Africa, Asia and Latin America) and the private sector over the first decade of this century.[86] The deals are often accompanied by human rights abuses: hundreds of hectares in the Guatemalan region of Alta Verapaz have been cleared for growing sugar cane. The crops are transformed into bioethanol, which is then poured into Europe's cars. About 3,200 people have been displaced in order to make way for the plantations.[87]

Evidence of the harm caused by the EU's biofuels target continues to pile up. For a long the time the Union not only remained committed to the target, it set additional objectives and indicated that generous subsidies will be granted to biofuels. In 2011, for example, the European Commission signed an accord with the energy and aviation industry aimed at providing 2 million tonnes of biofuels for use in air transport by 2020.[88] It wasn't until October 2012 that the Commission belatedly owned up to how its targets were having negative consequences and recommended that the proportion of road journeys undertaken with food-based biofuels should not exceed 5 per cent.[89]

At first glance, it might seem odd that oil salesmen are among the most gung-ho supporters of biofuels. If corn and sugar start competing with fossil fuels, then surely this will have an adverse effect on the oil industry's profits.

Some of the big players in that industry, however, have been shrewd enough to see the biofuels craze as an opportunity, rather than a threat. Shell's Graeme Sweeney has gone so far as to call biofuels 'a natural fit with our downstream business in transport fuels'.[90] Sweeney is clearly at ease extolling the 'virtues' of both carbon capture and storage and biofuels. When closely examined, his stance cannot be viewed as contradictory. He is making sure that Shell remains relevant no matter what type of energy predominates in the future.

The bulk of this chapter was written during a dreary July in Belgium. The absence of sunshine for a few consecutive weeks meant that the vegetables I tried to grow in my garden mostly failed to materialise. My barren harvest consisted of barely enough spinach for one vegetarian lasagne.

If I relied solely on the *Daily Telegraph* for news, I might have surmised that global warming is a hoax because my tomato plants were drowned by heavy rain. Yet while I was moaning about the wetter-than-usual summer in Brussels, I heard some of my friends in America complain that they could not cope with the heat. Meteorological data suggests that there were 4,313 record high temperatures across the US during July 2012.[91]

Doubtless, the condition of Greenland's ice sheet is a more reliable indicator of climate change than my soggy garden. NASA, the space agency, reported that for several days in July 2012, 'Greenland's surface ice cover melted over a larger area than at any time in over 30 years of satellite observation'. As much as 97 per cent of the ice sheet surface thawed at some point in the middle of that month.[92]

Climate change denial is not as prevalent in Europe as it is in the US. Charles and David Koch, the super-wealthy brothers who bankroll the anti-green lobby in America, haven't entirely ignored this continent. Koch Industries has tasked Thomas Dubois, its representative in Switzerland, with keeping an eye on the EU institutions.[93] He is a board member with the European Centre for Public Affairs (ECPA) in Brussels, a think tank set up in 1986 that claims to be dedicated to transparency.[94] Maria Laptev, the ECPA's director, told me that while the centre charges a corporate membership fee of €5,000 per year, it 'is not sector-specific nor does it engage in lobbying activity of any kind'.[95] Her centre certainly facilitates lobbying, however, by organising debates where invited guests have an opportunity to 'network' with EU policy-makers.[96]

Even if the Koch brothers do not have a major influence on this side of the Atlantic, their activities in Europe require further investigation. Given the firm's record in the US, it is impossible to believe that Koch Industries is checking out the Brussels scene solely to avail of the canapés served at think tank receptions. The limited ability of climate change deniers to buy votes on this continent does not mean that the EU deserves kudos for its environmental approach. Accepting that climate scientists are telling the truth is an empty gesture if you are not prepared to act on their advice lest a few pampered industrialists throw a tantrum.

Angela Merkel did not don her superhero costume for long. In 2008 – little more than a year after her 'five minutes after midnight' warning – she vowed to resist the 'destruction of German jobs because of an inappropriate climate policy'. Her backtracking on goals she had previously championed was motivated by the aforementioned fear of 'carbon leakage'.[97] To be clear, Merkel was not standing up for German jobs: promoting renewable energy would be a far better way to guarantee high levels of employment. Rather, she was protecting corporate profits. She was not alone in mollycoddling the polluters. When EU leaders got around to approving the final shape of a 'climate and energy package' in December 2008, they decided that the biggest energy guzzling industries could continue receiving free emissions licences in the absence of an ambitious international agreement to keep the earth's temperatures in check.[98]

The ambitious international agreement that EU leaders claim to desire remains elusive. Meanwhile, the latest data I found at the time of writing indicates that little effort is being made to conclusively end our fossil fuel addiction. In 2010, the Union's emissions rose by 2.4 per cent, compared to the previous year.[99] Emissions for the 27-country bloc fell by 3 per cent in 2011. This reduction is no cause for celebration: the per capita rate of CO_2 emissions in the EU remains higher than that of China. Our politicians, therefore, have no moral basis on which to justify their penchant for casting China as the chief villain.[100]

The EU's decision to only take the necessary action to address climate change if governments in other parts of the world do so amounts to an abdication of responsibility. But this is exactly the type of behaviour to expect when you put polluters in charge of saving the planet.

7
The malign legacy of Peter Mandelson

Robert Clive epitomised the worst excesses of the British Empire. A master, in his own words, of 'tricks, chicanery, politics and the Lord knows what', the head of the East India Company used mass starvation as a means of asserting control.

As well as plundering the Bengali treasury of its silver and gold reserves (transported out of India on over 100 boats), his firm pushed food prices to levels that the poor could not afford. One third of Bengal's population was wiped out in the famine that began in 1769; as their corpses rotted, wily British entrepreneurs hoarded the grain that would have saved numerous lives.[1]

Sharing many of Clive's personality traits, Peter Mandelson set out to reaffirm the influence of major corporations in India almost 250 years later. In his then role as a European Union commissioner, Mandelson was pictured smiling radiantly when he visited New Delhi in 2007 to launch talks aimed at reaching a 'free trade agreement'.[2] That 150,000 Indian farmers had committed suicide over the preceding decade (according to the New Delhi government's own data) because they found themselves indebted and unable to compete with the predatory tactics of Western food companies did not seem to trouble him.[3]

Mandelson's decision to make the opening up of India's markets a priority during his time in office was largely a response to pleas by the European Services Forum (ESF). An alliance of more than 30 corporations set up in 1999, it represents the collective interests of such titans of global finance as Goldman Sachs, Standard Chartered Bank and Deutsche Bank, as well as telecommunications providers like BT, Telefónica and Vodafone, and the French water, waste and transport firm Veolia. BusinessEurope is also part of the forum, along with 30 other federations of employers.[4]

In January 2006, the ESF took part in a conference that brought together the European Commission and business representatives. An internal Commission report drawn up following the event suggested that the Brussels institutions were not paying sufficient heed to ensuring that European firms had better investment opportunities abroad. The Commission expressed a preference for achieving a new international agreement for regulating (or, perhaps more accurately, deregulating) commerce through talks initiated in the Qatari capital, Doha, a little more than four years earlier. Yet it advocated a 'fall-back or complementary strategy' of seeking bilateral trade agreements with certain countries should the Doha round fail.

Pascal Kerneis, the ESF's representative at that meeting, vented frustration with how the EU had until then tended to enter protracted trade talks with regional blocs like the Gulf Cooperation Council and Mercosur in Latin America. It would be more productive, he hinted, if the EU was to concentrate on securing individual trade deals with 'key emerging markets' such as India, China, Brazil and South Africa, 'not the whole world'.[5]

The points made by Kerneis were fleshed out in March 2006 when the ESF wrote to Mandelson, arguing that 'EU trade policy has to be redefined to take into consideration the fact that the EU economy is now essentially a services based economy'. Signed by the forum's chairman Iain Vallance, a Liberal Democrat member of the House of Lords who was a leading figure in BT before joining the board of supervisors with the electronics firm Siemens, the letter complained that the European Commission had failed to grasp the importance of services until then. 'Only a very small section' was devoted to services in a discussion paper on future trade policy the previous year, Vallance noted.

Citing estimates that services accounted for 70 per cent of the EU's gross domestic product and that the Union was both the world's top exporter and importer of services, the ESF urged Mandelson to take a belligerent line in demanding that governments across the globe drop laws viewed as unnecessary by the captains of industry. A briefing paper accompanying Vallance's letter gave a list of such laws (or 'barriers' to investment, as the ESF termed them); they included capital requirements for banks, restrictions on multinational firms sending profits made in a particular country back to their headquarters and caps on equity holdings for foreign investors. It was 'extremely important to understand that EU service providers need trade negotiations to get increased market access in many countries,' according to the forum.[6]

TURBO-CHARGED TRADE

The key recommendations made by the ESF were copied and pasted into a blueprint for a new EU trade policy. Titled *Global Europe* and formally published by Mandelson in October 2006, the blueprint ran to a mere 20 pages. Yet a careful reading of its content indicated its publication was a gambit to make the European Commission lurch towards a more virulent form of capitalism than that to which it was already committed.

Global Europe stated: 'Our core argument is that rejection of protectionism at home must be accompanied by activism in creating open markets and fair conditions for trade abroad.' No longer, it added, would the Union's trade officials be simply striving towards persuading countries in the wider world to reduce or scrap the tariffs they levied on imports. 'Securing real market access in the twenty-first century will mean focusing on new issues and developing the tools of trade policy to achieve the types of opening that make a real difference,' it added. The two central planks of this bold agenda would be 'stronger engagement with major economies and regions' and 'a sharper focus on barriers to trade behind the border'. The paper acknowledged that challenging 'barriers' to investment can be 'sensitive because they touch directly on domestic regulation' of foreign countries. Identifying and tackling such obstacles would require 'new ways of working' inside the Commission and 'with others' such as EU governments and business interest groups.[7]

It is difficult to interpret *Global Europe* as being anything other than a manifesto for meddling in the internal affairs of sovereign nations. With remarkable hubris, it effectively warned countries beyond the EU that they would have to rewrite any laws that hampered the maximisation of profit. While there were some nods to the importance of social justice and caring for the environment in the paper, it is clear that they amounted to little more than sugar-coating. In his memoirs, Mandelson acknowledged that he spent much of his time in Brussels, working closely with José Manuel Barroso to ensure that the EU executive primarily promoted 'growth and jobs' (an Orwellian euphemism; the actual objective was to make it easier for large companies to shed jobs). Mandelson wrote: 'I helped José Manuel develop a programme that reflected this priority rather than social and environmental policy areas.'[8]

Moreover, the inferences in *Global Europe* that 'protectionism' was a blight on humanity betrayed either a fickle grasp of economic history or a ruthless determination to not allow reality to impede the waging of an ideological war. The *Oxford English Dictionary* defines protectionism as 'the theory or practice of shielding a country's domestic industry from foreign competition by taxing imports'. That is precisely the route that many European, American and

Asian countries followed in the past in order to stimulate economic development. The industrial triumphs of Mandelson's native Britain were the result of sustained protectionism from the 1720s until the 1850s. As Ha-Joon Chang has illustrated, Britain used high tariffs and subsidies to encourage textile manufacturing and nurture a number of other infant industries, only embracing what is today known as free trade when 'its industrial dominance was absolute' during the second half of the nineteenth century.[9]

Guided by a corporate coterie, Mandelson set out to deprive India of the possibility to use tactics that had proven indispensable towards realising the past economic development strategies of the West. BusinessEurope was an especially trusted accomplice for Mandelson and his minions.

EYEING UP INDIA

In February 2007, David O'Sullivan, then head of the Commission's trade department, wrote to BusinessEurope seeking its views on forthcoming trade talks with India. Sent nine months before the talks were formally launched, O'Sullivan's letter and an accompanying questionnaire signalled an enthusiasm 'to engage in a more regular consultation with industry' by the Commission. 'My colleagues are discussing with your colleagues the most practical ways and means to get organised in this respect,' O'Sullivan wrote to Philippe de Buck of BusinessEurope.[10]

De Buck later travelled to New Delhi for the official opening ceremony of the talks. Once the apparent euphoria of the occasion had worn off, he displayed an impatience over how the negotiations did not lead to swift results. On 6 March 2008, he contacted Mandelson to vent his frustration with how the talks 'appear to be encountering difficulties very early in the process' and how there had not yet been a formal exchange of offers made by each side. De Buck was particularly unimpressed with indications that the Indian government wished to exclude entire sectors of industrial production from the scope of the agreement. His organisation 'cannot accept' moves by India to prevent the reduction or elimination of taxes levied on goods viewed as important by European exporters, de Buck added.[11] Mandelson would soon express his appreciation for this input, stating that it gave a 'timely reinforcement' to his own views ahead of a meeting he held with Kamal Nath, then India's commerce minister, the following day.[12]

If the words of EU trade representatives are taken seriously, then it appears they were either misinformed about the reality of India or chose to misrepresent it as an economic equal for Europe. Attending an EU–India 'business summit' – where chief executives and senior politicians swapped notes – in Helsinki during 2006, Mandelson lauded India as 'a living embodiment of today's process of globalisation and dynamism'.[13] Similar sentiments continue to be expressed by corporate interests, though usually in more restrained terms. In 2009, a joint letter submitted to O'Sullivan by lobbyists for the car, chemicals, metal, paper and textile industries expressed strong hostility to the idea of 'accepting carve-outs', whereby certain types of industry in India could be cushioned from the full effects of liberalisation. The letter forecast that 'most Indian industrial sectors will be developed enough to face the full competition from the EU in a few years' time'.[14]

India cannot be compared to the EU, regardless of which indicator one examines. In 2010, India's gross domestic product stood at $1.7 trillion. At $3.3 trillion, Germany's GDP was almost twice that amount; France had a GDP of almost $2.6 trillion. India has a population exceeding one billion, whereas the EU's largest economies have a combined population of less than 147 million. While many of the EU's countries are categorised as 'high income' by the World Bank and other international bodies, India is categorised as 'lower-middle income'.[15]

By solely concentrating on India's economic growth in the early part of the twenty-first century, Mandelson and his aides were tearing up the policy commitments of the institution for which they worked. When stating its desire to have an 'enhanced partnership' with India in 1996, the European Commission emphasised that 'social development must be a parallel objective to economic development'.[16] While 30 or more of India's tallest buildings have been erected in the interim, the lot of its poorest citizens cannot be said to have improved; in some respects it has deteriorated. The marvellous writer Arundhati Roy summed up the enormous wealth disparities in her country following the 2008 attacks on luxury hotels in Mumbai. As newspapers brimmed with 'moving obituaries by beautiful people about the hotel rooms they had stayed in, the gourmet restaurants they loved', a small box in one daily told readers that India had slipped below Sudan and Somalia on the international hunger index.[17]

Mandelson and subsequent EU trade commissioners also stand accused of violating the Union's own laws. Although I am hugely critical of the neo-liberal orientation of the EU's treaties, it should be acknowledged that they contain some progressive principles. Under the Maastricht treaty of 1992, all of the EU's policies are supposed to be 'coherent' with the central aim of its development aid policy, namely to fight against poverty. A clause in the more recent Lisbon treaty is even more explicit in requiring the Union's trade activities to respect human rights, including rights of a social and economic nature. The absence of a proper mechanism for ensuring that these obligations are upheld has, however, enabled Mandelson and other senior politicians to effectively treat them as irrelevant.[18]

TRAMPLING ON FOOD RIGHTS

Access to healthy food is as much a basic human right – if not more so – than freedom of expression or assembly. The right to food has been enshrined in the International Covenant of Economic, Social and Cultural Rights, which came into effect in 1976 and has been ratified by all of the EU's member states. The steps required to realise this right were spelled out by a UN committee dealing with economic and social rights in 1999. The committee stressed that the right to food went beyond being guaranteed a minimum number of calories per day to include having a sustainable supply of food 'free from adverse substances'. A common misunderstanding is that the right to food simply means the right to be fed; instead, the UN has recognised that human beings have the universal right to feed themselves in a manner that protects their dignity.[19]

Paradoxically, those most at risk of having their right to food violated tend to be people who grow food for a living. Olivier de Schutter, the UN's special *rapporteur* on the right to food at the time of writing, has contended that 'smallholders in developing countries, cultivating small plots of land often with little or no public support, are the single most important group of those who are food insecure in the world today.' Because such farmers lack storage facilities and the wherewithal to market their own produce, they are extremely vulnerable to price fluctuations and competition from imports.[20]

India – the 'miracles' celebrated by Mandelson notwithstanding – remains an overwhelmingly agricultural economy. About 70 per cent of its inhabitants rely on farming to survive. And within that majority, more than 80 per cent of farmers have less than two hectares each.[21]

For a number of years, the European Commission has been conniving with the small number of firms intent on gaining complete, or near-complete, control of global food production to make the lot of India's small farmer even more perilous than it is now. Separate but related battles have been fought against the poor at the level of the World Trade Organisation (WTO) and in the bilateral EU–India negotiations. Efforts by the Indian government to ensure that an international agreement contained safeguards that could be triggered when imports of rice and other crops reached volumes that caused mass hardship for the country's farmers were vigorously resisted by the EU, at the behest of large agri-business companies.

The resistance was led by the Confederation of the Food and Drink Industries in the EU (known by its French acronym CIAA, it was later renamed FoodDrinkEurope). In May 2008, Jean Martin, the CIAA's president at the time, wrote to Mandelson, complaining about a draft paper for an agreement on the international food trade drawn up by Crawford Falconer, a New Zealand diplomat then chairing WTO discussions on agriculture. Martin's letter made clear his opposition to efforts by governments such as India to protect many types of food from all-out liberalisation. According to Martin, 'emerging economies' like India already benefited from 'generous protective provisions' and should not be allowed additional ones (he did not specify what the 'generous protective provisions' were).[22]

A few months later, India and China were blamed by the US for the failure to achieve a breakthrough on agriculture at a WTO ministerial conference in Geneva.[23] Mandelson declined to join America's blame game.[24] His reticence does not mean he was markedly more sympathetic to the plight of India's poor than Susan Schwab, the pugnacious trade representative for the George W. Bush administration. Correspondence between Mandelson and CIAA indicates that he was more attuned to the desires of snack producers in the West than the needs of Asian peasants. Replying to Jean Martin's letter, he suggested that he could only countenance special protections for subsistence farmers that were narrowly defined. The kind of safeguard mechanism sought by India is 'supposed to only cover staple food categories,' he wrote, adding: 'I share your view that current proposals go beyond this original objective and include some tariff lines unlikely to have any impact on subsistence farmers.'[25] Significantly, Mandelson's letter did not address one of the chief reasons cited by the Indian government for demanding a safeguard mechanism: to prevent farmers in poor countries (not just India) being destroyed by produce that can be sold cheaper because it had benefited from agricultural subsidies paid in America or Europe.[26]

While attending the Geneva conference, Mandelson was accompanied by Mariann Fischer Boel, the EU commissioner for agriculture at that time. A landowner and a recipient of the Union's farm subsidies, she is the granddaughter of Marius Boel, the reputed inventor of Danish blue cheese.[27] Her family connections to the dairy industry might explain why she undertook to sniff out opportunities for the agri-food business throughout the world. Just three days before talks aimed at reaching an EU–India free trade agreement opened in 2007, she addressed a seminar, attended by representatives of 78 food firms. Noting that the EU was traditionally a net importer of food but had become a net exporter to the rest of the world the previous year, she spoke of her conviction that an 'offensive strategy' for promoting agri-food interests was needed.

India, she emphasised, would feature prominently in that strategy. 'The Indian middle class is hungry for exciting food and drink experiences that go beyond Indian cuisine. And this middle class is growing at the rate of 35 million per year – in other words, by the population of a middle-sized European country. And that is why so many foreign companies are getting into position to increase their sales in India. We need a piece of the action.'[28]

To gain its 'piece of the action', the European agri-food industry wants to pressure India into dramatically cutting its tariffs, despite how they account for almost one-quarter of the country's entire tax revenue.[29] The European Dairy Association, a grouping that fights on behalf of yoghurt and chocolate makers like Yoplait, Müller and the ubiquitous Nestlé, has argued that tariffs charged on dairy imports by India are 'unreasonably high'.[30] While the CIAA has merely complained that the tariffs are 'very high', it has demanded that they be reduced 'to provide real new market opportunities'. In a 2009 submission to EU trade officials, the CIAA enthused that India 'presents a strong market potential for exports of jams, sugar confectionery, chocolate and fine bakery wares, as well as extracts of coffee and tea'.[31]

As tea is indigenous to India, the idea that it should have to import this crop from thousands of miles away appears perverse. Tea growing is one of many agricultural activities in which a high percentage of female labourers are employed. Overall, as much as 75 per cent of India's female workforce is engaged in agriculture, so any loss of jobs and earnings resulting from trade liberalisation will have particularly harsh effects for numerous women and the families they feed.[32] Those women have, however, been erased from the image of India that Mandelson and Fischer Boel present. The

Indians to whom they reach out are not hungry in the strict sense of that word; they are 'hungry for exciting food and drink experiences'.

The lure of India's middle class helps explain why Europe's distilleries are following the talks closely. EU trade officials attending a 2010 meeting with the Scotch Whisky Association and Pernod Ricard learned that India has the largest whisky market in the world but imported spirits account for just 1 per cent of those sales. There would be no 'meaningful access' for Western booze unless a free trade agreement called time on an 'exorbitant 150 per cent tariff', the officials were told.[33] Sections of India's press have allied themselves with the producers of absinthe and cognac. In an apparent reference to the John Lennon song 'Imagine', the *Business Standard* has reported that a free trade agreement with the EU could turn India into a 'Lennonesque Utopia' for lawyers, who after a long day's work 'could sit back in Delhi and enjoy a buttery glass of French wine without spending a month's wage on it.'[34]

The courting of the middle class is perhaps most pronounced in the determination of supermarkets to penetrate India. For the past few years, India has repeatedly occupied one of the top four rankings for the 30 'emerging markets' deemed most attractive for 'retail development' by the management consultants AT Kearney.[35] Yet chains such as Tesco and Carrefour have long been disgruntled by Indian regulations which restrict them to operating cash-and-carry wholesale stores directed at business owners, rather than the general public.[36] India has forbidden foreign investment in multi-brand retailing and placed a 51 per cent limit for the share of external ownership in sportswear shops and other outlets that sell just one brand.[37] In a detailed briefing paper sent to high-level Brussels trade officials in 2010, the European Services Forum bemoaned how opening up large Western-style supermarkets is 'virtually impossible' in India. 'A removal of these equity caps is essential,' according to the ESF.[38]

The same equity caps are themselves essential in securing a future for 35 million people who work in shops or as street vendors in India. After agriculture, retail is the largest source of employment in the country.[39]

Back in 1998, a study commissioned by the British government found that food shops lose up to 50 per cent of their business when a large supermarket is built on the edge of a town centre.[40] That finding related to the UK but it summarised the rapacious nature of Tesco and its ilk. Although the experience may not be replicated in exactly the same manner in India, it can still be assumed that huge job losses will result if hawkers and family stores are pitted against the masters of European retail.

CASINO CAPITALISM IN KOREA

In 2008, Mandelson made a surprise return to British domestic politics, when he was appointed business secretary in Gordon Brown's government. The vacancy he left in the European Commission was filled by Catherine Ashton, a protégé of Brown and his predecessor Tony Blair, who has never held elected office. Before formally taking up her new job, Ashton underwent a confirmation hearing in the European Parliament, in which she indicated that she would be mindful of the issues arising from the financial crisis spreading through the global economy, as well as climate change and the spike in food prices that had been experienced everywhere from Mexico to Mauritania that year. A 'negotiating style to overcome' these problems would have to be developed, she told MEPs.[41]

In truth, there was no discernible difference between Ashton's approach and that of Mandelson. Nor did the calamitous events witnessed in Wall Street lead her to question if the EU was justified in demanding that its trading 'partners' wield a machete over their banking regulations.

In December 2008, she expressed a determination to clinch a broad free trade agreement with South Korea, thereby setting a 'very useful precedent' for talks with other large countries.[42] Like India, Korea was identified as a prime target for increased business opportunities under the *Global Europe* strategy. Unlike India, the Korean government was amenable to signing an accord within a relatively short space of time. And so talks that were launched in 2007 led to the initialling of an actual agreement – running to nearly 2,000 pages – in October 2009.[43]

Ashton did not give Europe's corporate lobbyists everything that they wanted. She disappointed this continent's car-makers by agreeing to accommodate Korean concerns over its auto producers. As that proved something of a red line for Seoul, there would be 'no benefit' for the EU to jeopardise the agreement by proving inflexible over just one sector, she maintained.[44]

In contrast to the car-makers, the financial services industry was thrilled with the result. The European Banking Federation hailed the accord as 'the most comprehensive agreement ever negotiated by the EU'.[45] An analysis by TheCityUK, a group representing London's financial district, was similarly upbeat, noting that it was wider in scope than a free trade agreement that Seoul had signed with the US in 2007. Whereas the agreement with Washington only applied to 'financial institutions', the deal with the EU opened up Korea to 'financial services suppliers' such as asset management firms. Once the agreement came into effect, the 'products' offered by Europe's financial services industry could automatically be traded in Korea unless they had been subject to prior restrictions.[46] Casino capitalism had nabbed an important victory.

Moreover, the EU–Korea agreement contains an entire chapter devoted to resolving disputes. Under it, European firms who encounter 'obstacles' in Korea can effectively ask the EU to prosecute the Seoul authorities. Similarly, Korean entrepreneurs who are frustrated by European bureaucracy or regulation will be able to badger their government into suing the EU side. According to the European Commission, the relevant clauses are modelled on the dispute settlement mechanism provided for by the WTO but are intended to deliver faster results. Quarrels will be heard by an arbitration panel of three 'experts' chosen by the EU and Korea and its decisions – to be made within 120 days – will be binding.[47]

The eventual shape of the dispute settlement provisions closely reflected demands that Western corporations had been making for several years. In 2007, BusinessEurope complained to EU trade officials about a cap of 49 per cent on foreign ownership in Korea's telecommunications sector, as well as about limitations on investment in shipping, energy and banking. To overcome those hurdles, it argued that a binding arbitration procedure 'with clear-cut deadlines' should be introduced via a free trade agreement.[48] Responding to those demands, Peter Mandelson stated that an agreement with Korea 'will have to include satisfactory solutions to key EU concerns' such as a 'mediation and effective bilateral dispute settlement mechanism'.[49]

For quite a few months before the agreement was signed, European diplomats had been assessing ways of challenging Korean legislation deemed unhelpful to investors. Discussions held in the European Commission's embassy in Seoul during April 2009 dealt with the role of 'market access teams' who 'could serve as possible early warning systems by monitoring possible breaches' of the eventual agreement. Business representatives would be encouraged to take part in those teams, along with civil servants. Among the 'irritants' identified at that meeting was a tax imposed by Korea on imported water; revenue from the tax has been earmarked for improving the supply of public water.[50]

Water quality is a pressing concern in Korea due to poor maintenance of infrastructure and a high level of leakage. While cities and large towns enjoyed near universal access to tap water, the level of access was less than 38 per cent in some of Korea's fishing communities and rural areas, according to a 2007 report by the organisation Water Justice.[51]

Of course, the plight of isolated communities in Korea was not foremost on the minds of EU diplomats based in Seoul, at least not those diplomats tasked with identifying potential opportunities for Western corporations. Their discussions should be seen against the background of a wider effort to have water treated as a commercial commodity. In 2010, the United Nations general assembly voted to recognise water as a fundamental human right. No government had the temerity to oppose the resolution, yet 41 of them abstained. Eighteen of those abstainers were members of the European Union; they included Britain, Poland, Sweden, Denmark, the Netherlands and Ireland.

Interestingly, Korea also abstained.[52] This illustrated how the Seoul authorities shared a commitment to privatising water with a significant number of EU governments, as well as the European Commission. On the advice of large water firms such as Suez, Vivendi and RWE, the EU used negotiations on a planned international agreement on services liberalisation to request that 72 countries throughout the world allow unhindered access to their 'environmental services' markets for foreign investors in the first few years of the new millennium.[53] Initially, the EU tried to keep these requests secret; the controversy which ensued after they became public knowledge in 2003 eventually led to the Union specifying that drinking water would be excluded from the scope of the privatisation measures it was seeking.[54] Needless to say, the exemption was the result of outside pressure, not any moral hang-up on the part of EU officials about making the hard-pressed pay to quench their thirst.

As Korea was among the countries on the EU's wish list for water privatisation, it is logical that the Union is continuing to examine ways to achieve its objectives by other means.[55] A partial breakthrough was achieved with the signing of a free trade agreement, which allows Veolia (as Vivendi is now called) to bid for some sewage treatment contracts in Korea.[56] Veolia is unlikely to be content with being a bit player in the country, so nobody should be surprised if the EU exploits the opening it has won to wrest further control of Asian water.

SOVEREIGNTY SABOTAGED

When the Lisbon treaty entered into force in December 2009, the EU collectively acquired some important new powers. Already able to negotiate free trade agreements, the European Commission was now also tasked with thrashing out the kind of bilateral investment accords previously signed by the EU's national governments with countries throughout the world.[57]

Bilateral investment treaties – or BITs as they are known to specialists – have proven to be a boon for lawyers. Since the late 1990s, corporations have been using provisions in such treaties that allow them to litigate against entire states over regulatory decisions that affect (or are perceived to affect) their bottom line.[58] According to Gus Van Harten, a Canadian legal academic, the mushrooming of investor-state arbitration clauses in investment agreements has meant that nations are 'engaging in wars of attrition' with corporations.[59]

Few things are off limits in these wars. Philip Morris, the tobacco titan, moved in 2010 to sue Uruguay over stipulations that cigarette boxes should be in coloured or plain packaging and that 80 per cent of their surface area be devoted to health warnings. Availing of an investment agreement between Switzerland and Uruguay, Philip Morris alleged that its intellectual property rights were being breached.[60] Europe is by no means immune to litigation of this nature. Vattenfall, the Swedish electricity company, has started legal proceedings against Germany over its phasing out of nuclear power. The case is being taken under the Energy Charter Treaty, an investment agreement supposed to create 'stable' conditions for investors in power generation.[61]

The fact that decisions on the environment or public health have been approved by an elected parliament can be blithely dismissed by arbitrators handling these kinds of cases. Some lawyers argue that investment treaties are premised on 'protecting' foreign investors in ways that domestic laws don't. As most modern investment treaties follow an open-ended definition of investment, virtually every conceivable business activity is covered by them, in the opinion of WilmerHale, a law firm with a dedicated international arbitration unit.[62]

Big business seems to be both excited and slightly apprehensive by the transfer of responsibility for foreign investment from the capitals of EU countries to Brussels. The Federation of German Industries (BDI) has been arguing that investment treaties already in place should remain valid unless it is demonstrated that they are 'irreconcilable with EU legislation'. Yet in its correspondence with EU trade officials, the BDI has been emphatic that any new investment accords must allow corporations to sue nominally sovereign governments. The chief concern expressed by Werner Schnappauf, the federation's director-general, in 2010 was that there should be no weakening of 'investment protection' as a result of the changes ushered in by Lisbon.[63]

The potential 'weakening' that worried him was that principles relating to human rights or environmental protection might intrude on arcane discussions about commerce. Similar anxieties were voiced at a secretive meeting in December 2010. Hosted by the law firm Hogans Lovell, the meeting brought EU officials together with lobbyists from Shell, Alstom, GDF Suez, the European American Business Council and the Canada-EU Mining Council. The officials present, Colin Brown and Maria Alcover, promised that new investment clauses sought by the European Commission would provide the same level of 'protection' to corporations as the 1,200 or so bilateral treaties previously signed by individual EU governments. They were then warned by the lobbyists that such treaties 'might become meaningless if many social obligations are imposed on investors'.[64]

BLEEDING CANADA DRY

Corporate jitters notwithstanding, the Commission was formally given the go-ahead by EU governments to negotiate investment sections as part of free trade agreements in September 2011. However, the Commission's mandate was for the time being limited to negotiations with just three countries: India, Canada and Singapore.[65]

Canada's inclusion on the list was noteworthy. At a summit in Prague during May 2009, the EU and Canada kicked off talks with the objective of reaching a 'comprehensive economic and trade agreement' (CETA) between the two sides.[66] As its name suggests, CETA was never intended as a bog-standard deal. That much is evident from a blueprint for it issued a few months earlier by the Canada-Europe Roundtable for Business (CERT).

With a membership largely comprised of arms companies (including EADS, Bombardier and Bell Helicopters), CERT is chaired at the time of writing by Bill Emmott, a former editor of *The Economist* who backed the Anglo-American invasion of Iraq.[67]

The CERT paper warned that food safety and environmental standards 'can result in products being eliminated from the European and, to a lesser extent, Canadian markets'. To remedy this situation in a way that would accommodate profit maximisation, CERT recommended that dispute settlement procedures going beyond those provided for by the WTO should be introduced.[68] Xstrata, the mining company and a member of CERT, has been pressing for the agreement to introduce a dispute settlement mechanism with real 'teeth'. In a letter marked 'confidential', John Smillie of Xstrata Nickel argued that unless a Canada–EU deal enabled corporations to challenge environmental measures that ban certain chemicals 'it is just another tariff-based agreement and not the landmark, comprehensive and ambitious framework agreement that is being claimed and, we understand, both sides want'.[69]

CETA, according to some analysts, could be a carbon copy of the multilateral agreement on investment (MAI).[70] An initiative of that capitalist club, the Organisation for Economic Cooperation and Development (OECD), the MAI was intended to allow corporations litigate against governments over 'a lost opportunity to profit from a planned investment'.[71] Yet following an international campaign by activists for social and environmental justice, talks aimed at finalising the MAI were mothballed in 1998.[72] The core ideas floated in those talks, though, have remained on the agenda of major corporations, who have been crafty enough to resurrect them in other forums.

Michael Moore's film *Sicko* conveyed the impression that Canada has a model system of health care. Although Moore probably resorted to a little hyperbole, one reason why Canada is more decent towards the disadvantaged than its neighbour is that it has kept essential medicines affordable.

European confederations, particularly those in the pharmaceutical sector, have sniffed an opportunity in CETA to reverse the situation so that higher prices can be charged for drugs. MEDEF, the French employers' federation, has been particularly active in this respect. It has been urging that a trade agreement put an end to the preferential treatment given to generic medicines in Canada. In a detailed 2009 paper, MEDEF argued that a priority issue for the EU should be to persuade Canada to impose tougher standards of intellectual property for pharmaceuticals. MEDEF zoomed in on judicial practices regarding rows between generic drug companies and holders of patents for branded medicines. As things stand, corporations lack the possibility to appeal rulings in patent cases if the initial verdict favours the generic producer. As well as pressing for the chance to appeal in such cases, MEDEF wanted Canada to emulate an EU law allowing the extension of a monopoly on production once a pharmaceutical patent expires.[73] Canada did not have an equivalent to the 'supplementary protection certificates' issued in the EU and the US for medicines; these effectively lengthen the duration of patents by an extra five years, preventing the availability of cheaper generic versions of the drugs in question during that time.[74]

A study published by the Canadian Generic Pharmaceutical Association in 2011 predicted that the entry into force of CETA would delay the arrival of generic medicines on the Canadian market by an average of 3.5 years, causing a major increase in the medical bills paid out of public health budgets.[75] Heedless to such warnings, the European Commission has sided with Big Pharma against the patients of Manitoba and Quebec. During her brief stint as the EU's trade commissioner, Catherine Ashton complained about Canada's 'very poor IPR [intellectual property rights] enforcement'. CETA, she contended, aimed to tackle it and a few other 'longstanding issues that have marred our trade relationship in the past'.[76]

RESERVING MEDICINES FOR THE RICH

Robustly defending the patents held by Western corporations was one of the goals identified in the *Global Europe* strategy paper. The philosophy (if that is the correct word) behind the EU's stance on intellectual property was outlined by Mandelson when he visited China in 2007. 'Behind every innovative European product – whether it's a fashion shoe or a solar panel using new environmental technology or a medicine or a semiconductor – there is an idea that requires protection,' he said. 'But every day, in numbers that are getting higher every year, those ideas are being stolen.'[77]

Leaving aside the question of whether ideas require 'protection', there is an obvious difference between a fashion shoe and a medicine. Furthermore, there are differences between a pill intended to cure baldness and one for treating heart disease. Mandelson's absolutist stance, however, failed to draw any distinction between products of a frivolous nature and those necessary to keep people alive.

The argument that high standards of intellectual property are a prerequisite for the innovation of medicines that benefit all strata of society has been refuted authoritatively by the World Health Organisation. A 2006 probe by the WHO's Commission on Intellectual Property, Innovation and Public Health concluded that 'patents are not a relevant factor' in stimulating research into and the development of treatments for diseases that affect millions of the world's poor. 'In developing countries, the fact that a patent can be obtained may contribute nothing or little to innovation if the market is too small or scientific and technological capability inadequate,' the report added.[78]

Not liking the message, branded drug makers didn't quite try to shoot the messenger. Instead, they tried to render the messenger impotent. To follow up on the 2006 report, the government of Brazil proposed a resolution at the World Health Assembly (the WHO's decision-making body) the following year. The motion called for assistance to be given to those countries which planned to avail of flexibilities in international trade rules in order to override medical patents in cases of public health emergencies.[79]

Pharmaceutical lobbyists in Brussels tried to enlist the European Commission's help in thwarting the Brazilian initiative. Brendan Barnes from the European Federation of Pharmaceutical Industries and Associations (EFPIA) told EU officials that the WHO was not 'well-equipped' to deal with intellectual property. He also urged that the Union resist 'the expansion of the WHO's mandate' to patents. The subtext of his argument was that patents should be treated as a purely commercial matter, even when the lives of millions were at stake.[80]

Barnes was unable to prevent the Brazilian motion from winning a majority. But he and his colleagues did have an impact on the EU's position. Later in 2007, Portugal, then the holder of the EU's rotating presidency, submitted a paper to the WHO, effectively telling it not to become too active on patents as such issues are handled by the World Trade Organisation and the World Intellectual Property Organisation (WIPO).[81] As the names of the two latter bodies indicate, both are more focused on pandering to the captains of industry than curing tuberculosis or malaria.

Mandelson's hawkish stance on medical patents marked a departure from the positions taken by some of the EU's most powerful figures. In 2004, Jacques Chirac, then the French president, publicly stated his opposition to a US drive to reach a free trade agreement with Thailand that would, in his view, deprive people with AIDS of anti-retroviral drugs. Chirac described the pressure Washington was putting on Bangkok as 'tantamount to blackmail'.[82]

Within a few years, the European Commission was harassing the Thai government in a similar manner to that which angered Chirac.

In 2006 and 2007, Thailand circumvented patents on two drugs for treating AIDS by issuing compulsory licences to allow generic versions of them to be produced. It also issued a compulsory licence for a medicine to treat high blood pressure and indicated that it planned to do so for a heart disease drug, called Plavix.[83]

In July 2007, Mandelson wrote a menacing letter to the Thai ministries of health, foreign affairs and commerce. After noting that Bangkok had stated that drug companies wishing to do business in Thailand should not sell their products at prices more than 5 per cent above generic versions of them, he warned that continuing to disgruntle pharmaceutical corporations 'could lead to the isolation of Thailand from the global biotechnology investment community'.[84]

The letter revealed much about the mindset of Mandelson and his entourage. I recall asking one of Mandelson's then advisers about why he had threatened the Thais. The adviser told me that under a decision made by the World Trade Organisation, medical patents could only be overruled in cases of public health emergencies. Whereas AIDS 'meets anyone's definition of an urgent public health issue,' the adviser (who requested anonymity) said, 'something like heart disease, perhaps does not meet the criteria'.[85]

The WTO's decision was taken with the EU's support in 2005; it was designed to give permanent effect to a 2003 waiver from the terms of the organisation's trade-related intellectual property rights (TRIPS) agreement so that countries without the wherewithal to produce vital medicines could import generic versions of branded drugs by issuing compulsory licences. Contrary to what Mandelson's adviser indicated, the WTO decision was not limited to emergency situations or particular illnesses.[86]

Internal documents that I subsequently obtained show that Mandelson's advisers privately acknowledged that Thailand had not in any way breached the WTO decision. The reason why they had decided to put pressure on Bangkok to reverse its position was because they felt it had created a 'dangerous precedent' by circumventing patents on medicines other than those used to treat AIDS. Other countries could follow suit, they feared.[87] Despite accepting that Thailand had every right to take this course of action, EU officials decided to accuse the Bangkok government of breaking 'the spirit' of WTO commitments.[88] Mandelson kept on pressurising Thailand to change its public health policy at regular intervals. A briefing note prepared for a telephone conversation between him and a Thai minister in April 2008 recommended that he refer to Thailand's overruling of patents held by European firms on four breast and lung cancer drugs earlier that year. 'We are concerned about the Thai policy on compulsory licensing, where systematic recourse as a mere cost-cutting exercise is extremely worrying,' the note stated.[89]

From Mandelson's perspective, the cost of cancer or heart disease treatments in Thailand may not be something to lose sleep over. But around that time heart disease tablets manufactured by the corporation Sanofi were too expensive for 80 per cent of Thailand's population.[90] Cancer, meanwhile, was claiming around 30,000 Thai lives per year.[91]

Mandelson's missives closely resemble correspondence that the European Commission has received from EFPIA. In September 2010, EFPIA representative Louis-Nicolas Fortin alerted various Brussels officials about discussions underway in India. Fortin was troubled by a document from India's department of industrial policy, which raised the possibility that compulsory licensing could be used to increase the availability of generic medicines in the country. Among the 'considerations which raise key concerns for our industry,' Fontin wrote, was the 'possibility of broadening CL [compulsory licensing] grounds beyond public health emergencies'.[92]

In January 2012, a French MEP Kader Arif resigned as the European Parliament's point-man on the international Anti-Counterfeiting Trade Agreement (ACTA), protesting that the tough rules on intellectual property it contained could imperil the supply of generic medicines to the needy.[93] The European Commission has disputed his interpretation, insisting that there is nothing in ACTA that 'could directly, or indirectly, affect the legitimate trade in generic medicines or, more broadly, global public health'.[94]

The Commission's assurance was deceptive. Perusing ACTA's final text, I could not find anything in it that explicitly guarantees special treatment for generic medicines or that draws a clear distinction between fake imitations of copyrighted goods and generic versions of patented drugs. What I found instead were provisions allowing border authorities to impound goods regarded as 'suspect'.[95] As both Brazil and India have formally complained about several incidents in which generic medicines from their countries were seized in European ports (reportedly at the behest of large pharmaceutical firms) over recent years, it is logical to fear that such seizures could become more frequent if ACTA enters into force.[96] (Following many public protests, the European Parliament voted to reject ACTA in June 2012.[97] This is unlikely to be the end of the matter, though.

Recent history shows that 'free trade' advocates can find ways to resuscitate initiatives that once seemed moribund).

The worldview encapsulated by ACTA mirrors that of Big Pharma. So it should come as little surprise that the masters of medicine were fully behind efforts to have a new international regime on intellectual property that was more draconian than the one presided over by the WTO and WIPO. Pfizer and GlaxoSmithKline are among the companies belonging to the main corporate coalitions that have championed ACTA such as the International Chamber of Commerce (ICC) and the European Brands Association (known by its French acronym AIM).[98] At the beginning of the negotiations in 2008, the ICC and AIM distributed a joint memorandum to the governments and institutions taking part (including the US, Canada, Japan, the EU and Australia), outlining the core tenets they wished to see in an eventual deal. 'Intellectual property theft is no less a crime than physical property theft,' the memo insisted.[99]

Mandelson has been a stout ally for those pressure groups. Later in 2008, he told the Federation of German Industries that 'like you, I am convinced that in order to fight counterfeiting effectively, we need strong criminal sanctions as well'.[100]

AFRICA'S ALLY?

Arguably the worst thing Mandelson did during his time in Brussels was to bully some of the world's poorest countries into accepting trade arrangements that manifestly ran counter to the interests of their citizens.

When it suited him, Mandelson posed as a champion of Africa. He attended the Live8 concert organised by Bob Geldof in 2005 and called for 'continuing pressure and interest and attention not just to the issues of humanitarian aid and debt relief but trade'.[101] At the same time as he was hobnobbing with rock stars, Mandelson was the target of a public campaign urging him to display a little justice towards Africa. He refused to listen.

For much of his period as an EU commissioner, Mandelson was kept busy overseeing negotiations with almost 80 African, Caribbean and Pacific (ACP) countries. He appeared determined to convince their governments to sign comprehensive free trade deals with the EU by the end of 2007, maintaining that doing so was legally vital. His case for pushing that deadline rested on the fact that the preferential terms under which the ACP bloc could export its goods to the EU had been granted a waiver from WTO rules. Once the clock struck midnight on 1 January 2008, that waiver would expire.[102]

Adopting a patronising attitude, Mandelson told the ACP's governments that he was essentially helping them out by having his staff write complex trade pacts (labelled economic partnership agreements or EPAs) for them. He repeatedly claimed that Europe's top firms had no offensive interests in the EPA negotiations and that the pacts were designed as a tool for economic development. In an October 2007 opinion piece for the *Guardian*, he wrote: 'EU companies and investment are not trying to muscle in on markets. The problem is that EU companies and investors have too little interest in these regions, not that they have too much.'[103]

Correspondence between Mandelson and the European Services Forum indicates that he was saying different things in private. A day after that article appeared, the ESF sent a letter to Mandelson reminding him that 'the ACP includes 79 countries and therefore represents a large number of existing and potential markets and trading partners for our companies'. Iain Vallance, the forum's then chairman, said that his forum's members 'cannot agree that commitments on services can be left out of the EPA negotiations'. If the scope of the negotiations became narrower than what the EU originally desired, then the spirit of *Global Europe* would be broken, he argued.[104]

Mandelson didn't reply to the letter until March 2008. Yet his response was at odds with his earlier assurance that European firms were not trying to 'muscle in' on the ACP's markets. Mandelson drew the ESF's attention to how a comprehensive trade deal had been signed with the Caribbean region by the end of 2007 'covering not only market access in goods, but also services and establishment'. For the other regions, Mandelson had to take a 'pragmatic approach' and accept agreements that were limited to trade in goods. But those agreements were described as 'interim EPAs', meaning that both sides had given an undertaking to continue talks with a view to expanding them into other policy areas. 'You may have noted that all interim agreements contain provisions for the continuation of the negotiation of commitments in services and establishment throughout 2008,' Mandelson added. 'And I am committed to making progress in the services negotiations with those EPA regions who signed interim agreements.'[105] There is nothing in the letter to say that Mandelson only wanted to make progress for Africa's benefit.

The EPA talks were accompanied by the kind of spin-doctoring with which Mandelson is synonymous. Peeved by how they were failing to win support from Africa's home-grown private sector, officials working under Mandelson's direction engaged in a sleight of hand. They orchestrated and funded the establishment of an African business forum to give the impression that shrewd entrepreneurs throughout that continent wanted to see the EU's plans realised.[106] BusinessEurope (then called UNICE) provided less than subtle advice to Brussels officials about which trade associations in Africa it should co-opt. In one particular email message, Adrian van den Hoven, a senior lobbyist in BusinessEurope, recommended two African employer groups. 'Just call them and tell them they have to do it,' he wrote to EU official Robert Baldwin.[107]

This propensity for coercion appears to have been shared by Mandelson himself. A high-level source in a Southern African government told me of a meeting that Mandelson held with ministers and negotiators from that region in December 2007. There was strong opposition among the grouping present to how the draft trade agreement being touted by Mandelson contained a ban on taxing exports of raw materials (an instrument used by many countries to encourage processing of their resources at home), as well as a 'most favoured nation' clause, which stipulated that any preferences granted to economies with more than a 1 per cent share of world trade must automatically be extended to the EU as well. (The clause was mainly intended to stop China from being more dominant in Africa's markets than Europe).

Unwilling to compromise, Mandelson warned the Southern African governments that they would no longer be able to export goods to the EU under advantageous terms if they did not accept his conditions. 'It was a take it or leave it thing,' the source said. 'Mandelson put it quite abruptly. We went through a lot of issues, then Mandelson was saying 'I got to go'. He was asked 'when can we reconvene?' and he replied 'February' [after the end-of-year deadline]. Then he walked out. Some of the negotiators were begging him to come back. He did come back for a period of time and it was then that a large number decided to sign.'[108]

I contacted Mandeslon to request his side of the story. He did not respond.

EMBRACING OPPRESSION

The legacy bequeathed by Mandelson continues to have a marked effect on the direction of EU trade policy. The central objectives set out in the *Global Europe* paper are still being pursued with brio by Karel de Gucht, the EU's trade commissioner at the time of writing. In 2010, de Gucht (previously Belgium's foreign minister) published a 'vision' document that was presented as a sequel to *Global Europe*. With the ideological orientation of the two strategies almost identical, the only divergences were those of emphasis. De Gucht appears to be devoting more time to China than his predecessors did, for example; he also regards the question of ensuring 'unrestricted supply of raw materials' as increasingly urgent. Key to his argument is that the minerals and energy sources of poorer countries must be completely available to Western multinationals.[109]

Not only does de Gucht have a colonial mindset, he is influenced primarily by big business. His appointments diary for the first nine months of his new job indicated that he had 74 meetings with campaigners or lobbyists between taking up his post on 24 February 2010 and 8 December that year. Of those just seven meetings were with labour unions or organisations working in the public interest. The remaining 67 encounters were with corporate coalitions (including the European Chamber of Commerce in India and the EU–Canada Chamber of Commerce) or representatives of individual firms and banks such as HSBC, Unilever, Ikea, Telecom Italia and Alstom.[110]

When I contacted de Gucht and put it to him that there was a huge imbalance between the amount of time he spent listening to the defenders of the super-rich and the time he spent with anyone else, his spokesman replied that European Commission staff regularly see human rights activists that cannot be fitted into de Gucht's schedule. 'Ensuring human rights (social, economic or otherwise) are fully respected is not only central to Commissioner de Gucht's political beliefs and personal values but also a critical element he is obliged to respect to ensure a successful EU trade policy during his term in office,' the spokesman added.[111]

De Gucht is not, in fact, honouring his obligations. Each free trade agreement that the EU signs contains a clause saying that it is conditional on respect for human rights; Brussels officials are in the habit of describing the inclusion of this clause as non-negotiable. If de Gucht was actually taking his duties seriously, he would never have entertained the idea of a trade agreement with Colombia, where the right of workers to collective bargaining is routinely violated. The International Trade Union Confederation estimated in 2010 that a labour activist was murdered on average every three days in Colombia throughout the preceding two decades.[112] Yet while de

Gucht has received numerous pleas from human rights advocates to ditch a free trade agreement that EU officials have concluded with Colombia, he has brusquely dismissed their concerns. Speaking in September 2011, he contended that the Bogota government is 'acting in good faith in its efforts to curtail and eliminate violations of human rights'.[113]

Far from eliminating human rights violations, the administration of Juan Manuel Santos has taken steps to preserve and expand a culture of impunity. For example, it has sponsored a law to place all acts committed by the security services under the military justice system – an 'historic step backwards', according to UN staff based in Colombia.[114]

It is difficult to see how a European politician with a trade portfolio would have a clearer insight into what is actually happening in Colombia than dedicated human rights monitors living there. The conclusion that the EU is more determined to increase corporate dominance than to defend its much-vaunted values appears inescapable.

Conclusion
Taking Europe back

Each time the question of EU democracy is debated, it's a safe bet that someone will bemoan how Britons are more eager to have a say about who should win *Big Brother* than who their MEP should be.[1] The observation is often followed with a remark about how the European Parliament's powers have continuously increased, while participation in its elections has continuously fallen. Just 43 per cent of eligible voters throughout the Union took part in the 2009 poll.[2]

Who is to blame for this apparent apathy? Is it those of us who are more fascinated by 'reality TV' than the reality of how we are ruled? Is it an aloof assembly that doesn't invest enough time and effort in 'public relations'? Are we shunning the ballot box because we do not know enough about what politicians get up to? Or is the problem that we know too much: that politicians are engaged in a charade and power ultimately rests with forces we cannot control?

It would be wrong of me to claim that I can answer these questions definitively. But I find it hard to believe that the much-lamented 'democratic deficit' can be ascribed to simple laziness. It is more likely to reflect a deeper sense of impotence. With all of the dominant political parties committed to neo-liberalism, albeit to slightly varying degrees, the idea that we have genuine choice in either national or European elections is fanciful. Granting greater responsibility to MEPs may be a positive step *per se*. Yet its significance is limited if unaccountable bodies like the European Central Bank and the European Commission are running the show and, with some small exceptions, would not dare to do anything that discomfits corporations or banks. The significance is even more limited if our supposed representatives behave as ventriloquist dummies for big business.

Waiting for the European Union to change fundamentally seems futile. This is not to say that activists should never badger the Brussels bureaucracy. Despite its remote nature, the bureaucracy is not entirely cut-off from the world outside. Faceless mandarins do pay attention to complaints. Politicians often decide what to prioritise based on how many letters or email messages they receive about particular topics. While I respect many campaigners who try to engage with the EU politely, I am convinced that the time for timid interaction is over. What we need instead is a mass movement that confronts power directly. This confrontation does not have to be violent: the awesome uprisings in Tunisia and Egypt in 2011 showed how unarmed resistance can topple tyrants.

Fortunately, we do not have brutal dictators in the EU (at the moment). But we do have institutions that are essentially autocratic, including the ECB and the European Commission. Indeed, both of these institutions are becoming increasingly autocratic. Shortly before he stepped down as the ECB's president in 2011, Jean-Claude Trichet called for an end to all wage indexation agreements and 'when appropriate the privatisation of services today performed by the public sector'.[3] This can't be dismissed as merely a parting shot. As I explained earlier in this book, Trichet and his colleagues have pressurised Italy and some other countries into rapidly reshaping their economies.

Similarly, the European Commission has started to interfere more overtly in the internal affairs of EU states. When national elections were called in Ireland and Portugal in recent years, the Commission sent delegations to both countries.[4] The underlying message was that the main parties had been corralled. Irrespective of what manifestos may say, the incoming governments would have to dispense prescriptions written in Brussels and Frankfurt.

The European Commission and the ECB cannot be allowed to continue behaving in this manner. These institutions must either be placed under democratic control – and yes, that means giving ordinary people a say in who occupies their top posts and what policies they follow – or abolished. The notion that Europe cannot survive without them is bunkum. If anything, democracy will not survive if these institutions continue to bludgeon it.

There are signs that a mass movement against neo-liberalism is emerging. The huge anti-austerity protests witnessed in Greece, Spain, Romania, Italy and Portugal over recent years indicate that there is no shortage of people willing to stand up against the evisceration of our welfare states and to demand that governments cease worshipping financial markets. These protests should, of course, be seen as part of a wider international expression of outrage that has manifested itself everywhere from Chicago to Cairo. And they are best understood if one examines the bigger context of opposition to the slash-and-burn economic orthodoxy that unites the EU with the World Bank, World Trade Organisation and IMF.

The challenge mounted to those policies in Latin America – thanks to a combination of grassroots activism and the emergence of left-wing leaders who refuse to act as Washington's stooges – has exposed the mantra of 'there is no alternative' as a canard. The ability of Bolivia's poor to stymie attempts at water privatisation, for example, is an inspiring testament to how mighty corporations can be beaten.

While this book is focused on Europe, the companies I have examined mostly operate on a global basis. It follows that the best way to challenge their power is to build the largest alliance possible. To achieve this, trade unions should cease to see themselves as allies of big business as some union leaders in Europe appear to do (the EU institutions are officially committed to a concept called 'social partnership', which misleadingly implies a symmetry between the owners of industry and their employees). Instead, the organised left should accept that the bosses are trying to reverse gains that labour activists have made and therefore need to be opposed constantly. Trade unions need to reach out to youth, the unemployed and others who do not have organisations defending them.

A truly inclusive mass movement would embrace small farmers, feminists, gay rights activists, vegans, anti-road campaigners, pacifists, hackers, asylum-seekers and the homeless. Everyone would be welcome, provided they are committed to basic tenets of equality. The mass movement does not need to have a hierarchy or a rigid programme. But it should, in my view, unite around a set of demands. Having key objectives helps not only to ensure clarity, it also increases the likelihood that the movement will be effective.

As a small contribution to building such a movement, I've drafted a few demands that are designed to have a broad appeal. My five-point list is not intended as prescriptive but I hope it will provoke at least some debate.

1. Banks must serve society
One of the most obscene things about the financial crisis which erupted in 2008 is that governments rapidly found around $8.4 trillion for rescuing banks.[5] And then the banks were – with some minor tweaking of rules – allowed to carry on as if nothing had happened.

To date, I have not heard one convincing explanation why banks that were saved with public funds could not be fully taken into public ownership. Although I accept that swift action was necessary, I cannot see why the catastrophe could not have been turned into an opportunity. By starting afresh, debts accumulated through reckless gambling could have been written off; exotic 'products' like derivatives could have been banned, along with speculation on the prices of food and other commodities; and strict limits introduced on salaries paid in the financial sector. Steps like these might have helped destroy the myth that financial whizz-kids deal with 'other people's money'. The money that they play around with is ultimately ours; it is our schools and hospitals that have their budgets reduced when their gambling gets out of hand.

In the early hours of New Year's Day 2012, I saw a slogan that encapsulated the absurdity of the times we are living through better than any comment I have heard or read from economists. The slogan was written at the entrance to the Occupy Dame Street camp, on the plaza of the Central Bank in Dublin. 'Banks don't share their profits, so we won't share their losses,' it read (or words to that effect). The Occupy Dame Street camp was destroyed by police ahead of the St Patrick's Day celebrations in March that year.[6] And, of course, Occupy! camps in many other cities were dealt comparable blows. But this doesn't mean that Occupy! was in vain. On the contrary, it underscored that there are people from all walks of life who realise that banks need to be put at the service of society. They should be closely monitored to ensure they give young families loans that can be repaid without causing stress and hardship; that they assist small businesses; and that they facilitate investment in the real economy. To achieve this, banks have to be made accountable. In my view, this requires nationalising them and subjecting them to democratic oversight.

2. Tax justice
Progressive taxation is a simple matter: the richer you are, the more you pay. In most of the world today, this simple idea has been turned on its head. By availing of sweeteners and loopholes, corporations hand over a risibly low share of their profits to the governments of countries where they operate. The group UK Uncut has drawn much-needed attention to how Starbucks paid £8.6 million to the British exchequer between 1998 and 2012. That was a trifling sum, when you consider that the firm which brought a cornucopia of coffee varieties to the high street enjoyed sales worth more than £3 billion in Britain over that period.[7]

Richard Murphy, an authoritative campaigner on tax issues, has calculated that the EU has a 'shadow' economy in which illicit financial flows of €864 billion take place every year. This amount exceeds health expenditure throughout the Union. Tax avoidance by legal means amounts to a further €150 billion annually, he has estimated.[8]

It is patently unjust that the EU's governments and institutions are dramatically reducing social spending, while displaying a lackadaisical attitude to companies who welsh on paying tax. Politicians will not square up for a fight with big business on this or any other issue unless they are pressurised into doing so. That's where mass movements have to come in. Shaming individual firms has proven to be a worthwhile tactic and to have raised a huge amount of awareness. These efforts need to be stepped up.

3. Real action on climate

It wasn't until Hurricane Sandy hit the US in October 2012 that climate change featured as a topic in the campaign for that country's presidential election the following month. Here in Europe, we might think that we are more environmentally aware. But complacency would be foolish.

The combined weight of oil giants and energy-guzzling firms has succeeded in watering down the EU's policies on reducing greenhouse gas emissions to such an extent that they are only mildly stronger than those of other industrialised countries. Creative accounting has enabled the Union to avoid radical action at home and instead point to dubious 'clean development' schemes undertaken elsewhere as 'evidence' it is taking the attainment of its pollution control targets seriously.

As fossil fuel companies have five times more oil, gas and coal in reserve than scientists think is safe to burn, these companies cannot be allowed to determine the shape of climate change policies pursued by governments.[9] There are few tasks of greater urgency than fighting Shell, BP and other oil giants. North American green activists have been urging universities, churches and public authorities to divest from fossil fuels.[10] These efforts merit support from conscientious Europeans, but we should go further. Civil disobedience on an unprecedented scale might be the only way of preventing these corporations from frying our future.

4. Rethinking economics

Ben Bernanke, the Federal Reserve chairman, made an interesting comment in August 2012: 'The ultimate purpose of economics is, of course, to understand and promote the enhancement of well-being.'[11] His use of the term 'of course' hinted that all economists know this.

But do they? Most commentators I have encountered seem obsessed with 'competitiveness' and 'growth', two concepts that have at most a tenuous relationship with well-being. The fixation with flexibility – shorthand for dismantling labour laws – suggests that they want to reduce well-being, not enhance it.

To build a fairer system, it is vital to reassess what is important. Surely, it is time to rip up the rule that says every nation must maximise gross domestic product (GDP). Dating from the 1930s, this measure only tells us if an economy is busy. As John Perkins wrote in *Confessions of an Economic Hit Man*: 'Thanks to the biased "sciences" of forecasting, econometrics and statistics, if you bomb a city and then rebuild it, the data shows a huge spike in economic growth.'[12]

In his book *Prosperity Without Growth*, Tim Jackson noted that economists are not schooled to take account of resource limitations or damage to the environment. Macro-economics is, therefore, 'ecologically illiterate'.[13] Back in 2007, José Manuel Barroso said much the same thing when he pointed out that a ban on tropical hardwood may allow a forest to be conserved but that this benefit would not be registered in terms of GDP.[14] Sadly, Barroso has continued to wear blinkers with 'GDP' scrawled across them. In 2010, he published a European Commission paper which contained a commitment to 'smart, sustainable and inclusive' growth.[15] The hoped-for growth was to be measured with GDP, despite how Barroso had acknowledged two-and-a-half years earlier that this indicator was crude and flawed.

The economic thinking which prevails in Europe and beyond is based on neither social justice nor environmental sanity. We need a radical debate about how to replace it so that economics does indeed begin to take human well-being into account. The debate about a new form of economics is too important to be left to trained economists. The rest of us have to wade in.

5. Outlaw war

In *Letters to My Grandchildren*, Tony Benn writes: 'Every generation has to fight the same battles for peace, justice and democracy, and there is no final victory nor final defeat. Your generation will have to take up its own battles.'[16]

By arguing that a progressive movement should oppose war in all its forms, I leave myself open to accusations of stating the obvious. However, I feel that the obvious simply hasn't been stated enough.

Europeans voted with their feet against the invasion of Iraq in 2003. Yet when NATO bombed Libya in 2011, few of us took to the streets, even though the situation bore many parallels. Here again was a country with bountiful oil reserves being attacked because its leader had strayed outside the West's orbit.

Lower military expenditure in Europe than in the US should not delude us to the reality of how arms companies are influencing politicians in fiendishly clever ways. Most particularly, arms companies have succeeded in arguing that they should be nurtured as part of a general enterprise promotion or job creation policy. One key reason why they have been able to do this is that public awareness about their activities has been inadequate.

Weapons dealers deliberately shun the limelight. That's why it is so important that they be outed. Every grubby deal that they try to clinch should be challenged.

I've always been mystified as to why Human Rights Watch and Amnesty International – two organisations I mostly agree with – refuse to campaign against war in its entirety. Arms dealers rely on the killing of civilians to make profits. All wars involve denying the right to life, the right to freedom from fear and other elementary rights. *Ad hoc* initiatives aimed at banning landmines and cluster bombs have proven fruitful. So why can't we have a more comprehensive, long-term push against the arms industry?

No doubt, some readers will dismiss my five demands as Utopian. But the consequence of not striving for these objectives could be dystopian.

Unless strenuous efforts are made to thwart their plans, corporations will use whatever excuse they can find to widen inequalities and thrash the planet. Is it too late to stop them? Although much of the damage they have already caused to the natural world may be irreversible, I don't believe it is. For all their wealth and power, corporations and their cronies belong to a tiny club. Their greatest vulnerability is that they are outnumbered by ordinary people like you and me.

The first demonstration I attended as a youth in 1980s Ireland was against apartheid in South Africa. I can still recall one of the speakers at that demonstration declaring the fight against racism to be 'the moral issue of our age'. Racism certainly remains an enormous problem but considerable progress has been made in tackling it.

The fight against corporate power is, I believe, a key moral issue for the twenty-first century. It is inextricably linked to the anti-racist struggle which encouraged me to become politically active in the first place. Both scourges result from the successes made by an elite. The elite assumes an entitlement to lord it over everyone else based on a sense of superiority. But the elite is not invincible. With enough determination, it can be defeated.

Notes

INTRODUCTION

1. Ben Stein, 'In class warfare, guess which class is winning', *New York Times*, 26 November 2006.
2. Michael O'Sullivan & Richard Kersley, 'The Global Wealth Pyramid', *CreditSuisse.com*, 10 October 2012. https://infocus.credit-suisse.com/app/article/index.cfm?fuseaction=OpenArticle&aoid=368968&refresh=true&lang=EN.
3. Marco Riciputi, 'Europe's lobbies: Brussels comes second only to Washington', *cafebabel.com*, 19 August 2008. www.cafebabel.com.
4. Corporate Europe Observatory, *Brussels: The EU quarter*, September 2011, pp. 7–8. www.corporateeurope.org.
5. David Miller & William Dinan, *A Century of Spin: How Public Relations Became the Cutting Edge of Corporate Power*, London: Pluto Press, 2008, p. 32.
6. Elizabeth Martinez & Arnoldo Garcia, 'What is neo-liberalism? A brief definition for activists', Global Exchange website, 26 February 2000. www.globalexchange.org.
7. Interview with the author, March 2012.
8. Andrew Clark, 'Exxon Mobil profits slump to $19bn', *Guardian*, 1 February 2010.
9. Entry for ExxonMobil in European Commission's register of interest representatives, 8 November 2012. www.ec.europa.eu.
10. Entry for Greenpeace EU Unit in European Commission's register of interest representatives, 9 October 2012. www.ec.europa.eu.
11. Entry for Oxfam International EU Advocacy Office in European Commission's register of interest representatives, 13 July 2012. www.ec.europa.eu.
12. Entry for Burson-Marsteller in European Commission's register of interest representatives, 26 October 2012. www.ec.europa.eu.
13. Richard Wilkinson & Kate Pickett, *The Spirit Level: Why Equality is Better for Everyone*, updated ed., London: Penguin, 2010. p. 251.
14. Christophe Deloire & Christophe Dubois, 'L'avenir de l'Europe se discute à huis clos', *Le Monde diplomatique*, September 2012.
15. 'Euro MPs exposed in "cash for laws" scandal', *Sunday Times*, 20 March 2011.
16. Gaspard Sebag, 'AFCO rubber-stamps Buzek draft, gift provision weakened', *Europolitics*, 17 November 2011. www.europolitics.info.
17. Interview with the author, May 2012.
18. Stop the Wall, *European funding for Israeli actors that are complicit with violations of international law must not be allowed to continue*, May 2011, www.stopthewall.org.
19. European Commission, *Green Paper on a Common Strategic Framework for EU Research and Innovation Funding: Analysis of public consultation*, 2011.

20. Letter from Maros Sefcovic, European Commission, to various MEPs, 2011 (no precise date given). Document seen by the author.

21. European Parliament & European Commission, *Annual Report on the operations of the Transparency Register 2012*, p. 6. www.ec.europa.eu.

22. Rachel Tansey, 'EU transparency register still incomplete and inconsistent', *Public Service Europe*, 26 September 2012. www.publicserviceeurope.com.

23. Justin Greenwood, *Interest Representation in the European Union*, 3rd edn, Basingstoke: Palgrave Macmillan, 2011, p. 73.

24. Entry for the European Chemical Industry Council to European Commission's register of interest representatives, 13 September 2012. www.ec.europa.eu.

25. Ester Arauzo, Olivier Hoedeman & Erik Wesselius, *Dodgy data: Time to fix the EU's Transparency Register*, report by the Alliance for Lobbying Transparency and Ethics Regulation, June 2012, p. 11. www.alter-eu.org.

26. 'The headquarters in Brussels', BusinessEurope website, undated. www.businesseurope.eu.

27. Ellwood & Atfield, *Brussels Remuneration Report 2010–11*, pp. 4–10. www.ellwoodandatfield.com.

28. Entry for European Roundtable of Industrialists in European Commission's register of interest representatives, 11 June 2012. www.ec.europa.eu.

29. Rinus van Schendelen, *More Machiavelli in Brussels: The Art of Lobbying the EU*, 3rd edn, Amsterdam: Amsterdam University Press, 2010, p. 38.

30. 'About ERT', European Roundtable of Industrialists website, undated. www.ert.eu.

31. 'Origins', European Roundtable of Industrialists website, undated. www.ert.eu.

32. Profile of Etienne Davignon, *Forbes*, undated. www.forbes.com.

33. 'Inside the secretive Bilderberg Group', BBC News website, 29 September 2005. www.bbc.co.uk.

34. Interview with Etienne Davignon, France 24, 8 November 2011. www.france24.com.

35. European Roundtable of Industrialists, *Creating growth in Europe*, 16 January 2012. www.ert.eu.

36. 'Etienne Davignon, President of CSR Europe', CSR Europe website, undated. www.csreurope.org.

37. A full list of CSR Europe's members can be found on www.csreurope.org.

38. CSR Europe, *A Guide to CSR in Europe: Country insights by CSR Europe's national partner organisations*, October 2010, p. 4. www.csreurope.org.

39. Joel Bakan, *The Corporation: The Pathological Pursuit of Profit and Power*, 2nd edn, London: Constable & Robinson, 2005, p. 37.

40. 'Tackling tax fraud and evasion in the EU – frequently asked questions', European Commission website, 27 June 2012.

41. Michael Devereux, Christina Elschner, Dieter Endres & Christoph Spengel, *Effective Tax Levels Using the Devereux/Griffiths Methodology*, report written for the European Commission, October 2011. www.ec.europa.eu.

42. Oxford University Centre for Business Taxation, *Annual Report 2011–12*, p. 35. www.sbs.ox.ac.uk.

43. 'Vodafone in fresh corporation tax row', *The Huffington Post*, 10 June 2012. www.huffingtonpost.co.uk.

44. 'Deficit sinners' flags should fly at half-mast', *Spiegel Online International*, 9 September 2011. www.spiegel.de.

CHAPTER ONE

1. Paul Taylor & Janet McBride, 'France, Germany give Greece ultimatum on euro', Reuters, 2 November 2011.
2. 'Greece election announced for 6 May', BBC News website, 11 April 2012. www.bbc.co.uk.
3. Paul Mason, 'Italy: "hang on, lads, I've got a great idea"', BBC News website, 12 July 2011. www.bcc.co.uk.
4. Letter from Jean-Claude Trichet & Mario Draghi, European Central Bank, to Silvio Berlusconi, Italian prime minister, 5 August 2011. www.corriere.it.
5. Lisa O'Carroll, 'Silvio Berlusconi to resign after parliament approves austerity measures', *Guardian*, 12 November 2011.
6. Stacy Meichtry & Christopher Emsden, 'Italy premier appoints emergency government', *Wall Street Journal*, 17 November 2011.
7. Rachel Donadio, 'Italy's leader unveils radical austerity measures', *New York Times*, 4 December 2011.
8. 'Doorstep' interview with the author, April 2012.
9. Fiona Ehlers & Hans Hoyng, 'Interview with Italian Prime Minister Mario Monti: "A front line between North and South"', *Der Spiegel*, 8 June 2012. www.spiegel.de.
10. Notes taken by the author during European Business Summit, Brussels, 26 April 2012.
11. David Harvey, *A Brief History of Neoliberalism*, reprinted paperback edn, Oxford: Oxford University Press, 2011, pp. 22–23.
12. 'Mario Monti, honorary president', Bruegel website, undated. www.bruegel.org.
13. Bruegel, *Bruegel Annual Report 2006*, 22 May 2007, p. 2. www.bruegel.org.
14. Mario Monti, 'What Germany and France must rediscover', Bruegel website, 25 October 2005. www.bruegel.org.
15. Ulrich Müller, *Manufacturing a Neoliberal Climate: Recent Reform Initiatives in Germany*; in William Dinan & David Miller (eds), *Thinker, Faker, Spinner, Spy: Corporate PR and the Assault on Democracy*, London: Pluto Press, 2007, p. 168.
16. Charles Hawley, 'Angela Merkel's Achilles heel', *Spiegel Online International*, 13 September 2005. www.spiegel.de.
17. Sasha Lilley, 'On neoliberalism: an interview with David Harvey', *MRZine*, 19 June 2006. www.mrzine.monthlyreview.org.
18. Karl-Heinz Paqué, 'Minimum wages risk the accomplishments on the labour market', Initiative for a New Social Market Economy website, 9 November 2011. www.insm.de.
19. Christian Glossner & David Gregosz (eds), *60 Years of the Social Economy: Formation, Development and Perspectives of a Peacemaking Formula*, report published by Konrad Adenaeur Stiftung, December 2009, pp. 8–15. www.kas.de.
20. Naomi Klein, *The Shock Doctrine: The Rise of Disaster Capitalism*, London: Allen Lane, 2007, pp. 4–5.
21. Simon Carswell, *Anglo Republic: Inside the Bank that Broke Ireland*, Dublin: Penguin Ireland, pp. 3–294.
22. 'Reprieve for government as finance bill scrapes through', *thejournal.ie*, 26 January 2011. www.thejournal.ie.

23. John Walsh, 'Debt restructuring: Burn the bondholders?', *Business and Finance*, March 2011. www.businessandfinance.ie.

24. 'Fine Gael will make senior bondholders take a hit – Bruton', *Business and Finance*, 25 November 2010. www.businessandfinance.ie.

25. European Commission, briefing note on 'state of play regarding the implementation of financial assistance programme for Ireland', 7 December 2010. Document obtained under EU freedom of information law.

26. European Commission, briefing note titled 'Ireland – structure of government spending and revenue', 27 September 2010. Document obtained under EU freedom of information law.

27. European Commission, briefing note for Olli Rehn ahead of meeting with Brian Lenihan, Irish minister for finance, 15 February 2010. Document obtained under EU freedom of information law.

28. European Commission, speaking note for Olli Rehn ahead of 'meeting with Irish opposition leaders and social partners', Dublin, 9 November 2010. Document obtained under EU freedom of information law.

29. Eadaoin O'Sullivan, 'That bondholder list: cut out and keep version', *Politico*, 26 January 2012. www.politico.ie.

30. Olli Rehn, 'Reinforcing EU economic governance: relevance for Ireland', speech to Institute of International and European Affairs, Dublin, 9 November 2010. www.ec.europa.eu.

31. 'Funding', Institute of International and European Affairs website, undated. www.iiea.com.

32. Cormac McQuinn, 'Adviser denies leaving campaign due to tobacco links', *Irish Independent*, 10 October 2011.

33. Institute of International and European Affairs, *Sharing Ideas, Shaping Policy: Annual Report 2010*, pp. 11–12.

34. European Commission's register of interest representatives, searched 1 November 2012. www.ec.europa.eu.

35. Dieter Plehwe, *Paying the Piper: Think Tanks and Lobbying*; in Helen Burley et al. (eds), *Bursting the Brussels Bubble: The Battle to Expose Corporate Lobbying at the Heart of the EU*, Brussels: ALTER-EU, 2010, p. 53.

36. Karen Carstens, 'Germany and the US united in furthering Lisbon process', *European Voice*, 18 September 2003.

37. Christian Fischer & Sebastian Schronberg, *The competitiveness situation of the EU meat processing and beverage manufacturing sectors*, paper written for seminar of European Association of Agricultural Economists, Crete, 29 June–2 July 2006, p. 3. www.eaae.org.

38. Lisbon Council statutes, 31 August 2006. www.lisboncouncil.net.

39. Advisory board, Lisbon Council website, undated. www.lisboncouncil.net.

40. Ann Mettler, *From Why to How: Reflections on the Lisbon Agenda Post-2020*, 'e-brief' by the Lisbon Council, 7 November 2008, pp. 1–4. www.lisboncouncil.net.

41. Lucas Papademos, 'Determinants of growth and the role of structural reforms and macroeconomic policies in Europe', speech to Lisbon Council, Brussels, 9 December 2004. www.ecb.europa.eu.

42. Raghuram Rajan, 'Getting Europe moving again: concrete ideas for reform, prosperity and renewal', speech to Lisbon Council, Brussels, 8 December 2005. www.lisboncouncil.net.

43. Lorenzo Bini Smaghi, 'Growth and inflation in the euro area: the importance of productivity in the services sector', speech to Lisbon Council, Brussels, 28 October 2008. www.lisboncouncil.net.

44. 'Meet the eco-innovators', Lisbon Council website, undated. www.lisboncouncil.net.

45. European Roundtable of Industrialists, *Beating the Crisis: A Charter for Europe's Industrial Future*, December 1993, pp. 8–21. www.ert.eu.

46. Competitiveness Council, Council of the European Union website, undated. www.consilium.europa.eu.

47. European Roundtable of Industrialists, *ERT Highlights*, October 2010, pp. 87–90. www.ert.eu.

48. European Roundtable of Industrialists, *ERT's vision for a competitive Europe in 2025*, February 2010, pp. 4–5. www.ert.eu.

49. Council of the European Union, Conclusions of the European Council, 24–25 March 2012, p. 18. www.consilium.europa.eu.

50. European Roundtable of Industrialists, 'Industry leaders welcome "Pact for the Euro"', press statement, 11 March 2011. www.ert.eu.

51. European Roundtable of Industrialists, *Flexibility and Employability*, October 2011, p. 1. www.ert.eu.

52. *Curriculum vitae* for Valéry Giscard d'Estaing, undated. www.cvce.eu.

53. Historical note on Association for the Monetary Union of Europe held in French national archive, Paris, 2002.

54. 'The road to EMU; phrase three – the Delors report', European Commission website, 30 October 2010. www.ec.europa.eu.

55. Belén Balanyá, Ann Doherty, Olivier Hoedeman, Adam Ma'anit & Erik Wesselius, *Europe Inc.: Regional and Global Restructuring and the Rise of Corporate Power*, London: Pluto Press, 2000, p. 54.

56. Stefan Collignon, *Economic policy coordination in EMU: institutional and political requirements*, paper presented at the Centre for European Studies, Harvard University, May 2001, p. 31. www.stefancollignon.de.

57. Stefan Collignon, *Competitiveness and excessive imbalances: a balance sheet approach*, report for European Parliament's economic and monetary affairs committee, April 2012, p. 34. www.europarl.europa.eu.

58. European Commission, 'EU economic governance "Six Pack" regulation enters into force', memo, 12 December 2011. www.ec.europa.eu.

59. Mary Minihan, Rowan Gallagher & Stephen Collins, 'Creighton warns of No vote threat to tax rate', *Irish Times*, 23 May 2012.

60. 'Silent revolution', Open Europe blog, 18 June 2010. www.openeuropeblog.blogspot.com.

61. Email message from Christophe Houyoux, European Commission, to the author, 8 March 2012.

62. BusinessEurope, *Combining fiscal sustainability and growth: a European action plan*, March 2010, pp. 11–23. www.businesseurope.eu.

63. BusinessEurope, *Improving euro-area governance, securing the long-term success of the euro*, June 2010, pp. 4–6. www.businesseurope.eu.

64. BusinessEurope, *Going for growth: rethinking the role of the state*, Spring 2011, pp. 6–7. www.businesseurope.eu.

65. BusinessEurope, *Structural reforms: time to focus on implementation*, February 2012, pp. 5–31. www.businesseurope.eu.

66. Martin McKee, Marina Karanikolos, Paul Belcher & David Stuckler, 'Austerity: a failed experiment on the people of Europe', *Clinical Medicine*, 2012, Vol. 2, No. 4, p. 348. www.rcplondon.ac.uk.

67. 'Rajoy says Spain had no other option, it was between bad and worse', EITB, 18 July 2012. www.eitb.com.

68. Scott L. Greer, *The Changing World of European Health Lobbies*, in David Coen & Jeremy Richardson (eds), *Lobbying the European Union: Institutions, Actors and Issues*, reprinted edn, Oxford: Oxford University Press, 2011, pp. 192–8.

69. European Public Service Union, 'EU patient mobility legal basis left solely under single market rules in narrow European Parliament vote', press statement, 23 April 2009. www.epsu.org.

70. Gavin Mooney, *The Health of Nations: Towards a New Political Economy*, London: Zed Books, 2012, p. 78.

71. David Cronin, 'Neoliberals replace fascists', *Village*, July 2009.

72. Milton Friedman, *Free to Choose*, PBS, 1980. The series can be viewed on www.youtube.com.

73. Email message from Janina Clark, Insurance Europe, to the author, 18 June 2012.

74. CEA – Insurers of Europe, *Private medical insurance in the European Union*, January 2011, pp. 5–16. www.insuranceeurope.eu.

75. 'Healthcare: repeal and replace Obamacare', Mitt Romney website, undated. www.mittromney.com.

76. Wendell Potter, 'Keep Nataline's spirit of Christmas alive', *The Huffington Post*, 15 December 2011. www.huffingtonpost.com.

77. Email message from Wendell Potter to the author, 29 May 2012.

78. Email message from Anita Kelly, Fleishman-Hillard, to the author, 12 October 2012.

79. *Curriculum vitae* for John Bowis, European Parliament website, undated. www.europarl.europa.eu.

80. 'Former MEP/ex-UK health minister to advise Hanover in Brussels', *Public Affairs News*, 2 July 2010. www.publicaffairsnews.com.

81. Entry for Hanover in European Commission's register of interest representatives, 30 August 2012. www.ec.europa.eu.

82. Entry for Finsbury International Policy and Regulatory Advisers in European Commission's register of interest representatives, 4 October 2012. www.ec.europa.eu.

83. 'Who we are', Health First Europe website, undated. www.healthfirsteurope.org.

84. Interview with the author, March 2012.

85. Max Poinseillé & Paolo Giardano, *Patient mobility – what does it mean for the future?*, in Health First Europe, *2050 A Health Odyssey: Thought-Provoking Ideas for Policymaking*, August 2008, p. 48. www.healthfirsteurope.org.

86. Interview with the author, May 2012.

87. Colin Crouch, *The Strange Non-Death of Neoliberalism*, Cambridge: Polity, 2011, p. 84.

88. 'About', Paul Corrigan's website, undated. www.pauldcorrigan.com.

89. John Carvel, 'The quiet revolutionary', *Guardian*, 15 June 2005.

90. Paul Corrigan, John Higton & Simon Morioka, *Takeover: Tackling failing NHS hospitals*, report published by Reform, September 2012, pp. 36–7. www.reform.co.uk.

91. Reform, *Annual Review 2011*, p. 24. www.reform.co.uk.

92. Email message from Paul Corrigan to the author, 30 March 2012.

93. Stockholm Network, 'A new vision for the future of healthcare', programme for event held in Brussels, 28 March 2012. www.stockholm-network.org.

94. Steven Harkins & Melissa Jones, 'BMJ Lobby Watch – The Stockholm Network', *British Medical Journal*, 13 November 2010.

95. Stockholm Network, *Inspiring Growth: The Stockholm Network Annual Report 2007/08*, p. 16. www.stockholm-network.org.

96. Interview with the author, March 2012.

97. Exchange of email messages between Annika Ahtonen, European Policy Centre, and the author, March 2012.

98. European Patients' Forum, *A Strong Patients' Voice to Drive Better Health in Europe: Annual Report 2011*, pp. 5–41. www.eu-patient.eu.

99. Email message from Nicola Bedlington, European Patients' Forum, to the author, 20 April 2012.

100. 'Supporters', European Foundation for the Care of Newborn Infants website, undated. www.ecfni.org.

101. Baby Milk Action, *Briefing on Nestlé*, 24 April 2012. www.babymilkaction.org.

102. Email message from Silke Mader, European Foundation for the Care of Newborn Infants, to the author, 30 March 2012.

103. Costas Lapavitsas et al., *Crisis in the Eurozone*, London: Verso, 2012, pp. 120–1.

104. Letter from Siim Kallas, European Commission, to Michael O'Leary, Ryanair, 17 January 2012. Document obtained under EU freedom of information law.

105. Notes taken by the author during conference on air transport, Brussels, 12 April 2012.

106. Asbjørn Wahl, *The Rise and Fall of the Welfare State*, London: Pluto Press, 2011, pp. 67–92.

CHAPTER TWO

1. Joe Joyce & Peter Murtagh, *The Boss*, updated edn, Dublin: Poolbeg, 1997, p. 253.

2. 'McCreevy endorses legacy of Thatcher', RTE News, 20 December 2005, www.rte.ie.

3. David Marsh, *The Euro: The Battle for the New Global Currency*, updated edn, New Haven and London: Yale University Press, 2011, p. 331.

4. 'McCreevy defends support for Latvians', *The Local*, 26 October 2005. www.thelocal.se.

5. Pat Leahy, *Showtime: The Inside Story of Fianna Fáil in Power*, Dublin: Penguin Ireland, 2009, p. 126.

6. Catriona Cody, 'FitzGerald says crisis started with McCreevy', *Irish Independent*, 19 January 2009.

7. Jonathan Weil, 'The EU smiled while Spain's banks cooked the books', Bloomberg, 14 June 2012.

8. International Accounting Standards Committee Foundation, transcript of IASCF trustees and monitoring board meeting, 1 April 2009. www.iosco.org.

9. Charlie McCreevy, 'Capital Marketplace', *Wall Street Journal*, 5 March 2007.

10. Sebastian Mallaby, *More Money than God: Hedge Funds and the Making of a New Elite*, paperback edn, London: Bloomsbury, 2011, p. 23.

11. Sam Pizzigati, 'The hedge fund meltdown: another reason wealth needs spreading,' *AlterNet*, 26 October 2008, www.alternet.org.

12. Charlie McCreevy, speech to annual London Funds conference organised by Jersey Finance, 30 March 2010. www.jerseyfinance.je.

13. Photis Lysandrou, 'The primacy of hedge funds in the subprime crisis', *Journal of Post Keynesian Economics*, Winter 2011–12, Vol. 34, No. 2, p. 225.

14. Securities and Exchange Commission, 'SEC charges two former Bear Stearns hedge fund managers with fraud', press statement, 19 June 2008. www.sec.gov.

15. European Commission, *Report of the Alternative Investment Fund Expert Group: Managing, Servicing and Marketing Hedge Funds in Europe*, July 2006, pp. 36–8. www.ec.europa.eu.

16. Email message from Manica Hauptman, European Parliament, to various MEPs, 7 October 2009. Document seen by the author.

17. Corporate Europe Observatory, *Regulating investment funds: the power of filthy lucre*, November 2010, p. 10. www.corporateurope.org.

18. Interview with the author, April 2010.

19. European Commission, 'Directive on Alternative Investment Fund Managers: frequently asked questions', memo, 29 April 2009, www.ec.europa.eu.

20. John Rega, 'Hedge funds' "dangerous opponent" Rasmussen pushes EU crackdown', Bloomberg, 17 June 2009.

21. European Parliament, Committee on Economic and Monetary Affairs, *Report with recommendations to the Commission on hedge funds and private equity*, 19 September 2008. www.europarl.europa.eu.

22. Deutsche Bank, 'Comments on the Alternative Investment Fund Managers Directive', undated. Document seen by the author.

23. Nicholas Shaxson, *Treasure Islands: Tax Havens and the Men who Stole the World*, London: The Bodley Head, 2011, p. 17.

24. Richard Freeman, *London's Cayman Islands: The Empire of the Hedge Funds*, *Executive Intelligence Review*, 9 March 2007. www.larouchepub.com.

25. Jonathan Sibun & Louise Armistead, 'Mayor of London Boris Johnson takes hedge fund fight to Brussels', *Daily Telegraph*, 29 August 2009.

26. 'Hedge Fund Standards', Hedge Funds Standards Board website, undated. www.hfsb.org.

27. Hedge Fund Standards Board, comments on the Alternative Investment Funds Managers Directive, undated. Document seen by the author.

28. Exchange of email messages between Thomas Deinet, Hedge Fund Standards Board, and the author, April 2012.

29. Alternative Investment Management Association, 'Current regulation and the AIFM Directive', comments by Florence Lombard, executive director, undated. Document seen by the author.

30. Exchange of email messages between Sharon Bowles, European Parliament, and the author, April and May 2012.

31. 'Meeting with Sharon Bowles' office', Sharon Bowles' website, undated. www.sharonbowles.org.uk.

32. European Parliament, Committee on Legal Affairs, *Alternative Investment Funds Managers: how to regulate best*, programme for 'mini-hearing', 27 January 2010. www.europarl.europa.eu.
33. 'People', Re-Define website, undated. www.re-define.org.
34. Interview with the author, June 2012.
35. Poul Nyrup Rasmussen, 'Taming the private equity "locusts"', Project Syndicale, 4 April 2008. www.project-syndicale.org.
36. European Parliament, Committee on Legal Affairs, *Draft opinion on the 'proposal for a directive of the European Parliament and of the Council on Alternative Investment Funds Managers'*, Amendments 30–354, 1 March 2010. www.europarl.europa.eu.
37. 'Our lawyers: Klaus-Heiner Lehne – Partner', TaylorWessing website, undated, www.taylorwessing.com.
38. 'Our industries: private wealth', TaylorWessing website, undated, www.taylorwessing.com.
39. Joanne Harris, 'AIFM texts adopted by EU parliament and council', *Hedge Funds Review*, 18 May 2010. www.hedgefundsreview.com.
40. 'Financial power list 2008', *AccountancyAge*, 7 January 2008. www.accountancy.age.com.
41. A list of the International Accounting Standard Board's members can be found on www.ifrs.org.
42. Christian Aid, *'My Word is My Bond': Responsible Finance and Economic Justice*, November 2011, p. 3. www.christianaid.org.uk.
43. Keith Nuthall, 'McCreevy likens published accounts to "bikinis"', *AccountancyAge*, 19 April 2005.
44. 'The Forum's finances', European Parliamentary Financial Services Forum website, undated. www.epfsf.org.
45. Andy Rowell, *Too Close for Comfort? A report on MEPs, corporate links and potential conflicts of interest*, report by SpinWatch, July 2008, p. 19. www.spinwatch.org.
46. Alain Gourio, 'Mortgages in Europe: A practical approach of cross-border business', speech to European Parliamentary Financial Services Forum, 14 September 2005. www.epfsf.org.
47. Ryan Grim, 'Dick Durbin: Banks "frankly own the place"', *Huffington Post*, 30 May 2009. www.huffingtonpost.com.
48. Letter from Guido Ravoet, European Banking Federation, to Peter Mandelson, European Commission, 27 June 2006. Document obtained under EU freedom of information law.
49. European Commission, 'Agreement on *Sparkasse*', press statement, 6 December 2006. www.ec.europa.eu.
50. Matt Taibbi, 'The great American bubble machine', *Rolling Stone*, 9 June 2009.
51. European Commission, 'First meeting of the working party on derivatives', press statement, 5 November 2008. www.ec.europa.eu.
52. 'Warren Buffett on derivatives', edited excerpts from the Berkshire Hathaway annual report for 2002. www.fintools.com.
53. Financial Crisis Inquiry Commission, *The Financial Crisis Inquiry Report*, January 2011, p. xx. www.cybercemetery.unt.edu.
54. Interview with the author, April 2012.

55. Letter from George Handjinicolaou, International Swaps and Derivatives Association, to Charlie McCreevy, European Commission, 11 March 2009. www.ec.europa.eu.

56. European Commission, 'Financial services: Commission outlines ways to strengthen the safety of the derivatives markets', press statement, 3 July 2009. www.ec.europa.eu.

57. European Commission, *Communication from the Commission: Ensuring efficient, safe and sound derivatives markets*, 3 July 2009, p. 2. www.ec.europa.eu.

58. Kenneth Haar, Andy Rowell & Yiorgos Vassalos, *Would you bank on them? Why we shouldn't trust the EU's financial 'wise men'*, report by Corporate Europe Observatory, SpinWatch, Friends of the Earth Europe & Lobby Control, February 2009, pp. 5–8, www.corporateeurope.org.

59. Eurofi, 'The Eurofi High Level Seminar 2012', advertisement for conference held in Copenhagen, 29 March 2012. www.eurofi.net.

60. Patrick Jenkins & Megan Murphy, 'Goldman warns Europe on regulation', *Financial Times*, 30 September 2010.

61. European Commission, 'Commission proposal on OTC derivatives and market instruments – frequently asked questions', memo, 15 September 2010. www.ec.europa.eu.

62. European Commission, 'Commission delegated regulation on short selling and credit default swaps – frequently asked questions', memo, 5 July 2012. www.ec.europa.eu.

63. European Commission (Eurostat), *Report on the EDP Methodological Visits to Greece in 2010*, undated, pp. 16–17. www.epp.eurostat.ec.europa.eu.

64. Tracy Alloway, 'Goldman's Trojan currency swap', *Financial Times* (blog), 9 February 2010. www.ft.com.

65. Marc Roche, 'La franc-maçonnerie européenne de Goldman Sachs', *Le Monde*, 16 November 2011.

66. Stephen Foley, 'What price the new democracy? Goldman Sachs conquers Europe', *Independent*, 18 November 2011.

67. William D. Cohan, *Money and Power: How Goldman Sachs Came to Rule the World*, New York: Anchor Books, 2012, p. 9.

68. Letter from Michael Sherwood, Goldman Sachs, to Michel Barnier, European Commission, 4 March 2011. Document obtained under EU freedom of information law.

69. Letter from Michael Sherwood, Goldman Sachs, to Michel Barnier, European Commission, 11 April 2011. Document obtained under EU freedom of information law.

70. Letter from Michel Barnier, European Commission, to Michael Sherwood, Goldman Sachs, 9 June 2011. Document obtained under EU freedom of information law.

71. European Commission, *Social Business Initiative of the European Commission*, undated. www.ec.europa.eu.

72. 'Goldman Sachs vs. Occupy Wall Street: A Greg Palast investigation', Democracy Now!, 25 October 2011. www.democracynow.org.

73. 'Leading women steer through the crisis', *Wall Street Journal*, 14 September 2009.

74. Javier Blas, 'Commodities trading loses its Goldman queen', *Financial Times*, 12 January 2012.

75. 'Qui est Isabelle Ealet, la nouvelle patronne des métiers Titres chez Goldman Sachs', *eFinancialCareers*, 16 January 2012. www.efinancialcareers.fr.

76. Email message from Siân Smith, Goldman Sachs, to Michel Barnier, European Commission, 15 August 2011. Document obtained under EU freedom of information law.
77. Tim Jones, *The great hunger lottery: How banking speculation causes food crises*, report by World Development Movement, July 2010, p. 10. www.wdm.org.uk.
78. Walden Bello, *The Food Wars*, London: Verso, 2009, pp. 1–4.
79. Interview with the author, June 2012.
80. Institute of International Finance, *Financial investment in commodities markets: Potential impact on commodity prices & volatility*, IIF commodities task force submission to the G20, September 2011, pp. 14–17. www.iif.org.
81. Bruno Waterfield, 'Michel Barnier: the most dangerous man in Europe?', *Daily Telegraph*, 27 February 2010.
82. Louise Charbonneau & Emmanuel Jarry, 'Sarkozy wants summit to overhaul 'crazy' finance', Reuters, 23 September 2008.
83. Pascal Canfin, *Ce que les banques vous disent et pourquoi il ne faut presque jamais les croire*, Paris: Les petits matins, 2012, pp. 21–57.
84. Letter from Andre Villeneuve & Stuart Fraser, International Regulatory Strategy Group, City of London, to Michel Barnier, European Commission, 1 February 2012. Document obtained under EU freedom of information law.
85. European Commission, 'Commissioner Barnier appoints members of a high-level expert group on possible reforms to the structure of the EU banking sector', press statement, 22 February 2012. www.ec.europa.eu.
86. 'The Business on ... Carol Sergeant, chair of financial products steering group', *Independent*, 21 October 2011.
87. Damien Reece, Philip Aldrick & James Kirkup, 'Lloyds Bank strips 13 directors of more than £2 million in bonuses', *Daily Telegraph*, 20 February 2012.
88. European Parliament, 'Summary of hearing of Michel Barnier – internal market and services', 13 January 2012. www.europarl.europa.eu.
89. European Commission, *Proposal for a directive of the European Parliament and of the Council on the market in financial instruments repealing Directive 2004/39/EC of the European Parliament and of the Council*, 20 October 2011. www.ec.europa.eu.
90. Markus Henn, 'Food and commodity speculation: looming EU reforms', newsletter of the Centre for Research on Multinational Corporations, October 2011. www.somo.nl.
91. City of London, International Regulatory Strategy Group, *Key issues in the MiFID review: Summary report produced by the IRSG*, undated. Document obtained under EU freedom of information law.
92. Email message from Tim Binning, European Commission, to various colleagues, 7 July 2010. Document obtained under EU freedom of information law.
93. Email message from Tim Binning, European Commission, to various colleagues, 8 December 2010. Document obtained under EU freedom of information law.

CHAPTER THREE

1. Amnesty International, *Saudi Arabia: Repression in the name of security*, 1 December 2011, p. 6. www.amnesty.org.

2. 'Staff profile: Nick Witney', European Council on Foreign Relations website, undated. www.ecfr.eu.
3. 'Saudi defence deal probe ditched', BBC News website, 15 December 2006.
4. Interview with the author, April 2012.
5. John Pilger, *Distant Voices*, expanded edn, London: Vintage, 1994, p. 309.
6. Paul Waugh, 'East Timor vote: Row over use of Hawks to intimidate voters', *Independent*, 1 September 1999.
7. Campaign Against the Arms Trade, 'Saudi Arabia uses UK-made armoured vehicles in Bahrain crackdown on democracy protesters', press statement, 16 March 2011. www.caat.org.uk.
8. Interview with the author, April 2012.
9. Council of the European Union, Presidency conclusions, Thessaloniki European Council, 19–20 June 2003, p. 19. www.consilium.europa.eu.
10. Letter by Denis Ranque, Thales, Philippe Camus and Rainer Hertrich, EADS, and Mike Turner, BAE Systems, to selected newspapers, 15 June 2004. www.european-security.com.
11. Stockholm International Peace Research Institute, 'The SIPRI top 100 arms-producing and military services companies, 2010'. www.sipri.org.
12. Andrew Feinstein, *The Shadow World: Inside the Global Arms Trade*, London: Hamish Hamilton, 2011, p. 188.
13. Transcript of Prime Minister David Cameron's speech to the United Nations General Assembly in New York, 22 September 2011. www.number10.gov.uk.
14. 'Cameron defends arms sales mission', *Defence Management*, 24 February 2011. www.defencemanagement.com.
15. Letter from Claude-France Arnould, European Defence Agency, to Ian King, BAE Systems, 4 March 2011. Document obtained under EU freedom of information law.
16. Lewis Page, 'Army says farewell to UK's "bugger off" airbag drone', *The Register*, 26 March 2008. www.theregister.co.uk.
17. Principles of international law recognised in the charter of the Nuremberg tribunal and in the judgement of the tribunal, 1950. www.icrc.org.
18. Frost & Sullivan, *Study Analysing the Current Activities in the Field of UAV*, report written at the request of the European Commission, 2007, p. 27. www.ec.europa.eu.
19. Chris Cole, 'Drone Wars: A Briefing Document', *Nexus*, April–May 2012. www.nexusmagazine.com.
20. European Defence Agency, 'EDA awards contract for UAV air traffic insertion', press statement, 8 January 2008. www.eda.europa.eu.
21. Biographical note on David Kershaw, prepared for annual convention of Aerospace and Defence Industries Association of Europe, 6–7 October 2011. www.asd-europe.org.
22. Pieter Taal & Vassilis Tsiamis, 'Roadmap and implementation plan on precision-guided ammunition', European Defence Agency website, 7 March 2012. www.eda.europa.eu.
23. Bureau of Investigative Journalism, 'Covert War on Terror – The Data', undated. www.thebureauinvestigates.com.
24. 'Pieter Taal, EDA's industry and market assistant director, joined BAE Systems press briefing at DSEi 2011', European Defence Agency website, 15 September 2011. www.eda.europa.eu.

25. 'Saab admits R-24 million bribe paid to clinch arms deal', *Mail and Guardian*, 16 June 2011. www.mg.co.za.

26. Gerard O'Dwyer, 'Saab starts internal audit amid bribery claims', *DefenseNews*, 24 May 2011. www.defensenews.com.

27. Saab, *With a Mission to Keep People Safe: Defence and Security*, promotional brochure, June 2012, p. 19.

28. Data from the European Commission's register of 'interest representatives'. www.ec.europa.eu.

29. Email message from Saab to European Defence Agency, 12 March 2010. Document obtained under EU freedom of information law.

30. Email message from Saab to European Defence Agency, 15 December 2011. Document obtained under EU freedom of information law.

31. European Defence Agency, 'European Defence Agency calls for concerted action for future air systems', press statement, 13 September 2012. www.eda. europa.eu.

32. Email message from European Defence Agency to Saab, 2 March 2011. Document obtained under EU freedom of information law.

33. Minutes of meeting on Future Air Systems for Europe project, European Defence Agency headquarters, Brussels, 17 March 2011. Document obtained under EU freedom of information law.

34. Minutes of 'kick-off meeting' for Future Air Systems for Europe project, European Defence Agency headquarters, Brussels, 15 September 2010. Document obtained under EU freedom of information law.

35. Stephen Trimble, 'WikiLeaks shows US played AESA trick on Gripen in Norway', *Flightglobal*, 3 December 2010. www.flightglobal.com.

36. Series of email messages between Saab and European Defence Agency, September and October 2011. Documents obtained under EU freedom of information law.

37. Carlo Munoz, 'Saab takes shot at Navy drone deal', *AOL Defense*, 15 August 2011. www.defense.aol.com.

38. US Department of Defense, *Quadrennial Defense Review Report*, 6 February 2006, pp. ix–6, www.defense.gov.

39. Email message from Saab to European Defence Agency, 26 April 2012. Document obtained under EU freedom of information law.

40. European Commission, *Beyond the crisis, towards new goals: EU budget 2011* (brochure), 2010, www.ec.europa.eu.

41. David Cronin, *Europe's Alliance With Israel: Aiding the Occupation*, London: Pluto Press, 2011, pp. 86–105.

42. Notes taken by the author during conference titled 'Who's driving the agenda at DG Enterprise and Industry?', Brussels, 10 July 2012.

43. European Commission, *Security Industrial Policy: Action plan for an innovative and competitive security industry*, 26 July 2012, pp. 2–8. www. ec.europa.eu.

44. Email message from the European Defence Agency to Saab, 3 September 2010. Document obtained under EU freedom of information law.

45. 'Funding the SESAR JU', Single European Sky Air Traffic Management Research Joint Undertaking website, 16 May 2012. www.sesarju.eu.

46. 'Military needs and roles are unique in SESAR', *SESAR Magazine*, March 2010. www.sesarju.eu.

47. Treaty of Lisbon amending the Treaty of the European Union and the Treaty establishing the European Community, 13 December 2007. www.lisbontreaty2009.ie.

48. Ulrich Karock, *The European Defence Agency: Options for the Future*, briefing paper by the European Parliament's directorate-general for external policies of the Union, September 2011. Document seen by the author.

49. 'Lisbon Treaty: What they said', BBC News website, 30 September 2009. www.bbc.co.uk.

50. European Convention, *Final Report of Working Group VIII – Defence*, 16 December 2002, pp. 15–26. www.european-convention.eu.int.

51. Note by Claude-France Arnould, European Defence Agency, on EDA budget, April 2011. www.eda.europa.eu.

52. Minutes of meeting for Future Air Systems for Europe project, European Defence Agency headquarters, Brussels, 24 January 2012. Document obtained under EU freedom of information law.

53. Minutes of 'kick-off meeting' for Future Air Systems for Europe project, European Defence Agency headquarters, Brussels, 15 September 2010. Document obtained under EU freedom of information law.

54. 'La recherche en matière de sécurité dans le septième PCRD', speech by Antonio Tajani, European Commission, European Security Research Conference, Ostend, 22 September 2010. www.ec.europa.eu.

55. Minutes of first meeting of the FP7 Security Advisory Group, European Commission, Brussels, 9 November 2007. www.ec.europa.eu.

56. Uri Yacobi Keller, *Academic boycott of Israel and the complicity of Israeli academic institutions in occupation of Palestinian territories*, report published by the Alternative Information Centre, October 2009, p. 9. www.alternativenews.org.

57. Minutes of seventh meeting of FP7 Security Advisory Group, European Commission, Brussels, 7 January 2010. www.ec.europa.eu.

58. European Commission, Mandate for the Security Advisory Group for the Seventh Framework Programme, September 2009. www.ec.europa.eu.

59. Robin Tudge, *The No-Nonsense Guide to Global Surveillance*, Oxford: New Internationalist, 2010, p. 127.

60. European Commission, *Security Research Projects under the Seventh Framework Programme for Research: Investing in security research for the benefits of European citizens*, September 2011, pp. 3–190. www.ec.europa.eu.

61. Thales Group, 'Thales: Republic of China (Taiwan) arbitration', press statement, 9 July 2011. www.thalesgroup.com.

62. Jean Guisnel, *Armes de corruption massive: Secrets et combines des marchands de canons*, Paris: La Découverte, 2011, p. 206.

63. Briefing note prepared by Aerospace and Defence Industries Association of Europe for meeting with Günter Verheugen, European Commission, 23 March 2009. Document obtained under EU freedom of information law.

64. Ann Feltham, 'Cameron: BAE's arms-seller-in-chief', *CAAT News*, January–March 2013. www.caat.org.uk.

65. Letter from François Gayet, Aerospace and Defence Industries Association of Europe, to Heinz Zourek, European Commission, 19 January 2010. Document obtained under EU freedom of information law.

66. European Commission, *High-Level Expert Group on Key Enabling Technologies: Final Report*, June 2011, pp. 14–41. www.ec.europa.eu.

67. Rolls-Royce, *Annual Report 2011*, 8 February 2012, pp. 21–7. www.rolls-royce.com.
68. Larine Barr, 'Air Force plans to develop revolutionary engine', article published by Air Force Research Laboratory Public Affairs, 11 April 2007. www.wpafb.af.mil.
69. Defence Stakeholders Group, agenda for meeting, Brussels, 11 November 2009. Document obtained under EU freedom of information law.
70. Letter from Paul Weissenberg, European Commission, to various recipients, 8 October 2009. Document obtained under EU freedom of information law.
71. Bill Giles, 'Unwrapping the defence package', *ASD Focus*, Winter 2008–09. www.asd-europe.org.
72. Toby Vogel, 'EU seeks greater defence co-operation', *European Voice*, 22 March 2012. www.europeanvoice.com.
73. Letter from Paul Weissenberg, European Commission, to François Gayet, Aerospace and Defence Industries Association of Europe, 7 June 2010. Document obtained under EU freedom of information law.
74. Adrian Croft, 'BAE-EADS merger would advance Europe's military goals', Reuters, 16 September 2012.
75. Maria Leonor Pires, *Europe and United States Defence Expenditure in 2010*, report by European Defence Agency, 12 January 2012, pp. 2–10. www.eda.europa.eu.
76. Nick Witney, 'European defence: interests, strategies and the means to act', in Karl von Wogau (ed.), *The Path to European Defence: New Roads, New Horizons*, London: John Harper Publishing, 2009, p. 68.
77. Susan George, 'Europe deserves much better than the Lisbon treaty', Transnational Institute, 16 May 2008. www.tni.org.
78. Letter from Aerospace Industries Association of America to Barack Obama, US president, 3 December 2009. www.aia-aerospace.org.
79. Aerospace Industries Association of America, *Establishing more appropriate treatment of UAS technology under the Missile Technology Control Regime*, undated briefing paper. Document obtained under EU freedom of information law.
80. Email message from Gert Runde, Aerospace and Defence Industries Association of Europe, to Luigi Vitiello & James Copping, European Commission, 6 April 2010. Document obtained under EU freedom of information law.
81. Robert Gates, 'Reflections on the status and future of the trans-Atlantic alliance', brochure published by Security and Defence Agenda, 10 June 2011, pp. 4–5. www.securitydefenceagenda.org.
82. 'What we do', Security and Defence Agenda website, undated. www.securitydefenceagenda.org.
83. 'Who we are', Security and Defence Agenda website, undated. www.securitydefenceagenda.org.
84. Advisory board, Security and Defence Agenda website, undated. www.securitydefenceagenda.org.
85. Stanley Pignall et al., 'Eurostars', *Financial Times*, 3 June 2009.
86. Letter from Giles Merritt, Philip Morris Institute for Public Policy Research, to Alexander Lioutyi, British American Tobacco, 18 February 1998. www.legacy.library.ucsf.edu.

87. Programme for 'Europe's development policy comes of age', debate organised by European Development Forum, Brussels, 17 May 2011. www.friendsofeurope.org.

88. Giles Merritt, Robin Niblett, Narcis Serra, 'Debating Defence', Project Syndicale, 1 February 2010. www.project-syndicale.org.

89. Email message from Giles Merritt, Security and Defence Agenda, to the author, 16 May 2012.

90. Security and Defence Agenda, *After Chicago: Re-evaluating NATO's priorities*, brochure circulated at conference, Brussels, 25 May 2012.

91. Asa Winstanley & Frank Barat (eds), *Corporate Complicity in Israel's Occupation: Evidence from the London session of the Russell Tribunal on Palestine*, London: Pluto Press, 2011, pp. 134–63.

92. Notes taken by the author during Security and Defence Agenda conference titled 'After Chicago: Re-evaluating NATO's priorities', Brussels, 25 May 2012.

93. William D. Hartung, *Prophets of War: Lockheed Martin and the Making of the Military-Industrial Complex* (paperback edn), New York: Nation Books, 2012, pp. 193–213.

94. Letter from Edgar Breugels, Frontex, to Lockheed Martin UK Information Systems, 23 September 2011. Document obtained under EU freedom of information law.

95. Invoice sent by Connie Miller, Lockheed Martin UK Information Services, to Frontex, 2 December 2011. Document obtained under EU freedom of information law.

96. Human Rights Watch, *The EU's Dirty Hands: Frontex involvement in ill-treatment of migrant detainees in Greece, September 2011*, pp. 1–3. www.hrw.org.

97. United Nations, Convention relating to the status of refugees, 28 July 1951. www.unhcr.org.

98. Frontex, 'Management board designates fundamental rights officer', press statement, 27 September 2012. www.frontex.europa.eu.

99. 'Executive bios', Frontex website, undated. www.frontex.europa.eu.

100. Daniel Keenan, *Frontex: EU Agency for External Border Cooperation*, report by United States of America Department of Commerce, November 2011, pp. 1–3. www.export.gov.

101. Letter from Michael von Gizycki, Aerospace and Defence Industries Association of Europe, to Erik Berglund, Frontex, 14 June 2011. Document obtained under EU freedom of information law.

102. Letter from Paolo Pozzessere, Finmeccanica, to Ilkka Laitenen, Frontex, 12 May 2012. Document obtained under EU freedom of information law.

103. Finmeccanica, 'Selex Sistemi Integrati signed an agreement with Libya, worth €300 million, for border security and control', press statement, 10 July 2009.

104. Polly Pallister-Wilkins, 'Criticism of EU-Libyan migration policy is too little, too late', *openDemocracy*, 29 August 2011. www.opendemocracy.net.

105. Email message from Cecilia Malmström, European Commission, to the author, 30 May 2012.

106. European Defence Agency, 'Specifications attached to invitation to tender, 11.CAP.OP.133', document concerning call for tender launched on 26 August 2011. www.eda.europa.eu.

107. Ben Hayes & Mathias Vermuelen, *Borderline: The EU's new border surveillance initiatives*, report by Heinrich Böll Foundation, June 2012. www.boell.de.

CHAPTER FOUR

1. Jeanne Mager Stellman et al., 'The extent and patterns of usage of Agent Orange and other herbicides in Vietnam', *Nature*, 17 April 2003. www.nature.com.

2. Frank Susa, 'Improving healthcare and education for children with disabilities in Vietnam', UNICEF USA website, 10 October 2008. www.unicefusa.org.

3. 'Spina Bifida and Agent Orange', United States Department of Veteran Affairs website, 14 February 2012. www.publichealth.va.gov.

4. Email message from Thi Anh Nguyen, Monsanto, to Len Aldis, Britain–Vietnam Friendship Society, 20 August 2009. www.lenaldis.co.uk.

5. Dominic Rushe, 'Monsanto settles "Agent Orange" case with US victims', *Guardian*, 24 February 2012.

6. Wayne Dwernychuk and Charles Bailey, 'The difference between Agent Orange and dioxin', Agent Orange Record website, undated. www.agentorangerecord.com.

7. 'To Parma, the spoils', *The Economist*, 5 February 2004.

8. 'About EFSA', European Food Safety Authority website, undated. www.efsa.europa.eu.

9. Letter from Dirk Detken, European Food Safety Authority, to the author, 13 July 2012.

10. 'FAQ on genetically modified organisms', European Food Safety Authority website, undated. www.efsa.europa.eu.

11. Note by Per Bergman, European Food Safety Authority, 8 December 2009. Document obtained under EU freedom of information law.

12. Monsanto, *MON 87701 x MON 89788 Insect Protected and Herbicide Tolerant Soybean: Key facts*, July 2012, p. 2–3. www.europabio.org.

13. Letter from Per Bergman, European Food Safety Authority, to Monsanto Europe, 5 October 2009. Document obtained under EU freedom of information law.

14. Letter from Monsanto Europe to Per Bergman, European Food Safety Authority, 13 November 2009. Document obtained under EU freedom of information law.

15. Letter from Per Bergman, European Food Safety Authority, to Monsanto Europe, 8 December 2009. Document obtained under EU freedom of information law.

16. Letter from Per Bergman, European Food Safety Authority, to Monsanto Europe, 26 August 2009. Document obtained under EU freedom of information law.

17. Email message from Sonia Hernandez Valero, European Food Safety Agency, to Monsanto Europe, 26 January 2012. Document obtained under EU freedom of information law.

18. European Food Safety Authority, *Scientific opinion on application (EFSA-GMO-NL-2009-73) for the placing on the market of insect-resistant and herbicide-tolerant genetically modified soybean MON 87701 x MON 89788*

for food and feed uses, import and processing under Regulation (EC) No 1829/2003 from Monsanto, 15 February 2012. www.efsa.europa.eu.

19. European Food Safety Authority, *Scientific opinion on application (EFSA-GMO-NL-2008–52) for the placing on the market of herbicide tolerant genetically modified soybean A5547–127 for food and feed uses, import and processing under Regulation (EC) No 1829/2003 from Bayer CropScience*, 10 May 2011. www.efsa.europa.eu.

20. European Food Safety Authority, declaration of interests for Jean-Michel Wal, 27 July 2012. www.efsa.europa.eu.

21. European Food Safety Authority, declaration of interests for Harry Kuiper, 22 February 2012. www.efsa.europa.eu.

22. European Food Safety Authority, declaration of interests for Gijs Kleter, 10 April 2012. www.efsa.europa.eu.

23. 'ILSI Q&A', International Life Sciences Institute website, undated. www.ilsi. org.

24. International Life Sciences Institute, *ILSI Annual Report 2011*, p. 15. www. ilsi.org.

25. Programme for Twelfth International Symposium on Biosafety of Genetically Modified Organisms, St Louis, 16–20 September 2012. www.isbgmo.com.

26. Wellesley College Office for Public Affairs, '*Starved for Science*, new book by Robert Paarlberg, confronts reasons behind African poverty', press statement, 1 February 2008. www.wellesley.edu.

27. Frances Moore Lappe, 'Cheerleading for Monsanto? The shocking lack of difference between Oxford University Press and Fox News', *AlterNet*, 9 April 2012. www.alternet.org.

28. European Food Safety Authority, declaration of interests for Christoph Tebbe, 20 September 2012. www.efsa.europa.eu.

29. European Food Safety Authority, declaration of interests for Jeremy Sweet, 27 September 2012. www.efsa.europa.eu.

30. European Food Safety Authority, declaration of interests for Huw Jones, 19 September 2012. www.efsa.europa.eu.

31. Dave Keating, 'EFSA chairwoman resigns over conflict of interest', *European Voice*, 10 May 2012. www.europeanvoice.com.

32. Letter from Catherine Geslain-Lanéelle, European Food Safety Authority, to various members of the European Parliament, 8 May 2012. www.efsa.europa.eu.

33. European Court of Auditors, *Management of Conflict of Interests in Selected EU Agencies: Special Report No 15/2012*, October 2012, p. 26. www.eca. europa.eu.

34. Email message from James Ramsay, European Food Safety Authority, to the author, 31 October 2012.

35. Email message from Antonio Dumont Fernandez, European Food Safety Authority, to Monsanto Europe, 13 January 2012. Document obtained under EU freedom of information law.

36. European Food Safety Authority, minutes of 'scientific hearing with applicants', Parma, 21 March 2007. Document obtained under EU freedom of information law.

37. Gilles-Eric Séralini et al., 'Long term toxicity of a Roundup herbicide and a Roundup-tolerant genetically modified maize', *Food and Chemical Toxicology*, November 2012. www.sciencedirect.com.

38. Letter from Ladislav Miko, European Commission, to Catherine Geslain-Lanéelle, European Food Safety Authority, 26 September 2012. www.efsa.europa.eu.
39. European Food Safety Authority, 'EFSA publishes initial review on GM maize and herbicide study', press statement, 4 October 2012. www.efsa.europa.eu.
40. Hervé Kempf, *La guerre secrète des OGM*, (updated edn), Paris: Seuil, p. 17.
41. Email message from Monsanto Europe to Davide Arcella, European Food Safety Authority, 25 April 2012. Document obtained under EU freedom of information law.
42. A full list of members can be found on www.europabio.org.
43. Sarah Boseley, 'Anti-HIV drug made by GM plants begins trial in humans', *Guardian*, 19 July 2011.
44. Email message from European Association for Bioindustries to members of the European Commission, 20 July 2011. Document obtained under EU freedom of information law.
45. Letter from European Association for Bioindustries to John Dalli, European Commission, 14 July 2011. Document obtained under EU freedom of information law.
46. European Food Safety Authority, internal notes on workshop with applicants for authorisations of genetically modified foods, 13 December 2007. Document obtained under EU freedom of information law.
47. European Food Safety Authority, internal notes on 'technical meeting' with applicants for authorisations of genetically modified foods, 3 March 2009. Document obtained under EU freedom of information law.
48. European Food Safety Authority, report on 'stakeholder consultation workshop', Berlin, 16 June 2009. Document obtained under EU freedom of information law.
49. European Association for Bioindustries, note on 'stakeholder consultation workshop' organised by European Food Safety Authority, Berlin, 16 June 2009. Document obtained under EU freedom of information law.
50. 'Interview with Suzy Renckens, scientific co-ordinator of EFSA's GMO panel', *EFSA News*, May–June 2004. www.efsa.europa.eu.
51. Corporate Europe Observatory & Testbiotech, 'European Food Safety Authority admits failure', press statement, 18 April 2012. www.corporateeurope.org.
52. European Food Safety Authority, attendance list for 'stakeholder consultation' workshop, Berlin, 16 June 2009. Document obtained under EU freedom of information law.
53. Letter from Catherine Geslain-Lanéelle, European Food Safety Authority, to Nikiforos Diamandouros, European Ombudsman, 22 March 2012. www.testbiotech.de.
54. Entry by European Association for Bioindustries to the European Commission's register of interest representatives, 16 February 2012. www.ec.europa.eu.
55. Comment by Greenpeace EU unit on Twitter, 1 October 2012. www.twitter.com/GreenpeaceEU.
56. Letter from European Association for Bioindustries to Dorothée André, European Commission, 14 April 2011. Document obtained under EU freedom of information law.
57. Letter from European Association for Bioindustries to Paolo Testöri Coggi, European Commission, 14 January 2011. Document obtained under EU freedom of information law.

58. Letter from European Association for Bioindustries to Per Bergman, European Food Safety Authority, 20 July 2011. Document obtained under EU freedom of information law.

59. Marie-Monique Robin, *Le monde selon Monsanto: De la dioxine aux OGM, une multinationale qui vous veut du bien*, 2nd edn, Paris: La Découverte, 2009, p. 257.

60. Letter from Paolo Testöri Coggi, European Commission, to European Association for Bioindustries, 9 March 2011. Document obtained under EU freedom of information law.

61. David Cronin, 'Advantage GM in Europe', Inter Press Service, 18 May 2010. www.ipsnews.net.

62. European Commission, 'Commission announces upcoming proposal on choice for member states to cultivate or not GMOs, and approves five decisions on GMOs', press statement, 2 March 2010. www.ec.europa.eu.

63. Answer given by John Dalli, European Commission, to question from Michail Tremopoulos, European Parliament, 14 February 2012. www.europarl.europa.eu.

64. World Health Organisation, 'Twenty questions on genetically modified foods', undated. www.who.org.

65. LinkedIn profile for Mella Frewen, FoodDrinkEurope, undated. www.linkedin.com.

66. Letter from CIAA and other food and feed associations to various EU officials, 18 February 2010. Document obtained under EU freedom of information law.

67. Letter from CIAA and other food and feed associations to Androulla Vassiliou, European Commission, 24 June 2009. Document obtained under EU freedom of information law.

68. FoodDrinkEurope, *Annual Report 2011*, June 2012, p. 26. www.fooddrinkeurope.eu.

69. Internal note by Jan Peter Schoeffer Petricek, European Commission, 7 October 2010. Document obtained under EU freedom of information law.

70. Letter from Mella Frewen, CIAA, to Mario Milouchev, European Commission, 25 May 2010. Document obtained under EU freedom of information law.

71. Email message from Jan Peter Schoeffer Petricek, European Commission, to various EU officials, 12 November 2010. Document obtained under EU freedom of information law.

72. Email message from Jan Peter Schoeffer Petricek, European Commission, to Gerry Kiely, European Commission, 12 November 2010. Document obtained under EU freedom of information law.

73. Programme for CIAA congress, 18–19 November 2010. www.ciaacongress2010.eu.

74. Speech by John Dalli, European Commission, to CIAA congress, Brussels, 18 November 2010. www.ec.europa.eu.

75. European Commission, *High Level Group on the Competitiveness of the European Agro-Food Industry: Report on the Competitiveness of the European Agro-Food Industry*, 17 March 2009, pp. 28–77. www.ec.europa.eu.

76. Agenda for constitutive meeting of 'European food sustainable consumption and production roundtable', Brussels, 7 July 2009. Document obtained under EU freedom of information law.

77. Email message from APCO Europe to Martin Scheele, European Commission, 11 May 2009. Document obtained under EU freedom of information law.
78. List of members for European Platform on Diet, Physical Activity and Health, 4 September 2012. www.ec.europa.eu.
79. The full text of the pledge can be read on www.eu-pledge.eu.
80. IBF International Consulting, *Monitoring the European Platform for Action on Diet, Physical Activity and Health Activities: Annual Report 2012*, 21 September 2012, p. 36, www.ec.europa.eu.
81. Letter from Unilever to European Food Safety Authority, 22 February 2008. Document obtained under EU freedom of information law.
82. European Consumers' Organisation (BEUC), BEUC's Eight Priorities for the Hungarian Presidency, 6 January 2011, p. 28. www.beuc.org.
83. Dave Keating, 'Council rejects EFSA nominee', *European Voice*, 8 June 2012.
84. European Commission, *Proposal for a regulation of the European Parliament and of the Council on the provision of food information to consumers*, 30 January 2008. www.ec.europa.eu.
85. CIAA, *Position on food information*, 29 January 2010. www.fooddrinkeurope. eu.
86. Corporate Europe Observatory, *A red light for consumer information: The food industry 1 billion euro campaign to block health warnings on food*, June 2010, p. 6. www.corporateeurope.org.
87. Jennifer Rankin, 'Fear of information overload ahead of food labelling vote', *European Voice*, 11 March 2010.
88. CIAA, '"Statement of clarification" on CIAA activity in relation to the proposed EU food information to consumers regulation', press statement, 11 July 2010. www.fooddrinkeurope.eu.
89. Rebecca Smithers, 'MEPs reject "traffic light" food labelling system', *Guardian*, 16 June 2010.
90. European Alcohol Policy Alliance (Eurocare), *Eurocare position on the Commission proposal on the provision of food information to consumers*, September 2008, p. 3. www.eurocare.org.
91. Interview with the author, April 2012.
92. 'Lobbying zum "Vorschlag für eine Verordnung des Europaïschen Parlaments und des Rates betreffend die Information der Verbraucher über Lebensmittel"', note on Renate Sommer's website, 4 June 2010, www.renate-sommer.de.
93. World Health Organisation, *Alcohol in the European Union: Consumption, harm and policy approaches*, April 2010, p. 10. www.euro.who.int.
94. European Commission, *An EU strategy to support member states in reducing alcohol related harm*, 24 October 2006, p. 9. www.ec.europa.eu.
95. European Commission, *Charter establishing the European Alcohol and Health Forum*, 7 June 2007, pp. 10–11. www.ec.europa.eu.
96. 'About Us', European Forum for Responsible Drinking website, undated. www.efrd.org.
97. Email message from Alan Butler, Diageo, to the author, 11 April 2012.
98. European Commission, report on European Forum on Alcohol and Health plenary meeting, 26 April 2012. www.ec.europa.eu.
99. Brewers of Europe, 'Europe's brewers pledge increased action to combat alcohol misuse', press statement, 29 February 2012.
100. Stephen Rodgers, 'Drinks body tried to alter damning report', *The Irish Examiner*, 13 April 2012.

101. European Parliament Beer Club, 'Membership of the EP beer club', undated. www.epbeerclub.eu.
102. European Parliament Beer Club, 'Leading policy-makers mark Danish presidency with quality Danish beer', press statement, 15 May 2012. www.epbeerclub.eu.
103. Wine in Moderation, 'What is the Wine in Moderation programme and how will it work?', undated. www.wineinmoderation.eu.
104. Action Group on Erosion, Technology and Concentration, *Global seed industry concentration 2005*, September-October 2005, pp. 1–4. www.etcgroup.org.
105. Raj Patel, *Stuffed and Starved: From Farm to Fork, the Hidden Battle for the World Food System*, paperback edn, London: Portobello, 2008, p. 104.
106. Hope Shand, 'The Big Six: a profile of corporate power in seeds, agrochemicals and biotech', *The Heritage Farm Companion*, Summer 2012. www.seedsavers.org.
107. Action Group on Erosion, Technology and Concentration, *Who will control the green economy?*, November 2011, p. 22. www.etcgroup.org.
108. Pesticide Action Network Europe, *Meet (Chemical) Agriculture: The world of backdoors, derogations, sneaky pathways and loopholes*, April 2012, p. 8. www.pan-europe.info.
109. Pesticide Action Network Europe, *Disrupting Food: Endochrine disrupting chemicals in European Union food*, June 2012, pp. 5–6. www.pan-europe.info.
110. Marie-Monique Robin, *Notre Poison Quotidien: La responsabilité de l'industrie chimique dans l'épidemie des maladies chroniques*, Paris: La Découverte, 2011, pp. 104–5.
111. Claire Robinson, *Europe's pesticide and food safety regulators: Who do they work for?*, report by Earth Open Source, April 2011, p. 5. www.earthopensource.org.
112. European Food Safety Authority, declaration of interests for Theodorus Brock, 25 April 2012. www.efsa.europa.eu.
113. European Food Safety Authority, declaration of interests for Michael Klein, 7 October 2012. www.efsa.europa.eu.
114. European Food Safety Authority, declaration of interests for Daniel Pickford, 16 October 2012. www.efsa.europa.eu.
115. European Food Safety Authority, declaration of interests for Robert Smith, 11 April 2012. www.efsa.europa.eu.
116. 'About RRAG', Rodenticide Resistance Action Group website, undated. www.bpca.org.uk.
117. European Food Safety Authority, declaration of interests for Ettore Capri, 1 May 2012. www.efsa.europa.eu.
118. OPERA Research Centre, *Bee health in Europe: Facts & figures*, August 2011, pp. 1–42. www.operaresearch.eu.
119. United States Environmental Protection Agency, Memorandum on clothianidin, 2 November 2010.
120. Tom Philpott, 'Three new studies link bee decline to Bayer pesticide', *Mother Jones*, 29 March 2012. www.motherjones.com.
121. 'Bee health', European Food Safety Authority website, 20 September 2012. www.efsa.europa.eu.
122. 'What OPERA is', OPERA website, undated. www.operaresearch.eu.

123. Interview with the author, October 2012.
124. 'Frequently asked questions', European Food Information Council website, undated. www.eufic.org.
125. European Food Information Council, *Annual Report 2011*, pp. 28–32. www.eufic.org.
126. *Toxic Sludge is Good For You: The Public Relations Industry Unspun*, Northampton: Media Education Foundation, 2002. The film can be viewed on www.mediaed.org.

CHAPTER FIVE

1. European Commission, 'Press statement on behalf of the European Commission', 16 October 2012.
2. Alexandros Koronakis & Cillian Donnelly, 'John Dalli interview on OLAF, resignation, tobacco directive', *New Europe*, 17 October 2012. www.neurope.eu.
3. Sarah Boseley, 'Anti-smoking campaigners accuse tobacco lobby after office break-in', *Guardian*, 18 October 2012.
4. World Health Organisation, *Tobacco fact sheet*, May 2012. www.who.int.
5. US Department of Health and Human Services, *Ending the Tobacco Epidemic: A Tobacco Control Strategic Action Plan for the US Department of Health and Human Services*, 10 November 2010, p. 9. www.hhs.gov.
6. Matthew Boyle, 'BAT first-half profit growth checked by sterling's strength', Bloomberg, 25 July 2012.
7. World Health Organisation, WHO Framework Convention on Tobacco Control, updated reprint, 2005, p. 7. www.who.int.
8. Email message from Frédéric Vincent, European Commission, to the author, 14 November 2012.
9. World Health Organisation, *Guidelines for implementation of Article 5.3 of the WHO framework convention on tobacco control on the protection of public health policies with respect to tobacco control from commercial and other vested interests of the tobacco industry*, undated, pp. 3–9, www.who.int.
10. European Commission, minutes of meeting between European Commission and cigarette manufacturers, 2 December 2011. www.ec.europa.eu.
11. European Commission, minutes of meeting between John Dalli and 'representatives of the economic stakeholders active in tobacco products', 7 March 2012. www.ec.europa.eu.
12. Email message from Robert Madelin, European Commission, to the author, 13 November 2012.
13. Letter from Robert Madelin, European Commission, to Ben Stevens, British American Tobacco, 6 July 2005. The letter has been made public by Corporate Europe Observatory. www.corporateeurope.org.
14. Corporate Europe Observatory, *Obscured by the smoke: British American Tobacco's deathly lobbying agenda in the EU*, June 2009, p. 3. www.corporateeurope.org.
15. Letter from Jacek Siwek, Confederation of European Community Cigarette Manufacturers, to Robert Madelin, European Commission, 4 February 2010. Document obtained under EU freedom of information law.

16. Letter from Jack Bowles, British American Tobacco, to Robert Madelin, European Commission, 7 January 2010. Document obtained under EU freedom of information law.

17. Letter from Jack Bowles, British American Tobacco, to Antti Maunu, European Commission, 6 May 2010.

18. Acona, *British American Tobacco Stakeholder Dialogue: Harm Reduction, Smoking in Public Places, Anti-Illicit Trade*, 3 March 2010, pp. 2–11. www.batresponsibility.eu.

19. 'Our moderator', British American Tobacco website for 'EU social reporting', undated. www.batresponsibility.eu.

20. Pavel Telicka, introduction to *The Globe*, magazine of the Global Alcohol Public Health Alliance, 2004. www.ias.org.uk.

21. Biographical note on Pavel Telicka circulated at conference on EU–Turkey relations, Istanbul, 14–15 October 2005. www.britishcouncil.org.tr.

22. European Commission, high level group of independent stakeholders on administrative burdens, list of members, undated. www.ec.europa.eu.

23. Jeremy Fleming, 'Tobacco lobby focus switches from Dalli to Stoiber', *Euractiv*, 26 October 2012. www.euractiv.com.

24. Interview with the author, November 2012.

25. European Commission, minutes of meeting of the high level group of independent stakeholders on administrative burdens, 3 May 2012. www.ec.europa.eu.

26. European Policy Centre, *Annual Report 2011*, pp. 19–26. www.epc.eu.

27. 'Benefits and fees', European Policy Centre website, undated. www.epc.eu.

28. Simon Taylor, 'Obituary Stanley Crossick, 1935–2010: Passionate European integrationist', *European Voice*, 25 November 2010.

29. Stanley Crossick & Bruce Ballantine, *The Need for Cost-Benefit Analysis*, paper by European Policy Centre, September 1996, p. 2. www.legacy.library.ucsf.edu.

30. Fax message from Stanley Crossick, European Policy Centre, to Stuart Chalfen, British American Tobacco, 4 March 1998. www.legacy.library.ucsf.edu.

31. Action on Smoking and Health, *The smoke-filled room: How big tobacco influences health policy in the UK*, 2010, pp. 32–33. www.ash.org.uk.

32. Reply by Androulla Vassiliou, European Commission, to question by Godfrey Bloom, European Parliament, 1 October 2008. www.europarl.europa.eu.

33. Confederation of European Community Cigarette Manufacturers, *CECCM response to RAND Europe's interim report 'assessing the impacts of revising the tobacco products directive'*, 18 January 2010. Document obtained under EU freedom of information law.

34. Jan Tiessen et al., *Assessing the impacts of revising the Tobacco Products Directive*, report by RAND Europe, 2011, pp. xxii–xxxii. www.rand.org.

35. Letter from Jonathan Klick, University of Pennsylvania, to Paola Testori Coggi, European Commission, 17 December 2010. Document obtained under EU freedom of information law.

36. British American Tobacco, *Pack Regulation Briefing Note*, undated. Document obtained under EU freedom of information law.

37. 'Cigarette smoking', American Cancer Society website, 8 November 2012. www.cancer.org.

38. Letter from Jack Bowles, Confederation of European Community Cigarette Manufacturers, to Robert Madelin, European Commission, 24 February 2010. Document obtained under EU freedom of information law.

39. Imperial Tobacco, *Response to RAND questionnaire*, 5 February 2010. Document obtained under EU freedom of information law.

40. Letter from Solidarity representatives in Philip Morris plant, Krakow, to European Commission, 28 October 2010. Document obtained under EU freedom of information law.

41. Confédération Européenne des Détaillants en Tabac, *Tobacco Retailers Working Group Position on Possible TPD Revision: Position Paper*, undated. Document obtained under EU freedom of information law.

42. Robert Proctor, *Golden Holocaust: Origins of the Cigarette Catastrophe and the Case for Abolition*, Berkeley: University of California Press, 2011, p. 76.

43. Letter from Kristof Doms, Philip Morris International, to John Dalli, European Commission, 14 March 2012. Document obtained under EU freedom of information law.

44. 'Sweden renews vow to fight EU snus ban', *The Local*, 12 September 2012. www.thelocal.se.

45. Barnaby Feder, 'Philip Morris tries smokeless tobacco product', *New York Times*, 9 June 2007.

46. Sarah Wamala, 'Free trade of Swedish moist snuff in the EU', statement published by Swedish National Institute of Public Health. www.fhi.se.

47. A full list of European Smokeless Tobacco Council members can be found on www.estoc.org.

48. Letter from Patrick Hildingsson and Inge Delfosse, European Smokeless Tobacco Council, to Dominik Schnichels, European Commission, 25 November 2010.

49. World Health Organisation, 'Regulation urgently needed to control growing list of deadly tobacco products', press statement, 30 May 2006. www.who.int.

50. Letter from Inge Delfosse and Tomas Hammargren, European Smokeless Tobacco Council, to Antti Maunu, European Commission, 18 October 2010. Document obtained under EU freedom of information law.

51. European Commission Scientific Committee on Emerging and Newly Identified Health Risks, *Health Effects of Smokeless Tobacco Products*, 6 February 2008. pp. 93–115.

52. 'Our brands', Imperial Tobacco website, undated. www.imperial-tobacco.com.

53. Imperial Tobacco, *Imperial Tobacco comments on the RAND Europe Final Report: Assessing the Impacts of Revising the Tobacco Products Directive*, 21 December 2010.

54. Letter from Jeremy Hardy, International Chamber of Commerce, to John Dalli, European Commission, 15 December 2010. www.iccwbo.org.

55. 'CEO Group', Business Alliance to Stop Counterfeiting and Piracy, International Chamber of Commerce homepage, undated. www.iccwbo.org.

56. Programme for executive board meeting of Trans Atlantic Business Dialogue, 24–25 March 2011. www.tabd.com.

57. 'Membership', Trans Atlantic Business Dialogue website, undated. www.tabd.com.

58. Trans Atlantic Business Dialogue, Monthly Newsletter, July 2012. www.tabd. com.
59. Note on Jeffries Briginshaw, Tobacco Tactics website, 17 April 2012. www. tobaccotactics.org.
60. Letter from Jeffries Briginshaw and Kathryn Hauser, Trans Atlantic Business Dialogue, to Ron Kirk, US Trade Representative, and Karel de Gucht, European Commission, 27 May 2011. www.tabd.com.
61. 'Covert lobbying by the tobacco industry', *ASH Bulletin* (newsletter published by Action on Smoking and Health), June 2009. www.ash.org.uk.
62. Email message from Jeffries Briginshaw to the author, 3 April 2012.
63. 'About us', European Risk Forum website, undated. www.riskforum.eu.
64. Fax message from Stanley Crossick, European Policy Centre, to Vickie Curtis and Keith Gretton, British American Tobacco, 30 October 1997. www.legacy. library.ucsf.edu.
65. Entry for European Risk Forum in European Commission's register of interest representatives, 26 November 2012.
66. Email message from Dirk Hudig, European Risk Forum, to the author, 23 May 2012.
67. Exchange of email messages between the author and Henning Klaus, European Commission and Klaus Welle, European Parliament, March 2012. (Welle's reply was sent via his spokesman, Jaume Duch.)
68. European Commission, 'Questions and answers: towards a new EU law on tobacco products', 19 December 2012.
69. Dave Keating, 'Commission under fire over tobacco lobbying', *European Voice*, 10–16 January 2013.
70. Andy Carling, 'Borg: tobacco directive is balanced and ambitious', *New Europe*, 24 February–2 March 2013.

CHAPTER SIX

1. 'Europe divided over how to reach climate goals', *Spiegel Online*, 8 March 2007. www.spiegel.de.
2. Council of the European Union, Presidency Conclusions, Brussels European Council, 8–9 March 2007. www.consilium.europa.eu.
3. Raj Patel, *The Value of Nothing: How to reshape market society and redefine democracy*, paperback edn, London: Portobello, 2011, p. 173.
4. A full list of members can be found on www.europia.com.
5. European Petroleum Industry Association, *Position on the Commission's proposal on GHG emissions trading within the EU*, January 2002. www. europia.com.
6. European Commission, 'Emissions trading: EU Environment Commissioner Margot Wallström welcomes Council agreement as landmark decision for combating climate change', press statement, 10 December 2002. www. ec.europa.eu.
7. Organisation for Economic Cooperation and Development, Glossary of Statistical Terms, 25 September 2001. www.stats.oecd.org.
8. Charles Nicholson, 'Emissions trading: a market instrument for our times', speech to Royal Society of Arts, London, 28 October 2003. www.bp.com.
9. Andrew Simms & David Boyle, *Eminent Corporations: The rise and fall of the great British corporation*, London: Constable, 2010, p. 239.

10. Friends of the Earth Europe, *The EU Emissions Trading System: Failing to deliver*, October 2010, p. 3. www.foeeurope.org.

11. Letter from Isabelle Muller, European Petroleum Industry Association, to Günter Verheugen, European Commission, 28 March 2008. Document obtained under EU freedom of information law.

12. Ana-Maria Tolbaru, 'A refined approach to oil', *European Voice*, 11 November 2010.

13. Email message from Chris Beddoes, European Petroleum Industry Association, to several EU officials, 4 August 2010. Document obtained under EU freedom of information law.

14. European Commission, *Refining in Europe*, May 2009. Document obtained under EU freedom of information law.

15. Letter from Christine Berg, European Commission, to Isabelle Muller, European Petroleum Industry Association, 15 May 2009. Document obtained under EU freedom of information law.

16. Letter from Isabelle Muller, European Petroleum Industry Association, to Connie Hedegaard, European Commission, 25 March 2010. Document obtained under EU freedom of information law.

17. Letter from Isabelle Muller, European Petroleum Industry Association, to Philip Lowe, European Commission, 21 October 2010. Document obtained under EU freedom of information law.

18. A full list of members for the European Chemical Industry Council can be found on www.cefic.org.

19. European Chemical Industry Council, 'CEFIC input to public consultation in preparation of an "analytical report on the impact of the international climate negotiations on the situation of energy intensive sectors"', 12 April 2010. www.ec.europa.eu.

20. International Council of Chemical Associations, 'Policymaker invitation to workshop on reducing chemical industry energy & GHGs via catalysts', 23 January 2012. Document seen by the author.

21. Letter from Joachim Kreuger, European Chemical Industry Council, to Yvon Slingenberg, European Commission, 23 September 2010. Document obtained under EU freedom of information law.

22. European Commission, *High Level Group on the Competitiveness of the European Chemicals Industry – Final Report*, July 2009, p. 25. www.ec.europa.eu.

23. Email message from Francesca Ianni, European Chemical Industry Council, to Connie Hedegaard, European Commission, 1 March 2011. Document obtained under EU freedom of information law.

24. Letter from Giorgio Squinzi, European Chemical Industry Council, to Connie Hedegaard, European Commission, 9 March 2011. Document obtained under EU freedom of information law.

25. Ewa Krukowska, 'EU may set aside 800 million CO_2 permits by 2020, draft shows', Bloomberg, 16 February 2011.

26. Belén Balanyá & Oscar Reyes, *Caught in the cross hairs: how industry lobbyists are gunning for EU climate targets*, report by Corporate Europe Observatory and Carbon Trade Watch, June 2011, p. 4. www.corporateeurope.org.

27. Notes taken by the author during European Business Summit, Brussels, 26 April 2012.

28. Philippa Jones, 'EU's emissions bill changes hit chemical industry', *ICIS News*, 23 January 2008. www.icis.com.

29. European Chemical Industry Council, *Facts and figures 2011: The European chemical industry in a worldwide perspective*, p. 45. www.cefic.org.

30. Michael Grubb & Thomas Counsell, *Tackling carbon leakage: Sector-specific solutions for a world of unequal carbon prices*, report published by the Carbon Trust, February 2010, p. 2. www.carbontrust.com.

31. 'Our clients', Carbon Trust website, undated. www.carbontrust.com.

32. Notes taken by the author during conference titled 'Is the EU's approach to carbon markets the right solution for Durban?', Brussels, 22 November 2011.

33. Aurélien Bernier, *Comment la mondialisation a tué l'écologie: Les politiques environnementales piégées par le libre échange*, Paris: Mille et une nuits, 2012, p. 268.

34. Letter from Connie Hedegaard, European Commission, to Henry Derwent, International Emissions Trading Association, 19 October 2011. Document obtained under EU freedom of information law.

35. 'Our members', International Emissions Trading Association website, undated. www.ieta.org.

36. 'Blair's climate change man should have been handed two-year ban', *Click Green*, 3 December 2009. www.clickgreen.org.uk.

37. Jennifer Rankin, 'Fraud puts the brake on the emissions market', *European Voice*, 6 January 2011.

38. Letter from Henry Derwent, International Emissions Trading Association, to Connie Hedegaard, European Commission, 14 September 2011. Document obtained under EU freedom of information law.

39. Joshua Chaffin, 'Carbon trading: into thin air', *Financial Times*, 14 February 2011.

40. Letter from Connie Hedegaard, European Commission, to Henry Derwent, International Emissions Trading Association, 19 October 2011. Document obtained under EU freedom of information law.

41. Interview with the author, July 2012.

42. Email message from Simone Ruiz, International Emissions Trading Association, to Thomas Bernheim, European Commission, 30 September 2011.

43. Email message from Thomas Bernheim, European Commission, to Simone Ruiz, International Emissions Trading Association, 30 September 2011. Document obtained under EU freedom of information law.

44. 'Court fines firm £250,000 for radioactive leak', *Guardian*, 21 February 2006.

45. AEA, *Study on the integrity of the Clean Development Mechanism (CDM)*, December 2011, pp. 13–39. www.aeat.co.uk.

46. Ricardo Coelho, *Green is the Colour of Money: The EU ETS failure as a model for the 'green economy'*, report published by Carbon Trade Watch, June 2012, p. 11. www.carbontradewatch.org.

47. Tamra Gilbertson & Oscar Reyes, *Carbon Trading: How it works and why it fails*, report published by Dag Hammarskjöld Foundation, November 2009, p. 11. www.dhf.uu.se.

48. Environmental Investigation Agency, *HFC-23 offsets in the context of the EU emissions trading scheme*, briefing paper, 14 July 2010, pp. 1–2. www.cdm-watch.org.

49. Soumitra Ghosh & Subrat Kumar Sahu, *The Indian Clean Development Mechanism: Subsidising and legitimising corporate pollution*, report by

National Forum of Forest People and Forest Workers, November 2011, pp. 71–82. www.dishaearth.org.

50. European Commission, Directorate-general for climate action, 'Business roundtable: draft notes on key messages', 18 May 2010. Document obtained under EU freedom of information law.

51. Andrew Simms, *Ecological Debt: Global Warming and the Wealth of Nations*, 2nd edn, London: Pluto Press, 2009, p. 195.

52. Camillus Eboh & Felix Onuah, 'UN slams Shell as Nigeria needs biggest ever oil clean-up', Reuters, 4 August 2011.

53. Email message from Hans van der Loo, Shell, to various EU officials, 17 May 2011. Document obtained under EU freedom of information law.

54. Promotional leaflet for Comment:Visions, distributed at corporate events in Brussels during 2012.

55. Email message from Martin Deloche, Euronews, to the author, August 2012.

56. Email message from Tim King, *European Voice*, to the author, September 2012.

57. Comment:Visions, report of debate titled 'Putting carbon capture and storage into action', European Parliament, Brussels, 25 February 2009. www.commentvisions.com.

58. For a full list of members, see www.zeroemissionsplatform.eu.

59. European Commission, project description of Zero Emissions Platform Support Secretariat, 31 October 2011. www.cordis.europa.eu.

60. European Technology Platform for Zero Emission Fossil Fuel Power Plants, *Strategic Deployment Document*, August 2006, pp. 5–39. www.zeroemissionsplatform.eu.

61. European Commission, *NER300 – Moving towards a low carbon economy and boosting innovation, growth and employment across the EU*, 12 July 2012, p. 6. www.ec.europa.eu.

62. Alstom UK, 'Alstom confirms joint application for CCS project funding', press statement, 10 February 2011. www.alstom.com.

63. 'Alstom to construct pilot in Poland', *Carbon Capture Journal*, 10 December 2008. www.carboncapturejournal.com.

64. Carbon Capture and Storage Association, *A Strategy for CCS in the UK and Beyond*, September 2011, p. 16. www.ccsassociation.org.

65. 'Companies chase Davies's billions', blog post on Chris Davies' website, 4 July 2011. www.chrisdaviesmep.org.uk.

66. Michael Gillard & Andy Rowell, 'How BP drafted Brussels' climate legislation', report by Spinwatch, 15 December 2010. www.spinwatch.org.

67. Corporate Europe Observatory & Spinwatch, *EU billions to keep burning fossil fuels: The battle to secure EU funding for carbon capture and storage*, December 2010, pp. 5–14. www.corporateeurope.org.

68. 'Our members', Carbon Capture and Storage Association website, undated. www.ccsassociation.org.

69. Entry for Paul Adamson on SourceWatch website, undated. www.sourcewatch.org.

70. Edelman, 'Edelman expands global public affairs network through merger with The Centre in Brussels', press statement, 22 March 2010. www.edelman.com.

71. Exchange of email messages between Martin Porter, Edelman:The Centre, and the author, June 2012.

72. David Cronin, 'Europeans pay companies to pollute more', Inter Press Service, 11 December 2009.
73. European Parliament, 'MEPs give green light to EU economic recovery plan', 6 May 2009. www.europarl.europa.eu.
74. United Nations Environment Programme, European Patent Office & International Centre for Trade and Sustainable Development, *Patents and clean energy: Bridging the gap between evidence and policy*, 30 September 2010, pp. 9–31, www.epo.org.
75. Letter from Philippe de Buck, BusinessEurope, to Karel de Gucht, European Commission, 14 April 2011. Document obtained under EU freedom of information law.
76. Letter from Philippe de Buck, BusinessEurope, to Karel de Gucht, European Commission, 1 September 2011. Document obtained under EU freedom of information law.
77. European Environment Agency, *Opinion of the EEA Scientific Committee on the environmental impacts of biofuel utilisation in the EU*, 10 April 2008. www.eea.europa.eu.
78. April Streeter, 'Amsterdam edging ahead of Copenhagen as most bike-loving Euro-capital?', *treehugger*, 1 February 2009. www.treehugger.com.
79. European Commission, *Biofuels in the European Union: A vision for 2030 and beyond, Final report of the Biofuels Research Advisory Council*, April 2006, pp. 30–1. www.ec.europa.eu.
80. 'EBTP steering committee', European Biofuels Technology Platform website, undated. www.biofuelstp.eu.
81. European Biofuels Technology Platform, *Strategic Research Agenda & Strategic Deployment Document*, January 2008. www.biofuelstp.eu.
82. Jean Ziegler, *Destruction Massive: Géopolitique de la faim*, Paris: Seuil, 2011, p. 284.
83. Klaus Deininger & Derek Byerlee, *Rising global interest in farmland: Can it yield sustainable and equitable benefits?*, report published by the World Bank, September 2010, p. 15. www.worldbank.org.
84. Bettina Kretschmer, Catherine Bowyer & Allan Buckwell, *EU Biofuel use and agricultural commodity prices: A review of the evidence base*, report published by Institute for European Environmental Policy, June 2012, p. 5. www.ieep.eu.
85. ActionAid, *Biofuelling the global food crisis: Why the EU must act at the G20*, June 2020, p. 9. www.actionaid.org.uk.
86. Claire Provost, 'New international land deal reveals rush to buy up Africa', *Guardian*, 27 April 2012.
87. John Vidal, 'Guatemala farmers losing their land to Europe's demand for biofuels', *Guardian*, 5 July 2012.
88. Victoria Bryan, 'Airlines in EU biofuels pact to cut pollution', Reuters, 22 June 2011.
89. 'Commission makes proposals to minimise the climate impact of biofuels', European Commission website, 17 October 2012. www.ec.europa.eu.
90. 'Graeme Sweeney reveals Shell's biofuels strategy', *Bloomberg Businessweek*, 15 April 2009.
91. 'July heat sets 4,313 records', *The Buckeye Lake Beacon*, 4 August 2012. www.buckeyelakebeacon.net.

92. Maria-José Viñas, 'Satellites see unprecedented Greenland ice sheet surface melt', NASA website, 24 July 2012. www.nasa.gov.

93. 'International news', *Discovery – The Quarterly Newsletter of Koch Companies*, January 2010. www.kochind.com.

94. 'About us', European Centre for Public Affairs website, undated. www.theecpa.eu.

95. Exchange of email messages between Maria Leptev, European Centre for Public Affairs, and the author, May 2012.

96. European Centre for Public Affairs, Programme for ECPA annual debate, 20 March 2012, www.theecpa.eu.

97. 'La crise économique menace l'accord sur la paquet énergie-climat', *Euractiv*, 22 September 2008. www.euractiv.fr.

98. Council of the European Union, 'Energy and climate change – elements of the final compromise', note from general secretariat, 12 December 2008. www.eu2008.fr.

99. European Environment Agency, 'Higher EU greenhouse gas emissions in 2010 due to economic recovery and cold winter', press statement, 30 May 2012. www.eea.europa.eu.

100. Jos Olivier, Greet Janssens-Maenhout, Jeroen Peters, *Trends in global CO2 emissions: 2012 report*, report by PBL Netherlands Environmental Assessment Agency, July 2012, pp. 10–15. www.pbl.nl.

CHAPTER SEVEN

1. Piers Brendon, *The Decline and Fall of the British Empire, 1781–1997*, London: Vintage, 2008, pp. 30–4.

2. Devinder Sharma, '"Free" trade killing farmers in India', *bilaterals.org*, November 2007. www.bilaterals.org.

3. Palagummi Sainath, 'Nearly 1.5 lakh farm suicides in 1997–2005', *The Hindu*, 12 November 2007.

4. A full list of members can be found on the European Services Forum website, www.esf.be.

5. European Commission, *External Aspects of Competitiveness*, report on consultation of EU business federations, 18 January 2006. Document seen by the author.

6. Letter from Iain Vallance, European Services Forum, to Peter Mandelson, European Commission, 21 March 2006. Document obtained under EU freedom of information law.

7. European Commission, *Global Europe: Competing in the World*, October 2006, pp. 6–7. www.ec.europa.eu.

8. Peter Mandelson, *The Third Man*, London: HarperPress, updated edn, 2011, p. 395.

9. Ha-Joon Chang, *23 Things They Don't Tell You About Capitalism*, London: Allen Lane, 2010, p. 70.

10. Letter from David O'Sullivan, European Commission, to Philippe de Buck, BusinessEurope, 20 February 2007. Document seen by the author.

11. Letter from Philippe de Buck, BusinessEurope, to Peter Mandelson, European Commission, 6 March 2008. Document seen by the author.

12. Letter from Peter Mandelson, European Commission, to Philippe de Buck, BusinessEurope, 18 March 2008. Document seen by the author.

13. European Commission, *Report of the 7th EU–India Business Summit*, 12 October 2006. Document seen by the author.

14. Letter from representatives of car, chemicals, paper, textiles, metal industry representatives to David O'Sullivan, European Commission, 24 November 2009. Document seen by the author.

15. Data on World Bank website. www.data.worldbank.org.

16. Christa Wichterich, *Economic Growth Without Social Justice: EU–India Trade Negotiations and their Implications for Social Development and Gender Justice*, report published by Women in Development Europe (WIDE), 2007, p. 3. www.wide-network.org.

17. Arundhati Roy, *Listening to Grasshoppers: Field Notes on Democracy*, London: Penguin, 2nd edn, 2010, p. 182.

18. European NGO Confederation for Relief and Development (CONCORD), *Spotlight on EU Coherence for Development*, November 2011, p. 14. www.coherence.concordeurope.org.

19. United Nations Office of the High Commissioner for Human Rights, *The Right to Adequate Food*, April 2010, pp. 2–4. www.ohchr.org.

20. Olivier de Schutter, *Agribusiness and the Right to Food*, report to Human Rights Council of the United Nations General Assembly, 22 December 2009, p. 11. www.srfood.org.

21. Armin Paasch et al., *Right to Food Impact Assessment of the EU–India Trade Agreement*, report by Misereor and several other organisations, December 2011, p. 43. www.misereor.de.

22. Letter from Jean Martin, CIAA, to Peter Mandelson, European Commission, 30 May 2008. Document obtained under EU freedom of information law.

23. Heather Stewart, 'Tariffs: WTO talks collapse after India and China clash with US over farm products', *Guardian*, 30 July 2008.

24. 'India, China not to blame for WTO talks collapse: Mandelson', *India Today*, 30 July 2008.

25. Letter from Peter Mandelson, European Commission, to Jean Martin, CIAA, 8 July 2008. Document obtained under EU freedom of information law.

26. 'Trade: Kamal Nath explains how the Geneva talks failed', Third World Network website, 31 July 2008. www.twnside.org.sg.

27. Martin Banks, 'Farmers' sensitive friend', *European Voice*, 14 October 2004.

28. Mariann Fischer Boel, 'Going on the offensive: a new approach to agri-food exports', speech to European Commission seminar for agri-food exporters, 25 June 2007. www.ec.europa.eu.

29. Traidcraft, *The EU–India Free Trade Agreement: What MEPs Need to Know*, August 2009, p. 2. www.traidcraft.co.uk.

30. David Cronin, 'Indian farmers won't say cheese', Inter Press Service, 3 May 2010.

31. CIAA, 'CIAA priorities for the negotiations of a free trade agreement with India', 16 March 2009. Document obtained under EU freedom of information law.

32. Roopam Singh & Ranja Sengupta, *The EU–India FTA in Agriculture and Likely Impact on Indian Women*, report by Consortium for Trade and Development and Heinrich Böll Stiftung India, December 2009, p. 3. www.in.boell.org.

33. European Commission, minutes of meeting with CEPS (European Spirits Producers' Organisation), 25 May 2010. Document seen by the author.

34. Pallavai Aiyar, 'EU–India FTA suffers the ennui of vested interests', *Business Standard*, 8 July 2009.
35. Hana Ben-Shabat, Mike Moriarty & Deepa Neary, *Retail Global Expansion: A Portfolio of Opportunities*, report published by AT Kearney, pp. 9–10. www.atkearney.com.
36. Pulkhit Agarwal, *Foreign Direct Investment in India: An Analysis*, Legal India website, 24 November 2011. www.legalindia.in.
37. Pia Eberhardt & Dharmendra Kutar, *Trade Invaders: How big business is driving the EU–India free trade negotiations*, report by Corporate Europe Observatory and India FDI Watch, September 2010, p. 22. www.corporateeurope.org.
38. Letter from Christoffer Taxell, European Services Forum, to Karel de Gucht, European Commission, 6 December 2010. Document obtained under EU freedom of information law.
39. Armin Paasch, *Human Rights in EU Trade Policy: Between Ambition and Reality*, report by Misereor and several other organisations, December 2011, p. 12. www.misereor.de.
40. George Monbiot, 'My town is menaced by a superstore. So why are we not free to fight it off?', *Guardian*, 10 August 2009.
41. 'Ashton backs Doha rescue in Q&A with MEPs', European Parliament website, 21 October 2008. www.europarl.europa.eu.
42. Letter from Catherine Ashton, European Commission, to Christoffer Taxell, European Services Forum, 15 December 2008. Document obtained under EU freedom of information law.
43. European Commission, 'EU and South Korea initial free trade deal', press statement, 15 October 2009. www.trade.ec.europa.eu.
44. Email message from Andres Garcia Bermudez, European Commission, to various EU officials, 20 November 2008. Document seen by the author.
45. Letter from Guido Ravoet, European Banking Federation, to Vital Moreira, European Parliament, 22 June 2010. www.ebf-fbe.eu.
46. TheCityUK, *The EU–South Korea Free Trade Agreement*, 28 June 2011, pp. 3–4. www.thecityuk.com.
47. European Commission, *EU–South Korea Free Trade Agreement: A Quick Reading Guide*, October 2010, pp. 10–11. www.ec.europa.eu.
48. BusinessEurope, *BusinessEurope position on the EU–Korea free trade agreement*, 18 July 2007, pp. 6–8. www.businesseurope.eu.
49. Letter from Peter Mandelson, European Commission, to Philippe de Buck, BusinessEurope, 10 September 2007. Document seen by the author.
50. European Commission, Report of the meeting of the Market Access Team-Working Group on SPS/TBT [sanitary phytosanitary measures/technical barriers to trade], Seoul, 23 April 2009. Document seen by the author.
51. Water Justice, *Problems of Water Privatisation and Responses in Korea*, 6 May 2007, pp. 1–2. www.waterjustice.org.
52. United Nations General Assembly, 'General Assembly adopts resolution recognising access to clean water, sanitation', press statement, 28 July 2010. www.un.org.
53. Corporate Europe Observatory, *WTO and Water: The EU's Crusade for Corporate Expansion*, March 2003, www.corporateeurope.org.
54. Corporate Europe Observatory and Transnational Institute, *The EU's FTA Talks: Is Water Included?*, 25 July 2008. www.corporateeurope.org.

55. Copies of the EU's requests for services liberalisation can be found on www. gatswatch.org.
56. Christian Oliver, 'Trade agreement: Landmark deal with Europe to cut tariffs', *Financial Times*, 10 November 2010.
57. Marc Maes, 'While the EU member states insist on the status quo, the European Parliament calls for a reformed investment policy', *Investment Treaty News*, 1 July 2011. www.iisd.org/itn.
58. Latha Jisnu, 'Investment Terror', *Down to Earth*, 31 January 2012. www. downtoearth.org.in.
59. Notes taken by the author at conference on investment treaties, Brussels, 5 November 2011.
60. Raphael Lencucha, 'Philip Morris versus Uruguay: health governance challenged', *The Lancet*, 11 September 2010.
61. 'Vattenfall suing Germany over nuke phaseout', *The Local*, 3 November 2011. www.thelocal.se.
62. Steven Finizio, Ethan Shenkman & Julian Davis Mortenson, 'Recent developments in investor-state arbitration: effective use of provisional measures', *The European Arbitration Review 2007*, p. 15. www. globalarbitrationreview.com.
63. Letter from Werner Schnappauf, Federation of German Industries, to Karel de Gucht, European Commission, 20 July 2010. Document seen by the author.
64. European Commission, *Report on EU Foreign Direct Investment Roundtable*, 21 December 2010. Document seen by the author.
65. Council of the European Union, '3,109th Council Meeting, General Affairs, 12 September 2011', press statement. www.consilium.europa.eu.
66. Canada–EU Summit declaration, 9 May 2009. www.canadainternational. gc.ca.
67. Bill Emmott, 'A long goodbye', *The Economist*, 30 March 2006.
68. Canada–Europe Round Table for Business, *CERT Policy Priorities for a Canada–EU Trade and Investment Agreement*, March 2009, p. 13. www. canada-europe.org.
69. Email message from Jason Langrish, Canada–Europe Roundtable for Business, forwarding a letter from Xstrata Nickel to various EU officials, 13 July 2011. Document obtained under EU freedom of information law.
70. Stuart Trew, 'Dinosaur economics: Why a free trade pact with the European Union is an (old) bad idea', *Canadian Perspectives*, Spring 2010, www. canadians.org.
71. Organisation for Economic Cooperation and Development, *The Multilateral Agreement on Investment: Commentary on the Consolidated Text*, 22 April 1998, p. 38. www.oecd.org.
72. Phillip Hudson, 'The Multilateral Agreement on Investment faces indefinite postponement', *The Age*, 25 April 1998.
73. Mouvement des Entreprises de France (MEDEF), *Recommandations de MEDEF sur un accord entre l'Union européenne et le Canada*, April 2009, p. 3. www.gfie.fr.
74. European Commission, 'Supplementary protection certificates for medicinal products', information note, 24 September 2009. www.ec.europa.eu.
75. Kathie Lynas, 'Canada's generic drug sector could face more change from Ontario court ruling and possible Canada-EU trade deal', *Canadian Pharmacists Journal*, March/April 2011. www.cpjournal.ca.

76. Letter from Catherine Ashton, European Commission, to Philippe de Buck, BusinessEurope, 1 April 2009. Document seen by the author.

77. Carla Johnson, 'Peter Mandelson speaks on IP protection in China', *Tax News*, 28 November 2007. www.tax-news.com.

78. World Health Organisation, *Public Health, Innovation and Intellectual Property Rights*, report of the Commission on Intellectual Property Rights, Innovation and Public Health, 2006, p. 22. www.who.int.

79. World Health Assembly, 'Public health, innovation and intellectual property', 24 May 2007. www.who.int.

80. Email message from Brendan Barnes, European Federation of Pharmaceutical Industries and Associations, to various EU officials, 23 May 2007. Document obtained under EU freedom of information law.

81. Portuguese Presidency of the European Union, 'EU answer to 2nd Public Hearing of the IGWG [Intergovernmental Working Group] on Public Health, Innovation and Intellectual Property', 2007. www.who.int.

82. Rohit Malpani & Sophie Bloemen, *Trading away access to medicines: how the European Union's trade agenda has taken a wrong turn*, report published by Health Action International and Oxfam, October 2009, p. 13. www.haiweb.org.

83. David Cronin, 'EU opposes cheap medicines for AIDS in Thailand', Inter Press Service, 28 August 2007.

84. Letter from Peter Mandelson, European Commission, to Krirk-krai Jirapeat, minister of commerce, Thailand, 10 July 2007. A copy of the letter can be found on www.keionline.org.

85. David Cronin, 'EU split arises over Thai effort to obtain cheaper patented drugs', *Intellectual Property Watch*, 5 September 2007. www.ip-watch.org.

86. World Trade Organisation, 'Compulsory licensing of pharmaceuticals and TRIPS', fact sheet, September 2007. www.wto.org.

87. European Commission, briefing note on 'compulsory licences of pharmaceutical patents in Thailand', 9 February 2007. Document obtained under EU freedom of information law.

88. European Commission, briefing note on 'compulsory licensing in Thailand', 5 July 2007. Document obtained under EU freedom of information law.

89. European Commission, briefing note prepared for Peter Mandelson ahead of telephone call with Thai commerce minister, 17 April 2008. Document obtained under EU freedom of information law.

90. James Love, 'What does democrats.com have against poor people in Thailand getting affordable medicines?', *The Huffington Post*, 25 April 2007. www.huffingtonpost.com.

91. Ministry of Public Health, Thailand, *The 10 burning questions on the government use of patents on the four anti-cancer drugs in Thailand*, February 2008, p. 2. www.moph.go.th.

92. Email message from Louis-Nicolas Fortin, European Federation of Pharmaceutical Industries and Associations, to various EU officials, 23 September 2010. Document obtained under EU freedom of information law.

93. Charles Arthur, 'ACTA goes too far, says MEP', *Guardian*, 1 February 2012.

94. European Commission, 'Ten Myths about ACTA', fact sheet, January 2012. www.ec.europa.eu.

95. Anti-Counterfeiting Trade Agreement, 2011, p. 9–10. The text of the agreement can be found on www.international.gc.ca.

96. 'Brazil, India take EU to WTO over generic drug seizures', *EUbusiness*, 12 May 2010. www.eubusiness.com.

97. Charles Arthur, 'ACTA down, but not out, as Europe votes against controversial treaty', *Guardian*, 4 July 2012.

98. Pfizer and GlaxoSmithKline both belong to the International Chamber of Commerce, for full membership see www.iccwbo.org; GSK is also part of the European Brands Association, for full membership see www.aim.be.

99. Concerned business groups operating in ACTA nations, memo to ACTA negotiators, 3 June 2008. The text of the memo can be found on www.eff.org.

100. Letter from Peter Mandelson, European Commission, to Walter Schnappauf, Federation of German Industries, 8 September 2008. Document seen by the author.

101. 'Live8 success hailed by Geldof', BBC News website, 3 July 2005. www.bbc. co.uk.

102. European Commission, 'Statement by Commissioner Peter Mandelson following the General Affairs and External Relations Council', 10 December 2007. www.ec.europa.eu.

103. Peter Mandelson & Louis Michel, 'This is not a poker game', *Guardian*, 31 October 2007.

104. Letter from Iain Vallance, European Services Forum, to Peter Mandelson, European Commission, 1 November 2007. Document obtained under EU freedom of information law.

105. Letter from Peter Mandelson, European Commission, to Christoffer Taxell, European Services Forum, 12 March 2008. Document obtained under EU freedom of information law.

106. Julio Goodoy, 'EC manufactured bogus "African business" support for EPAs', Inter Press Service, 7 May 2009.

107. Email message from Adrian van den Hoven, Union of Industrial and Employers' Confederation of Europe, to Robert Baldwin, European Commission, 5 October 2006. Document seen by the author.

108. Interview with the author, February 2012.

109. European Commission, *Trade, Growth and World Affairs: Trade policy as a core component of the EU's 2020 strategy*, 9 November 2010, pp. 4–11. www.trade.ec.europa.eu.

110. European Commission, list of meetings for Karel de Gucht, 24 February 2010 to 8 December 2010. Document seen by the author.

111. Email message from John Clancy, European Commission, to the author, 4 February 2012.

112. Cecilia Olivet & Paulina Nova, *Time for Europe to put values and human rights above commercial advantage: Why EU–Colombia/Peru free trade agreements should not be ratified*, report by Transnational Institute, March 2011, p. 5. www.tni.org.

113. European Parliament, debates, 27 September 2011. www.europarl.europa.eu.

114. International Office for Human Rights – Action on Colombia, 'The EU must request that Colombia withdraws the expansion of military jurisdiction from its reform of the justice system', press statement, 26 January 2012, www. oidhaco.org.

CONCLUSION

1. Stephen Mulvey, 'The EU's democratic challenge', BBC News website, 21 November 2003.

2. Elitsa Vucheva, 'European elections marked by record low turnout,' *EUobserver*, 8 June 2009. www.euobserver.com.

3. Antoine Dumini & François Ruffin, 'Enquête dans le temple de l'euro', *Le Monde diplomatique*, November 2011.

4. Patricia Kowsmann, 'Portugal opposition demands voice on aid', *The Wall Street Journal*, 12 April 2011.

5. Duncan Green, 'The global bank bailout is enough to end (that's "end", not just halve) global poverty for 50 years', Oxfam website, 1 April 2009. www.oxfamblogs.org.

6. Orla Tinsey, 'The rise and fall of Occupy Dame Street', *Irish Times*, 17 March 2012.

7. Louise Lucas, Barney Jopson & Vanessa Houlder, 'Starbucks ground down', *Financial Times*, 8–9 December 2012.

8. Richard Murphy, *Closing the tax gap*, report by Tax Research, February 2012, pp. 2–21. www.taxresearch.org.uk.

9. Bill McKibben, 'Global warming's terrifying new math', *Rolling Stone*, 19 July 2012.

10. Coral Davenport, '"Man who crushed Keystone" is targeting fossil fuels in anti-apartheid style campaign', *National Journal*, 6 November 2012.

11. Brendan Greeley, 'Bernanke to economists: more philosophy, please', *Bloomberg Businessweek*, 6 August 2012.

12. John Perkins, *Confessions of an Economic Hit Man*, paperback edn, London: Ebury, 2006, p. 216.

13. Tim Jackson, *Prosperity Without Growth: Economics for a Finite Planet*, paperback edn, London: Earthscan, 2011, p. 123.

14. Speech by José-Manuel Barroso to 'Beyond GDP' conference, Brussels, 19 November 2007. www.beyond-gdp.eu.

15. European Commission, *Europe 2020: A strategy for smart, sustainable and inclusive growth*, 3 March 2010. www.ec.europa.eu.

16. Tony Benn, *Letters to My Grandchildren: Thoughts on the Future*, London: Hutchinson, 2009, p. 4.

Index

Abengoa Bioenergy, 122
AccountancyAge, 41
ActionAid, 122–3
Adamson, Paul, 119
Aerospace and Defence Industries
    Association of Europe (ASD), 63,
    67, 71
Aerospace Industries Association of
    America (AIA), 67
Afghanistan, 57, 61
Africa, 52, 54, 71, 75, 81, 114, 116,
    123, 145–9
African, Caribbean and Pacific (ACP)
    countries, 145–9
Agent Orange, 73
Ahtonen, Annika, 31
AIDS, 25, 52, 78, 142–3
alcohol, 31, 85–9, 95, 134
Alcohol Beverage Federation of Ireland
    (ABFI), 88
Alcover, Maria, 139
Alliance for Lobbying Transparency
    and Ethics Regulation (ALTER-EU),
    7
Alstom, 118, 139, 148
Alternative Investment Management
    Association (AIMA), 39
Amnesty International, 51, 156
Anglo Irish Bank, 15–17
Annan, Kofi, 122
Anti-Counterfeiting Trade Agreement
    (ACTA), 144–5
apartheid, 57, 62, 156
APCO, 83
Arab uprisings, 52–3, 71, 151
Arif, Kader, 144
Arkema, 110
Armack, Alfred-Müller, 14
arms industry, 9, 31, 51–72, 139,
    155–6
Arnould, Claude-France, 53, 65, 68
Ashton, Catherine, 135, 141

Association for the Monetary Union of
    Europe (AMUE), 21–3
asylum-seekers, 62, 70–2, 152
AT Kearney, 134
Atomic Energy Authority (AEA), 114
Australia, 103, 145
Austria, 43
Aviva, 30
Axa, 28–9, 45

Bacardi-Martini, 87
BAE Systems, 51–5, 60, 62, 65–7
Baldwin, Robert, 147
Bakan, Joel, 9
Bánati, Diána, 76
Bank of Ireland, 17
Barclays, 17, 43
Barnes, Brendan, 142
Barnier, Michel, 46–9
Barroso, José Manuel, 23, 36, 78,
    80–1, 104, 128, 155
BASF, 76, 80–1, 90
Bavaria, 96
Bayer, 75–6, 78, 90
Bear Stearns, 36
Beddoes, Chris, 108
Bedlington, Nicola, 31
bees, 90–1
Belgium, 8, 24, 28, 60–1, 69, 74, 79,
    82, 123–4, 148
Bell Helicopters, 139
Belmont, 96–7
Berès, Pervenche, 41–2
Bergman, Per, 74
Berlusconi, Silvio, 11
Bernanke, Ben, 154–5
Bernays, Edward, 2
Berkshire Hathaway, 43
Beugels, Edgar, 70
Bevan, Nye, 26
Bilderberg Group, 8
Binning, Tim, 50
biofuels, 48, 120–3

Biofuels Research Advisory Council (BIOFRAC), 121–2
biotechnology, 7, 74–83, 89–91, 122, 126, 143
Blair, Tony, 30, 51–2, 68, 97, 112, 119, 135
Blankfein, Lloyd, 45
Bloom, Godfrey, 97
BNP Paribas, 17, 42–4
Boel, Marius, 133
Bohan, Niall, 36
Bolivia, 152
Bombardier, 139
Bowis, John, 28–9
Bowles, Jack, 95
Bowles, Sharon, 39
bovine spongiform encephalopathy (BSE), 74
Boyle, David, 108
BP, 76, 107–9, 112, 116–17, 119, 122, 154
Brazil, 74, 127, 142, 144
Brewers of Europe, 88
Briginshaw, Jeffries, 103
Britain, 10, 24, 26, 28–30, 38–9, 44–6, 49, 51–5, 58, 61, 63, 74, 78, 84, 90, 95, 97, 103, 112–14, 118–20, 122–3, 126–7, 129, 134–5, 137, 139, 153
British American Tobacco (BAT), 22, 92–9, 101–3
British Sugar, 122
Brock, Theodorus, 90
Brown, Colin, 139
Brown, Gordon, 135
Bruegel, 13
Bruton, Richard, 15
BT, 17, 126–7
Buffett, Warren, 1, 43
Bundesbank, 17
Bureau of Investigative Journalism, 54
Burson-Marsteller, 3–4
Bush, George W., 57, 68, 70, 106, 132
Bushke, Hakan, 54
Business Alliance to Stop Counterfeiting and Piracy (BASCAP), 102–3
BusinessEurope, 7–8, 12, 22–4, 103, 110, 120–1, 126, 129, 147
Business Standard, 134

Butler, Alan, 87

Cadbury, 83
Cameron, David, 30, 46–7, 52–3
Campbell, Nick, 110–11
Canada, 138–41, 145, 148
Canada-EU Mining Council (CEUMC), 139
Canada-Europe Roundtable for Business (CERT), 139–40
Canadian Generic Pharmaceutical Association (CGPA), 141
Capri, Ettore, 90
carbon capture and storage (CCS), 115–21, 123
Carbon Capture and Storage Association, 119
Carbon Trust, 112
Cargill, 9
Carrefour, 134
Carss, Joanna, 48
Carswell, Simon, 15
Cayman Islands, 38
Central Intelligence Agency (CIA), 54
Centre for Research on Multinational Corporations (SOMO), 50
Chang, Ha-Joon, 128
chemical industry, 7, 40, 73–82, 89–91, 97, 109–13, 130
China, 60, 110, 115, 120, 125, 127, 132, 141, 147–8
Chirac, Jacques, 142
Christian Aid, 41
Christian Democratic Union (CDU), 14, 39
Cigna, 22, 27–8
City of London, 38–9, 46, 48–50, 135
Clark, Alan, 51
Clark, Janina, 26–7
Clark, John, 58
clean development mechanism (CDM), 114–15, 154
Clifford Chance, 104
Climate Action Network, 119
climate change, 4, 48, 64, 103, 106–25, 135, 154
Clinical Medicine, 24–5
Clive, Robert, 126
Coca-Cola, 83, 91, 97, 112
Colombia, 148–9

Collignon, Stefan, 22–3
Comment:Visions, 116–17
competitiveness, 1, 9, 18–20, 23, 25, 55, 58, 63, 83, 107–8, 110, 115, 155
Confederation of European Community Cigarette Manufacturers (CECCM), 94–5, 97–9
Conservative Party, 26, 28–9, 117
Cook, Allan, 63
Cooper, Robert, 68
Copenhagen, 4, 116
corporate social responsibility (CSR), 9–10
Corrigan, Paul, 30
Council of Ministers, viii, 84, 107, 119, 142
Credit Suisse, 1–2
Cromme, Gerhard, 20
Crossick, Stanley, 96–7, 103
Crouch, Colin, 30
CSR Europe, 9
Cyprus, viii
Czech Republic, 95–6, 139

Dáil Eireann, 34
Daily Telegraph, 49, 124
Daily Universal Register, 117
Dalli, John, 81–3, 92, 96, 104
Danone, 9
Dassault, 9
Davies, Chris, 118–19
Davignon, Etienne, 8–9
Davos, 18
de Buck, Philippe, 23, 120–1, 129
Defence Stakeholders Group, 64–5
Defence Systems and Equipment International (DSEi), 54
de Gucht, Karel, 148–9
de Hoop Scheffer, Jaap, 68
Deinet, Thomas, 38
de Jong, Dennis, 5
de Larosière, Jacques, 44
Deloche, Martin, 117
Deloitte & Touche, 41
Delors, Jacques, 22
de Meeûs, Ferdinand, 1, 8
Denmark, 37, 40, 55, 66, 88, 115–16, 120, 133, 137

derivatives, 39, 43–50, 112–13, 153
Derwent, Henry, 112–13
de Schutter, Olivier, 131
Deutsche Asset Management, 17
Deutsche Bank, 22, 36–40, 43, 112, 126
Development Policy Forum, 68
Devereux, Michael, 10
Diageo, 17, 86–7
Disney, Helen, 30–1
Doha round (trade negotiations), 120, 127
Doms, Kristof, 100
Dow, 78, 90, 97, 112
Draghi, Mario, 11, 46
drones, see unmanned aerial vehicles
Dubois, Thomas, 124
Dumont Fernandez, Antonio, 76–7
DuPont, 89
Durbin, Dick, 42

EADS, 52, 60, 66, 139
Ealet, Isabelle, 47
Earnshaw, David, 3–4
East India Company, 126
East Timor, 51
economic growth, 1, 9, 19, 24, 128, 130, 155
Economist, 117, 139
Edelman:The Centre, 119
Egypt, 53, 71, 151
Ellwood and Atfield, 7
Eli Lilly, 29
Emmott, Bill, 139
emissions trading scheme (ETS), 106–15, 118–19, 125
Engström, Jan, 41
Environmental Protection Agency (EPA), 90
Erhard, Ludwig, 13
EU-Canada Chamber of Commerce, 148
EU Platform on Diet, Physical Activity and Health, 83
Eurofi, 45
Euronews, 116–17
European Alcohol and Health Forum (EAHF), 87–8
European Alcohol Policy Alliance (Eurocare), 85–6

European American Business Council (EABC), 139

European Association for Bioindustries (EuropaBio), 78–80, 122

European Banking Federation (EBF), 42–3, 135

European Biodiesel Board (EBB), 122

European Bioethanol Fuel Association (eBIO), 122

European Biofuels Technology Platform (EBTP), 122

European Brands Association (AIM), 145

European Business Circle (EuBC), 14

European Central Bank (ECB), ix, 11, 19, 44, 46, 150–1

European Centre for Public Affairs (ECPA), 124

European Chamber of Commerce in India, 148

European Chemical Industry Council (CEFIC), 7, 90, 109–13

European Commission, viii–ix, 5–6, 8–10, 15–16, 18–19, 22–3, 25, 32–3, 34–7, 43–4, 46–7, 49–50, 53, 57–72, 77–7, 92–105, 107–23, 126–51, 155

European Committee of Wine Companies (CEEV), 88–9

European Confederation of Tobacco Retailers (CEDT), 99–100

European Consumers' Organisation (BEUC), 84

European Court of Auditors, 76

European Court of Human Rights, 70

European Court of Justice, 33

European Crop Protection Association (ECPA), 90

European Dairy Association (EDA), 133

European Defence Agency (EDA), 51–72

European Federation of Pharmaceutical Industries and Associations (EFPIA), 142–4

European Food Information Council (EUFIC), 91

European Food Safety Authority (EFSA), 73–84, 89–90

European Forum for Responsible Drinking (EFRD), 87–8

European Foundation for the Care of Newborn Infants (EFCNI), 31–2

European Low Fares Airline Association (ELFAA), 32–3

European Observatory on Sustainable Agriculture (OPERA), 90–1

European Parliament, viii–ix, 3–5, 7, 17, 23, 28, 32, 34–42, 49–50, 59, 76, 84–6, 88, 97, 104, 116, 118–19, 135, 144, 150

European Parliamentary Financial Services Forum (EPFSF), 41–2

European Patients' Forum (EPF), 31

European Petroleum Industry Association (EUROPIA), 107–9

European Policy Centre (EPC), 31, 96–7, 103

European Risk Forum (ERF), 103–4

European Roundtable of Industrialists (ERT), 8, 20–1

European Seed Association (ESA), 7

European Services Forum (ESF), 126–8, 134, 146

European Smokeless Tobacco Council (ESTOC), 101–2

European Union constitution (*see also* Lisbon treaty), 59

European Union of Private Hospitals (UEPH), 29

European Voice, 116–17

Eurostat, 45–6

ExxonMobil, 4, 7, 107, 109

Facebook, 88

Falconer, Crawford, 132

Federal Reserve, 154–5

Federation of German Industry (BDI), 138–9, 145

Feinstein, Andrew, 52

Fianna Fáil, 15

Fiat, 20

financial crisis, ix, 2, 11, 13, 15, 20, 34–50, 55–6, 65, 118, 135, 152–3

Financial Services Authority (FSA), 43

Financial Times, 45, 68

Fine Gael, 15

Finland, 24, 71, 73, 130

Finmeccanica, 71

Finsbury International Policy and
    Regulatory Advisers (FIPRA), 28–9
Fiscal treaty, 24
Fischer Boel, Mariann, 133
Fleishman-Hillard, 28–9
FN Herstal, 61
FoodDrinkEurope, 81–6, 132–3
food price speculation, 47–50, 126,
    153
food safety, 73–91, 140
Fortin, Louis-Nicolas, 144
France, viii, 5, 13, 17, 21, 24, 29, 43,
    47–51, 53, 59, 62, 77, 86, 110,
    118, 120, 126, 130, 140–2, 144
Frankfurt Trust Investments, 17
Fraunhofer, 90
Free Democrats, 13
Frewen, Mella, 81–4
Friedman, Milton, 14, 26
Friends of the Earth, 108
Frontex, 70–2
Frost & Sullivan, 53
Fulgham, Chad, 69
Fullerton, John, 39
Futures and Options Association, 43

Gaddafi, Muammar, 71, 156
Gates, Robert, 67–8
Gaza, 57
GDF Suez, 7, 139
Geldof, Bob, 145
General Electric (GE), 13, 112
genetically modified organisms
    (GMOs), 74–83, 89, 126
Germany, 5, 13–14, 16–17, 20–1,
    39–40, 43, 75, 81, 85–6, 90, 96,
    106, 120, 123–5, 127, 130, 138–9,
    145
Geslain-Lanéelle, Catherine, 76, 79, 89
Ghana, 122–3
Giardano, Paolo, 29
Giles, Bill, 65
Giscard d'Estaing, Valéry, 21, 59
GlaxoSmithKline (GSK), 30, 76, 145
Global Europe, 128–49
Goldman Sachs, 13, 17, 22, 36, 39,
    43–50, 112, 126
Google, 17, 103
Gourio, Alain, 42

Greece, 8–11, 19, 24, 45–6, 52, 70,
    151
Greenland, 124
Green Party, 15
Greenpeace, 4, 18, 79
Greenwood, Justin, 7
Group of 20 (G20), 38, 48
Guardian, 78, 146
Guatemala, 123
Gulf Cooperation Council, 127
Gulf of Mexico, 108

Halligan, Brendan, 17
Hanlon, John, 32–3
Hanover, 28
Hardy, Jeremy, 102
Harris, Scott, 68
Hartung, William, 70
Harvard University, 22–3
Haun, Frank, 66
Hayek, Friedrich, 44
Health First Europe, 29
health insurance, 22, 24–30
Hedegaard, Connie, 109, 111–13,
    115–16
hedge funds, 35–41, 43
Hedge Funds Standards Board (HFSB),
    38
Heinz, 112
Hofheinz, Paul, 18
Hogans Lovell, 139
Honeywell, 13
Horizon 2020, 59
House of Lords, 127
HSBC, 148
Hudig, Dirk, 103–4
Hudson, Linda, 67
Human Rights Watch, 70, 156

IBM, 19
Ikea, 148
ILA Berlin, 55
Imperial College London, 30
Imperial Tobacco, 99–102
India, 110, 115, 120, 126–7, 129–35,
    139, 144, 148
Indonesia, 51
Initiative for a New Social Market
    Economy (INSM), 13

Institute for European Environmental Policy (IEEP), 122
Institute of International and European Affairs (IIEA), 17
Insurance Europe, 26–7, 39, 42
intellectual property, ix, 102–3, 120–1, 138, 140–5
International Accounting Standards Board (IASB), 41
International Chamber of Commerce (ICC), 102–3, 110, 145
International Emissions Trading Association (IETA), 112–14
International Institute of Finance (IIF), 48
International Life Sciences Institute (ILSI), 75–7
International Monetary Fund (IMF), 14–17, 19, 44, 151
International Swaps and Directives Association (ISDA), 39, 43
International Trade Union Confederation (ITUC), 148
Iraq, 53, 57, 70, 139, 156
Ireland, 14–17, 24, 34, 59, 86, 88, 95, 137, 151, 153, 156
Issing, Otmar, 44
Israel, 6, 57, 61–2, 69
Israel Institute of Technology (Technion), 61
Italy, 11–13, 24, 29, 46, 60–1, 71, 73, 90, 110, 151

Jackson, Bruce, 69–70
Jackson, Tim, 155
Japan, 145
Japan Tobacco, 102
Johansson, Leif, 21
Johnson & Johnson, 31
Johnson, Boris, 38
Jones, Huw, 76
Joseph, Keith, 12
J.P. Morgan, 39

Kelly, Anita, 28
Kerneis, Pascal, 127
Kershaw, David, 54
Keynes, John Maynard, 12
King, Ian, 53
King, Tim, 117

Kirchhof, Paul, 13
Klaus, Henning, 104
Klein, Michael, 90
Klein, Naomi, 14
Kleter, Gijs, 75
Klick, Jonathan, 98
Koch, Charles, 124
Koch, David, 124
Koch Industries, 124
Konrad Adenaeur Stiftung, 14
KPMG, 41
Kraft, 91
Krauss-Maffei Wegmann, 66
Kuiper, Harry, 75
Kyoto protocol, 106
Kyprianou, Markos, 85

Labour Party (Britain), 3, 30, 113, 119
Labour Party (Ireland), 17
Laitenen, Ilkka, 71
Lapavitsas, Costas, 32
Laptev, Maria, 124
Latvia, 34
Laval, 34
Le Grand, Julian, 30
Lehne, Klaus-Heiner, 39–40
Lennon, John, 134
Lenihan, Brian, 16
Liberal Democrats, 26, 39, 118, 127
Libya, 64, 71, 156
Lisbon Council for Economic Competitiveness and Social Renewal, 18–20
Lisbon strategy, 18, 20
Lisbon treaty, 17, 59, 67, 131, 138–9
Lloyd's, 49
Lobbycontrol, 18
Lockheed Martin, 52, 68–70
Lombard, Florence, 39
Lower East Side People's Federal Credit Union, 47

Maastricht treaty, 46, 131
McCarthy, Callum, 44
McCreevy, Charlie, 34–7, 41–4
McDonald's, 83, 91
McKee, Martin, 25
Madelin, Robert, 80, 93–5
Mader, Silke, 32
Major, John, 117

Mallaby, Sebastian, 35
Malmström, Cecilia, 71–2
Malta, 92
Mandelson, Peter, 126–49
Mann, Erika, 88
Mapei, 110
Marchis, Alexandru, 91
Mars, 97
Martin, Jean, 132
Marx, Karl, 19
Maunu, Antti, 95
Mauritania, 135
Meadows, Damien, 112
Mercosur, 127
Merck, 28, 31
Merkel, Angela, 5, 11, 13–14, 106, 117, 124–5
Merritt, Giles, 68–9
Mettler, Ann, 18–20
Mexico, 135
Milburn, Alan, 30
Moët Hennessy, 87
Le Monde diplomatique, 5
Monsanto, 73–8, 81, 89
Monti, Mario, 11–13, 46
Montreal protocol, 115
Moore, Michael, 140
Morgan Stanley, 36, 43, 112
Movement of the Enterprises of France (MEDEF), 140–1
Mubarak, Hosni, 51
Müller, 133
Muller, Isabelle, 108–9
multilateral agreement on investment (MAI), 140
Murdoch, Rupert, 5
Murphy, Richard, 153–4

nanotechnology, 64
Nath, Kamal, 129
National Aeronautics and Space Administration (NASA), 124
National Forum of Forest People and Forest Workers (NFFPFW), 115
National Health Service (NHS), 26, 30
Nestlé, 20, 31–2, 83, 91, 133
Nestlé, Henri, 32
Netherlands, 24, 50, 55, 59, 84, 121, 137
New Zealand, 132

Nice treaty, 17
Nicholson, Charles, 107
Nigeria, 116
North Atlantic Treaty Organisation (NATO), 53, 55, 64, 67–70, 88, 156
Norway, 55
Nuffield, 31
Nuremberg principles, 53

Obama, Barack, 66–8
obesity, 83–6
Occupy! movement, 1, 43, 153
Occupy Wall Street, 43
Oettinger, Günter, 108
oil industry, 4, 7, 17, 22, 76, 106–25, 154, 156
Oireachtas, 15, 34
O'Leary, Michael, 32–3
Organisation for Economic Cooperation and Development (OECD), 140
O'Sullivan, David, 129
Oxfam, 3–4
Oxford University Centre for Business Taxation, 10

Paarlberg, Robert, 75
Pakistan, 54
Panavision, 7
Papademos, Lucas, 19, 46
Papandreou, George, 8–9, 11
Parker, Richard, 64
Patel, Raj, 107
Pepsi, 91
Perkins, John, 155
Pernod Ricard, 83, 87, 134
pesticides, 74, 77, 79, 89–91
Petards, 61
Petite, Michel, 104
Pfizer, 29, 31, 145
pharmaceutical industry, 29, 30–1, 76, 81, 121, 140–5
Philip Morris, 68, 96, 99, 100–4, 138
Philip Morris Institute, 68
Pickford, Daniel, 90
Pilger, John, 51
Pioneer Investments, 17
Plain English Campaign, 58
Plehwe, Dieter, 18

Poinsillé, Max, 29
Poland, 4, 55, 71, 99, 118, 137
Policy Action, 29
Porter, Martin, 119
Portugal, 24, 142, 151
Potter, Wendell, 27–8
Powell, Colin, 61
Pozzessere, Paolo, 71
Prats, Lluís, 57–8
private equity, 36–7, 40
Private Finance Initiative (PFI), 117
Proctor, Chris, 97
public relations industry, 1, 19, 28–9, 41, 83, 91, 119, 150

Qatar, 120, 127
QinetiQ, 61

Rajan, Raghuram, 19
Rajoy, Mariano, 24–5
Ramsay, James, 76
RAND, 98–9
Rasmussen, Anders Fogh, 88
Rasmussen, Poul Nyrup, 37, 40
Ravoet, Guido, 42
Reagan, Ronald, 33, 35, 69–70
Re-Define (think tank), 39
Reform (think tank), 30
Rehn, Olli, 15, 23
Reid, John, 30
Renault, 9
Renckens, Suzy, 79
right to food, 47–50, 122–3, 131–5
Rodenticide Resistance Action Group (RRAG), 90
Rolling Stone, 43
Rolls-Royce, 64
Romania, 151
Romney, Mitt, 27
Rose, Chris, 39
Rothamsted, 76
Rowell, Andy, 42
Roy, Arundhati, 130
Royal Air Force (RAF), 58
Ruiz, Simone, 113–14
Russia, 70, 109, 111
RWE, 137
Ryanair, 32–3

Saab, 54–7, 67

Sanofi, 144
Santos, Juan Manuel, 149
Saudi Arabia, 51
Sarkozy, Nicolas, 5, 11, 49
Schmidt, Helmut, 21
Schnappauf, Werner, 139
Schwab, Susan, 132
Scotch Whisky Association (SWA), 134
Securities and Exchange Commission, 36
Security and Defence Agenda, 68–9
security research, 52, 57–66
Sefcovic, Maros, 6
Sellafield, 114
Séralini, Gilles-Eric, 77–8
Serbia, 53
Serco, 30
Sergeant, Carole, 49
Serra, Narcis, 68
Shaxson, Nicholas, 38
Shell, 7, 17, 76, 97, 107, 109, 112, 116–20, 122–3, 139, 154
Sherwood, Michael, 46
Siemens, 22, 61, 127
Simms, Andrew, 108
Singapore, 139
Single European Sky Air Traffic Management Research (SESAR), 58
Siwek, Jacek, 94–5
Skar, Mariann, 85
Smaghi, Lorenzo Bini, 19–20
Smillie, John, 140
Smith, Robert, 90
Social Democrats (European Parliament), 41
Social Democrats (Germany), 13
Socialist Party, 41
social market, 13–14
Société Générale, 17
Société Générale de Belgique, 8
Sodexo, 30
Solana, Javier, 68
Solidarity (trade union), 99
Somalia, 130
Sommer, Renate, 85–6, 88
South Africa, 54, 121, 127, 156
South Korea, 135–7
Spain, 10, 24–5, 34–5, 57, 68, 86, 116, 151
Sparkasse, 43

Der Spiegel, 12
SpinWatch, 42
Squinzi, Giorgio, 110
Standard Chartered Bank, 126
Starbucks, 153
Statoil, 107
Stauber, John, 91
Stevens, Ben, 94
Stockholm Network, 30–1
Stoiber, Edmund, 96
Stricker, Jeff, 64
Sudan, 130
Suez, 137
Sunday Times, 5
Sweden, 34, 41, 54–7, 92, 100–2, 110, 116, 137–8
Swedish Match, 92
Sweeney, Graeme, 117, 123
Sweet, Jeremy, 76
Switzerland, 18, 79, 124, 138
Syngenta, 78–9, 89, 90

Taal, Pieter, 54
Taibbi, Matt, 43
Taiwan, 62
Tajani, Antonio, 60–1
Tanzania, 52
tax avoidance and evasion, 10, 37–41, 153–4
TaylorWessing, 40
TDC, 40
Tebbe, Christoph, 75–6
Telecom Italia, 148
Telefónica, 126
Telicka, Pavel, 95–6
Tesco, 97, 112, 134
Testöri Coggi, Paola, 80
Thailand, 142–4
Thales, 52, 61–2
Thatcher, Margaret, 12, 19, 34
think tanks, 2, 13–14, 17–20, 30–1, 45, 55, 68–9, 75–7, 90–1, 96–7, 103–4, 119, 124
ThyssenKrupp, 20
Times, 30
tobacco, 3, 17, 22, 31, 68, 81, 86, 92–105, 138
Total, 22, 107–9, 112, 117, 119, 122
Toyota, 9, 112
trade policy, 10, 126–49

Trans Atlantic Business Dialogue (TABD), 102–3
Trichet, Jean-Claude, 11, 151
Tunisia, 71, 151
Turkey, 70

unmanned aerial vehicles (UAVs), 53–4, 56–7, 60, 62, 67, 70–2
Unilever, 9, 20, 83–4, 91, 148
United Kingdom Independence Party (UKIP), 97
UK Uncut, 153
United Nations, 4, 48, 52–3, 122, 131, 137, 149
United Nations Children's Fund (UNICEF), 73
United Nations Conference on Trade and Development (UNCTAD), 4
United Nations Environment Programme (UNEP), 116, 120
United States, 1–2, 20–1, 24, 27–8, 31, 35–6, 41–4, 47, 49–50, 52–7, 61–2, 64, 66–71, 73–5, 78, 82, 90–1, 98, 101, 103, 108, 122, 124, 132, 135, 139–42, 145, 151–2, 154–5
United States Air Force (USAF), 64
United States Navy, 56
United States Senate, 42
University of Caen, 77
University of Pennsylvania, 98
Uruguay, 138

Vallance, Iain, 127, 146
van den Hoven, Adrian, 147
van der Loo, Hans, 116, 119
Van Harten, Gus, 138
van Schendelen, Rinus, 8
Vassiliou, Androulla, 94, 97
Vattenfall, 138
Veolia, 126, 137
Verheugen, Günter, 108
Vietnam, 73
Vincent, Frédéric, 93
Vodafone, 10
Volkswagen, 9, 21, 122
Volvo, 20–1, 41, 122

Wal, Jean-Michel, 75
Walesa, Lech, 99

Wall Street, 39, 43
Wall Street Journal, 35
water, 24, 126, 136–7
Water Justice, 137
Watson, Graham, 26
Weissenberg, Paul, 65–6
Welle, Klaus, 104
welfare state, 1, 9–33
West Bank, 57
WilmerHale, 138
WikiLeaks, 55
Witney, Nick, 51–2
World Bank, 122, 130, 151
World Development Movement
    (WDM), 47

World Economic Forum, 18
World Health Organisation (WHO),
    81, 86, 92–5, 97, 101, 104, 141–2
World Intellectual Property
    Organisation (WIPO), 142, 145
World Trade Organisation (WTO),
    132–3, 136, 142–3, 145, 151

Xstrata, 140

Yoplait, 133

Zero Emissions Platform (ZEP),
    117–19
Ziegler, Jean, 122